Ulfried Reichardt, Regina Schober (eds.)
Laboring Bodies and the Quantified Self

American Culture Studies | Volume 27

Ulfried Reichardt (Prof. Dr.), born in 1956, teaches American literature and culture at the University of Mannheim. He was principal investigator of the research project "Probing the Limits of the Quantified Self" as well as founder and speaker of the graduate school "Formations of the Global". His research also focuses on American philosophy and music as well as the uses of time in literature.

Regina Schober (Prof. Dr.), born in 1980, teaches American studies at the Heinrich-Heine-University Duesseldorf. She received her dissertation from the University of Hannover in 2009 and her habilitation from the University of Mannheim in 2019. Her research focuses on literary conceptions of networks, data fiction, and the intersections of failure and knowledge. With Ulfried Reichardt, she was principal investigator of the research project "Probing the Limits of the Quantified Self".

Ulfried Reichardt, Regina Schober (eds.)
Laboring Bodies and the Quantified Self

[transcript]

We would like to thank the Deutsche Forschungsgemeinschaft (DFG) for funding our research project "Probing the Limits of the Quantified Self: Human Agency and Knowledge in Literature and Culture of the Information Age" and also for funding the publication of this volume. Likewise, we want to thank the University of Mannheim for generously providing the necessary infrastructure as well as Katrin Ramseier and Su Montoya for their invaluable support in proofreading the manuscript of this volume for publication. A great thanks also to Juliane Straetz who suggested the theme of the volume.

Bibliographic information published by the Deutsche Nationalbibliothek
The Deutsche Nationalbibliothek lists this publication in the Deutsche Nationalbibliografie; detailed bibliographic data are available in the Internet at http://dnb.d-nb.de

© 2020 transcript Verlag, Bielefeld

All rights reserved. No part of this book may be reprinted or reproduced or utilized in any form or by any electronic, mechanical, or other means, now known or hereafter invented, including photocopying and recording, or in any information storage or retrieval system, without permission in writing from the publisher.

Cover layout: Maria Arndt, Bielefeld
Printed by Majuskel Medienproduktion GmbH, Wetzlar
Print-ISBN 978-3-8376-4921-5
PDF-ISBN 978-3-8394-4921-9
https://doi.org/10.14361/9783839449219

Printed on permanent acid-free text paper.

Contents

Introduction: Laboring Bodies and the Quantified Self
Ulfried Reichardt and Regina Schober 7

Command and Control: The Quantified Self and Biomedical Transhumanism
Stefan Danter 15

Reconsidering Agency and Choice: The Office, the Wall, and the Tax Code (Herman Melville, "Bartleby" and David Foster Wallace, *The Pale King*)
Ulfried Reichardt 41

"To Be Reckoned in the Gross": Corporate Storytelling and Quantified Selves in Joshua Ferris's *Then We Came to the End*
Stefanie Mueller 61

Racialized Self-Improvement: Advice in Black and White Self-Help of the Interwar Years
Kristina Graaff 81

The Solipsism of the Quantified Self: Working Bodies in David Foster Wallace's Body of Work
Dominik Steinhilber 103

Reading Chick Lit through Numbers: Postfeminist Self-Quantification in Helen Fielding's *Bridget Jones's Diary* and Karyn Bosnak's *What's Your Number?*
Regina Schober 123

"I Track my Cycle Religiously": Representations of Fertility
Tracking and Childlessness in Contemporary Graphic Memoirs
Dorothee Marx 141

Compulsive Self-Tracking: When Quantifying the Body Becomes
an Addiction
Katharina Motyl 167

The Portable Peoplemeter Initiative: Wearable Sensor
Technologies and Embodied Labor
Jennifer Hessler 189

Instant Nerve-Ana: Biofeedback as Quantified Self Avant la Lettre
Philipp Hauss 215

Contributors 239

Introduction: Laboring Bodies and the Quantified Self

Ulfried Reichardt and Regina Schober

> "You're generating big numbers," he said, peering at the screen. "I was out there only two and a half minutes. That's how many seconds?"
> "It's not just you were out there so many seconds. It's your whole data profile. I tapped into your history. I'm getting bracketed numbers with pulsing stars."
> "What does that mean?"
> "You'd rather not know." (Don DeLillo, *White Noise* 140)

The use of data in conceptualizing the human body has been present in narratives of the self for much longer than current discourses on self-quantification would suggest. What Don DeLillo depicts in his 1984 novel *White Noise* already indicates the measurability of biometric data in relation to individual risk assessment, while it may not be self-tracking as we know it today. Jack Gladney, the protagonist of DeLillo's novel, exposed to toxic fumes, tries to reach certainty about his health status – a desire that is denied to him. The novel thus exemplifies a central paradox in relation to quantified self-experience: Although numbers may seem reliable, they simultaneously create more uncertainty. While numbers provide the illusion of objectivity, like DeLillo's protagonist, we are always left with the question of "What does this mean?" Personal data has to be interpreted to generate meaningful narratives about ourselves. Yet, what this passage also addresses is the ambivalence of probabilistic knowledge and the incalculable effects of predictions on individuals. How much data do we want to aggregate about our bodies? Under which circumstances can too much data generate problems (for example, when a prediction becomes a self-fulfilling prophecy)? The Covid19 pandemic that is keeping the entire world in check as we write these words also raises the important question of when individual data turns into a social and even political concern. To what extent can apps that track individual behavior help contain a global health hazard and when do they begin to restrict individual rights?

These questions have become increasingly pressing in the last decades, in particular in the context of an all-encompassing digitalization. As part of this development, the body has become central to practices of self-tracking and self-improvement. We optimize our bodies by quantifying ourselves, for example by counting steps and calories, by tracking sleep patterns, heart rate, blood pressure etc. New sensor and analytic technologies have made it easier and thus more pervasive to monitor and control the body as a project. Although, of course, self-improvement through quantification can enhance physical performance and well-being, many users are unaware of the economic value of their data that is generated at the same time. While providing access to a 'deeper' knowledge of the self, our own data and by extension, our body, is turned into a commodity, particularly when data is correlated to create specific marketing profiles, or when quantification is used to adjust the body to normative standards. This quantified data of the self is instrumental in unlocking the body's potential as a laboring body, and in turn, disciplining the individual according to market demands and biopolitical agendas. In this volume, we want to draw critical attention to the role that the laboring body plays in practices, discourses, and literary as well as other cultural representations of the quantified self. Moreover, the essays in this book shed light on the ways that data collection and production redefine what passes as labor, including notions of immaterial and free labor in an increasingly virtual work environment. Of particular interest is the relationship between quantitative and qualitative knowledge, between data and narrative, between measuring and interpretation. We understand this relationship not as one that is mutually exclusive but rather as one that is complementary or, put into a nutshell: Counting without recounting is blind and, arguably, recounting without counting is empty.

US American culture and literature is at the center of the critical investigations in this volume. Indeed, self-tracking has already been a decisive component of individual self-formation in the US for a long time. We can, for example, detect early forms of self-tracking in Benjamin Franklin's Autobiography (1793). His chart of virtues attests to a view of the individual as striving for control and discipline by way of externally datafying and monitoring internal processes. In the late 19th century, insurance companies used personal data on a large scale to assess risk, with large corporations aiming at turning data into profit. The self as a project, then, has been a well-known topos and practice for a long time, and self-enhancement or self-optimization has a long cultural and economic history. In recent self-tracking practices driven by digital culture, however (ironically, perhaps), the body has come center stage and has become the main target of enhancement and control.

In current social, technological, and economic debates, the 'quantified self' – the product of self-tracking – is understood primarily as the collection, aggregation, and analysis of personal data via digital technologies. In a narrower sense, the term 'quantified self' refers to a movement originating in the US with an active and global community that, with the slogan "Self-Knowledge Through Numbers," has propagated personal self-optimization through the use of self-measuring technologies (www.quantifiedself.com). While this movement itself is an interesting social phenomenon, the aim of this book is rather to explore larger cultural, aesthetic, theoretical, political, and historical dimensions of monitoring the self. How do we know ourselves through numbers, and more precisely: What version of the 'self' do we know, get to know or better 'construct' numerically? What is the relation between numbers and subjectivity? An important question in this context concerns the effects of quantification, of using numbers and algorithms, on processes of 'knowing' oneself. The quantified self turns into an object to be observed, known, and shaped by a controlling mind. Yet, going beyond the time-worn dualism of mind/body, a posthumanist conception regards the human body, human mind, and machine or technology as connected in a continuum. A posthumanist approach to self-tracking emphasizes the agency that tracking devices (including smartphone apps but also analog media like writing) possess and therefore also explores the effects of these technologies on the subject.

As references to DeLillo's *White Noise* and Franklin's *Autobiography* suggest (one could also mention the rigorous self-disciplining chart mentioned in F. Scott Fitzgerald's *The Great Gatsby*, 1925), literature (and culture, for that matter) has widely explored the links between numbers and the self, between measuring and subjectivity. A core concern of many essays in this volume is the question of what literature and culture can tell us about these new forms of self-exploration. An increasingly urgent problem in this context is data surveillance and the phenomenon of 'sousveillance', the unknowing but active participation of the individual in the act of surveillance. As data have become a valuable currency in the emerging digital economy, the practice of 'prosumption', defined as the often inevitable merging of consumption and production, has come to define the entanglement between on- and offline activities.

The essays in this collection take a particular interest in the role that the laboring body has played in practices, discourses, and literary as well as other cultural representations of the quantified self. The essays focus on the relations between quantification, the body, and labor in US American literature and culture. Therefore, they also consider the tension between quantification and (self-) measurement on the one hand and narrative on the other. The collection sheds light on the ways in which discourses on data collection and production are instrumental in redefining concepts of labor, including notions of immaterial and free labor in an increasingly virtual work environment. More specifically, the contributions examine the functions of quantification in conceptualizing the body as a laboring body and examine how quantification contributes to disciplining the body. By doing so, they also inquire how practices of self-tracking, self-monitoring, and self-optimization have evolved historically.

In the opening essay of this volume, "Command and Control: The Quantified Self and Biomedical Transhumanism," Stefan Danter describes and discusses current self-tracking gadgets and apps, before he moves to an analysis of literary representations of such devices. In his interpretation of Eric Garcia's *Repossession Mambo* and Gary Shteyngart's *Super Sad True Love Story*, he investigates how literature reflects recent developments in the field of medicine, (bio)technology, and Big Data. Both novels, Danter argues, show how current biomedical and technological developments can result in distinctly dystopian scenarios. With a stronger emphasis on economic dimensions and the formation of the 'corporate self', Ulfried Reichardt, in "Reconsidering Agency and Choice: The Office, the Wall, and the Tax Code" examines the intersection of the economic sphere and subjective experience in the ways in which laboring bodies and subjectivities are shaped in Herman Melville's "Bartleby, The Scrivener" and David Foster Wallace's *The Pale King*. His reading of these narratives traces how work situations in organizations produce specific versions of the self, and in how far characters are actively involved as free individuals. The connection between corporations and self-quantification, particularly in the creative economy, is also explored in Stefanie Mueller's "'To be Reckoned in the Gross': Corporate Storytelling and Quantified Selves in Joshua Ferris's *Then We Came to the End*." In her reading of Ferris's novel, Mueller shows how the narrative voice of corporate storytelling firmly places the novel within a neoliberal agenda. By demonstrating how this novel fits into an older tradition of anti-corporate rhetoric, she argues that it effectively celebrates labor and selfhood under entrepreneurial capitalism.

Kristina Graaff, in "Racialized Self-Improvement: Advice in Black and White Self-Help of the Interwar Years" historicizes self-tracking practices, while investigating the dimension of race in this context. Looking at two self-help manuals of the 1920s and 1930s, "The Way to Health" and Dale Carnegie's bestseller *How to Win Friends and Influence People*, Graaff examines how the 'optimization scripts' of self-help catered to both white and African American mass audiences. Her essay argues that these self-help manuals intended to standardize subjects in relation to the emerging age of automization and mass production. At the same time, they had a large share in prescribing normative standards of able-bodiedness/able-mindedness. Drawing on both Dis/ability Studies and Critical Race Theory, Graaff discusses these texts in relation to the racialization of ability and the ableism inherent to processes of racialization. In recourse to Ludwig Wittgenstein's public language philosophy, Dominik Steinhilber's essay "The Solipsism of the Quantified Self: Working Bodies in David Foster Wallace's Body of Work" examines the problematics of self-optimization within a neoliberal regime. In discussing David Foster Wallace's *Infinite Jest*, Steinhilber demonstrates how the novel critiques the commodification of bodies in the game of tennis, bodies that are continuously ranked. Self-quantification, the essay argues, seems to inhibit the formation of stable selves, instead enforcing solipsism.

The disciplining demands of neoliberalism are also central to the literary genre of 'chick lit'. Regina Schober, in "Reading Chick Lit through Numbers" explores the functions of self-quantification in Helen Fielding's *Bridget Jones's Diary* and Karyn Bosnak's *What's Your Number?* As the essay shows, numbers and statistics contribute significantly to the genre's ambiguous politics. As forms of narrative rupture, the data charts expose and critically subvert the logic of a competitive rating culture, while at the same time confirming some of their underlying normative assumptions. Numbers in chick lit, Schober argues, both discipline and liberate female characters as well as readers, thereby informing the postfeminist agenda of these novels to a considerable extent. Female self-discipline is also a core concern of Dorothee Marx's "'I Track my Cycle Religiously': Representations of Fertility Tracking and Childlessness in Contemporary Graphic Memoirs." Reading fertility tracking apps next to two contemporary graphic memoirs about infertility, Marx discusses the implications of these apps for women who are trying to conceive. She argues that the self-disciplining inherent in fertility tracking practices mirrors the surveillance of pregnant women. Looking at two contemporary graphic memoirs, *Good Eggs* by Phoebe Potts and *Broken Eggs* by Emily Steinberg, she examines in how far cultural representations of the female body are related to current practices of self-quantification and the image of the docile body created by these practices.

Considering the discourse of self-disimprovement, Katharina Motyl, in "Compulsive Self-Tracking: When Quantifying the Body Becomes an Addiction," argues that self-optimization can turn into a form of compulsion. Self-tracking's addictive potential, she claims, seems to be intensified by the competitive nature of fitness apps as well as by the immersive nature of online environments. While some may consider compulsive self-tracking an excessive aberration from an otherwise beneficial practice, Motyl contends that compulsive self-tracking takes the rationale underlying the practice of self-tracking in capitalist societies to its logical conclusion: self-tracking represents a "technology of the self" (Foucault 1988). Users mobilize quantifying bodily data to discipline their bodies in accordance with the ideological regimes of productivity and beauty concomitant to the capitalist economic order.

The following two essays propose regarding mid-20th century technologies as prefiguring current self-tracking practices. In "The Portable Peoplemeter Initiative: Wearable Sensor Technologies and Embodied Labor," Jennifer Hessler provides insight into 1980s television rating technologies, with a special focus on Nielsen's peoplemeter technology. She argues that the peoplemeter entrenched users within a surveillance enclosure, implicating even activities that are unrelated to television viewing under corporate surveillance, thus turning the body into a round-the-clock technology of commodification. This technology's compliance with the body influenced contemporary logics of mobile self-tracking and body attachment. Philipp Hauss, in "Instant Nerve-Ana: Biofeedback as Quantified Self Avant la Lettre," sheds light on another historical example of self-monitoring that can be regarded as a precursor to current self-tracking practices. The biofeedback movement of the 1960s and 1970s, Hauss explains, aimed at accessing and monitoring the body via electronic feedback technology in order to recognize and control bodily processes and reactions. Reading biofeedback against the backdrop of digital self-quantification, the essay illuminates the historical continuities and discontinuities of feedback technologies and practices as well as their biopolitical implications in relation to our body.

The essays collected in this volume underline the intricate relationship and entanglement of quantification and measuring routines, technologies, in particular digital ones, and recent forms of subject formation. That the body figures so prominently in this process and that it is the laboring body that is foregrounded may be regarded as a significant signature of our current era.

Command and Control: The Quantified Self and Biomedical Transhumanism

Stefan Danter

Before sitting down to write this article, I walked a total of 5,743 steps, a number that the Health App on my iPhone conveniently counted using a variety of motion sensors before displaying the data in an aesthetically pleasing graph. The question, however, is what I can do with this quantified information now that I have it, or rather what it could teach me about my walking habits. A quick Google search reveals that the number of steps is below the optimal of 10,000 steps that one should supposedly take each day in order to reach a healthy level of exercise. While I am of course free to ignore all of this, the implied message of the Health App and its automatic transformation of my physical movements into quantified digital data is that in order to lead a 'good' life, I should literally step it up. This impression is explicitly reinforced by the message, displayed at the top of the "Activities" section of Apple's Health App, which greets users with an almost commanding tone to "Sit down less, move more, and exercise," accompanied by a video whose thumbnail features a bicycle. Because who doesn't want to live a long, healthy, and carefree life?

The fact that the health app's data confronted me with my apparent lack of sufficient exercise is also a symptom of a broader logic of quantification that has far-reaching consequences for the 21st century subject and its agency. While it is my decision whether or not I will exercise (or in this case: walk) more, seeing that kind of data nevertheless exerts pressure. This pressure can be traced to a growing cultural affinity towards mechanisms that ensure and constantly increase the possibilities of both small-scale and large-scale control. As a result of the constant flow of innovative gadgets, software, and hardware that emerge out of breeding grounds such as Silicon Valley and their combination with the increasingly sophisticated algorithms and technologies of Big Data, it is safe to say that we find ourselves firmly in an age of numbers. And while it is easy to get carried away by the appeal of all these shiny new objects and their promise of improving our lives, turning us into numerical beings or Quantified Selves, the speed at which development and innovation progress also creates the uneasy feeling of being carried along by a technoscientific wave which does not grant us the possibility of properly reflecting on its consequences. In order to provide an overview of technological developments alongside their literary reflection, this analysis consists of two stages. In a first step, I will analyze current self-tracking gadgets and apps, focusing specifically on their communication and marketing strategies. Later, I will use Eric Garcia's *Repossession Mambo* (2009) and Gary Shteyngart's *Super Sad True Love Story* (2010) to demonstrate how literature reflects and reacts to contemporary developments in the field of medicine, (bio)technology, and Big Data. Both novels show how current biomedical and technological developments can result in distinctly dystopian scenarios. It is in this high-speed context that literature can play an important role as a medium of deceleration, allowing its readers to assume a position of second-order observation, emphasizing consequences, and exploring possible negative outcomes of these developments. There are two other points the example above demonstrates. One, the practices that can be summarized under the label of self-tracking are becoming ever more pervasive and subtle. While just a few years ago, it was mostly athletes and avid exercise fanatics who used tracking systems, software, or gadgets like the FitBit, technological developments and their implementation into smartphones exponentially increased the number of people who are willingly and also unwillingly quantified through tracking technology. Apple's Health app mentioned above is a good example for this: signified by a red cartoon heart on a white background, the app and its corresponding step tracker are turned on by default, meaning the system is designed to require the user to 'opt-out' rather than to 'opt-in'. In the past, these two mechanisms were best known from E-Mail newsletters, where users were often automatically subscribed once they used their E-mail address to register somewhere, and would receive the electronic newsletter until they actively decided to cancel it. The case of the Health App is different because upon buying an iPhone, the user will be tracked immediately, even if they never open the app and do not care about a daily step count. Since every iPhone owner is required to create an Apple-ID by using a valid E-Mail address, however, the data could immediately be collected and ascribed to a specific user. Furthermore, 'opting out' is not made easy, as the user has to navigate through the confusing structure of the phone's settings and manually forbid the app from collecting data, a task made more difficult by the lack of transparency regarding the workings of the app and the permissions it has by default. The impression that Apple might have an interest in this data is additionally underlined by the fact that when Apple began to allow users to delete the 'integrated' apps that are pre-installed on every phone, including apps like Maps, Music, FaceTime, or the contact list, the Health app was curiously excluded from that list and has remained so until this day.

As a result of the developments outlined above, a few theoretical thoughts about the Quantified Self (henceforth abbreviated as QS) and practices of self-tracking are required before delving deeper into literary engagements with these technologies. An important side note here is of course that the practice of tracking in and of itself is not a 21st century novelty. From the keeping of diaries to surveys to the daily act of stepping on a scale, self-tracking activities have always been important in highlighting the relationality of a subject with the world surrounding it. In other words, human subjects have always relied on 'technologies' of tracking, storing knowledge, and improving their efficiency while operating in the world, whether it was planting crops or going on a diet. For example, Michel Foucault (1998) traced this behavior as far back as ancient Greece in his lectures on the "Technologies of the Self," and Dan Bouk (2015) presented a convincing analysis of the role of life insurance companies in the emergence of the so-called "statistical self." This is just to name two short examples. What has fundamentally changed are the technological means to conduct tracking as well as the reasons behind it, which seem to become more and more personal. From a theoretical standpoint, studies and explanations of self-tracking and the QS movement are still few and far between, with academic interest slowly growing and catching up with the fast-paced development of the industry. The most common understanding of the term appears synonymously with the movement of the same name that was started by Gary Wolf and Kevin Kelly in 2007. In his 2010 TED Talk in Cannes, Wolf advocated that sensors and measuring devices should also be seen as mirrors pointing inward that can be "useful for self-improvement, self-discovery, self-awareness, self-knowledge" (2010), before concluding that while the self serves as operation center and moral consciousness, "if we want to act more effectively in the world, we have to get to know ourselves better" (2010). For Wolf and many other proponents of self-quantification, the idea that quantified data will improve the quality of our lives conforms to the basic idea that sensors and measuring devices present an objective account of reality. The self-asserting logic behind this is that these technologies can be used not only to increase our knowledge about the immediate environment, but also to motivate subjects to optimize their surroundings and, more importantly, their individual bodies. It is interesting that Wolf's rhetoric already opens the door for a critical engagement with practices of quantification when he asserts that Kelly and he "noticed that people were subjecting themselves to regimes of quantitative measurements and self-tracking that went far beyond the ordinary familiar habits such as stepping on a scale" (2010). It is precisely the danger of quantification being abused by governments or of becoming a powerful apparatus that subjects individuals to its logic, surveillance, and control, that the overly positive assessments made by proponents of this technology tend to gloss over.

Indeed, the process of measuring and constantly tracking the body is rarely presented in a negative light, as a look at the QS website as well mission statements and advertisements by companies producing QS gadgets shows. Quantification is marketed as the key to a deeper knowledge about the self and as a means to gain access to a numerical, and thus, by extension, objective truth. The knowledge generated by these practices is thematically tied to issues of personal health, medical treatment, and lifestyle. As such, it employs language evoking qualities such as positivity, progress, improvement, and development. While FitBit describe themselves as "a passionate team dedicated to health and fitness who are building products that help transform people's lives" (2019), their competitors Spire Health proclaim that "Our mission is to harness the power of algorithms and sensors to improve health outcomes by empowering patients and physicians with useful and actionable data" (2019). Thus, the culture and practices of quantification seem to be primarily concerned with health, increasing efficiency and performance, the minimization of risk, and the ability to foresee and adapt to near-future developments. In other words, tracking technologies are always connected to issues of control, with ideal numbers or statistics often depending on who is in command and able to define the norm. This is not to say, however, that quantification and self-tracking are universally negative. The technologies mentioned here are helpful in enabling the subject to observe itself from a distance, thus helping to overcome blind spots, revealing previously unknown or overlooked patterns, and assisting people in achieving some of their goals. Furthermore, tracking and quantification technologies have proven effective in various areas of medical treatment and health care, for instance in the treatment of diabetes, blood pressure issues, or heart disease. In those cases they greatly improved the quality of life and independence of patients. It is when QS-practices become fused too tightly with neoliberal ideology and threaten to pressure subjects into conformity that they become problematic. The goal is not to vilify quantification per se, but to reveal and critically reflect problematic tendencies.

One example for the increasing ubiquity of quantification is the tracking app Beeminder, which under the slogan "Engineer Yourself" proclaims on its website that "your goals can be anything quantifiable – weight, pushups, minutes spent on Facebook, points on Duolingo. Answer with your number when Beeminder asks – or connect a device/app below to auto-report – and we'll show your progress and a Yellow Brick Road to follow to stay on track" (2019). The unique aspect of the app, however, is that it is built on a strict punishment system which penalizes users for veering off track by charging them an amount of money they pledged before starting to track their progress. In a blog post on the company's website, its founder Daniel Reeves explains that the idea behind the app was inspired by *akrasia*, a concept he adopted from Greek philosophy which according to Reeves includes "procrastination, lack of self-control, lack of follow-through, and any kind of addictive behavior" (2011). Reeves sees the solution for problems of this nature in so called "commitment devices," a game theory term that in this context is meant to serve "a way of changing one's own incentives to make an otherwise empty threat or promise credible." The ultimate goal, he reveals later on in his blog post, is for the present-day self to combat its own, lazy future-self, thus ensuring the success of long-term goals and commitments:

> The myopic future self that thwarts your intentions is every bit as smart as your current, forward-looking self. You can make lists and set rewards and break tasks into small chunks, or plan diets and buy treadmills and establish routines, but mostly your future self will see right through all the tricks and just won't give a damn. That version of yourself just wants to surf the web and/or eat pie. (2011)

By portraying the relationship between rational, goal-oriented thinking and behavior as a fierce battle taking place within the subject, and by attesting that every subject is prone to laziness, gaining weight, and procrastination, Reeves depicts the contemporary subject as fundamentally flawed. It reveals an underlying neoliberal logic that Beeminder does not appear to reflect critically at all. This is underlined by the fact that it requires its users to sign a contract before they can start tracking. The wording of this contract leaves no doubt about the strictness of the regime that users of the app, albeit voluntarily, subject themselves to:

> I, ____, will stay on my Yellow Brick Road *every day* until I reach my goal or forfeit $___. If I'm in the wrong lane I'm risking going off the road tomorrow and losing. In this way my long-term goal is broken down into something I'm forced to work towards gradually every day. In general, I promise to abide by the spirit of this commitment and not weasel or abuse loopholes. (2019, original emphasis)

In a move that ties back to the Puritan tradition of self-analysis and introspection that formed early roots of quantification practices, Beeminder is designed to function as a sort of externalized conscience pressuring the subject into exhibiting 'proper' behavior, taking and keeping the money pledged should the user fail to adhere to his/her own standards. As the name of the app suggests, what the user gets in return is an incentive to become a diligent worker bee that works hard and is always focused on achieving his/her predetermined goals. Although there is a possibility to archive a tracked goal and thus get off the hook, the general tenor of the app's ideology is designed to motivate people to stay on course by appealing to their sense of self-worth and well-being, a strategy well known from other neoliberal and capitalist attempts at disciplining the individual. It is also strikingly similar to the "machinery for adding up and capitalizing time" (157) that Foucault located within the disciplinary governmentalities of the school or the military. Accordingly, docile, disciplined bodies were produced through the constant observation and recording of individuals and their actions, a task which has been made substantially easier by technology.

In other words, what concepts such as the Quantified Self, but also lifelogging, self-measuring, personal informatics, and self-monitoring have in common is the fact that they describe a practice, as sociologist Deborah Lupton defined it, "in which people knowingly and purposively collect information about themselves, which they then review and consider applying to the conduct of their lives" (2016: 2). She also notes that the practices of self-tracking have evolved beyond the individual and become relevant in a variety of social, cultural, as well as political contexts (ibid: 3). A similar observation was made by Nora Young, who identified contemporary digital culture as one of the main factors facilitating the proliferation of tracking practices. Digital culture is taking the subject "out of the here and now. It is precisely this disembodied, distracted, digital life we lead, [she argues], that is creating the urge to document the physical body" (2012: 3). Young claims that the extreme focus on the body has to be understood in the context of and as a response to the disembodiment and decontextualisation (in terms of space as well as time) of lives lived in constant digital communication and self-monitoring. Young highlights the fact that self-tracking has evolved from being a mere practice of improving oneself to one that actually helps create a sense of self and endow it with substance and physicality (ibid: 51). The self is then created at least in part through its documentation, a practice which bears the inevitable risk of objectifying the body.

In *Seeing Ourselves Through Technology*, Jill Walker Rettberg similarly argues that tracking apps represent a new form of the diary, a self-image written by and seen through the eyes of the machine. Contemporary technology thus represents "a diary that writes itself automatically, without needing your input" (2014: 46). In this context it is important to point out that technology follows its own set of rules and that the user is rarely able to see, much less edit, its settings or parameters. If one agrees with this assessment, a critical approach to digital life-logging and the power of the algorithm needs to take into account the possibility of the machine 'seeing' the user differently from how they see themselves. This is problematic precisely because the machine's perspective is supposedly objective by virtue of being based on the rationality of calculations and measurements, when in reality its perspective follows predetermined rules, is influenced by context, and can be manipulated. Rettberg argues that this is a fact that developers of apps and devices choose to hide or at the very least will not openly address. In other words, the confidence that self-tracking devices and apps emanate about the accuracy of their findings is often misleading, at least in part because the data that users can see only represents a small, carefully filtered portion of the whole.

Rettberg maintains that filters have become a universal presence in digital culture and self-tracking practices because the infinite and unfathomable amounts of data we produce are not useful if not arranged around a specific question, or at least condensed and somewhat simplified for interpretation. Rettberg aims to raise awareness for the limiting and structuring influence of filters, which she categorizes as simple visual/photo filters, technological filters, and cultural filters. While the definition of photo filters is straightforward, and easily underlined by the popularity of beautifying, or playfully de-humanizing and alienating filters on apps like Instagram and Snapchat, cultural filters are understood as the foundation of widespread behavioral norms, beauty standards, expectations, or discursive strategies (ibid: 24). Concerning technological filters, Rettberg stresses that within every app, social media platform, or even programming language, there are settings in place that allow for certain actions while disallowing/preventing others. This includes filtering certain content based on knowledge gained through algorithmic correlation and the tracking of user behavior. Ultimately, Rettberg contends,

> We cannot represent our lives or our bodies without adapting, resisting, and pushing against filters that are already embedded in our culture, whether those filters are cultural or technological.... We can and often do resist or change cultural filters, but most of the time we simply act according to the logic of the filter without even realizing that is what we are doing. (ibid: 24)

The example that perhaps best illustrates technological filtering is the selective process underlying the display of news and political opinions on social media platforms, such as Twitter and Facebook. The how, why, and extent to which Facebook, the biggest and most pervasive social network, has been used to influence voter opinion and thus sway the outcome of the 2016 US presidential election has been fiercely and extensively debated.[1] From a purely technological point of view, the Facebook algorithms were merely doing what they had been programmed to do: showing users, whose preferences they sometimes appear to know better than they do, the type of content that is assumed to be agreeable to them. Facebook is only one prominent example for a broader development of economic practices that has been summarized under the label 'attention economy'. Due to the overwhelming number of ways for users to spend their time online, companies developed an interest in maximizing the time users spend on their platforms and websites, actively trying to incite them to interact (e.g. like, comment, share) with other people. As Tiziana Terranova put it, "If information is bountiful, attention is scarce because it indicates the limits inherent to the neurophysiology of perception and the social limitations to time available for consumption" (2). Of course this is not part of an elaborate social experiment, but follows the singular goal of using that time to collect more data and sharpen the picture about them, their personalities, preferences, and behavioral as well as decision making patterns. This

---

[1] The implicit dangers of everyday online activity and how it could be misused is also analyzed in the documentary *The Great Hack* (2019) by Karim Amer and Jehane Noujaim. While the overall apocalyptic tone of the documentary feels overdone at times, it still is successful in providing a detailed look at the role Cambridge Analytica played in the 2016 election and demonstrating the possibilities of Big Data technology on a broader level.

highly valuable information is especially lucrative because it can be used to both optimize the algorithms and 'user experience' of Facebook and be sold to advertisers aiming to target specific cohorts of people. One only needs to take a look at "Blue Feed, Red Feed," a website and project developed by Jon Keegan (2016) for the *Wall Street Journal*, to understand the magnitude of these technological filters and their influence on people's opinion. The project juxtaposes liberal and conservative Facebook news feeds using hourly updates and lets users filter them by topics such as President Trump, gun control, abortion, immigration, or health care. It offers a real-time look into the formation of the states of intellectual isolation that activist Eli Pariser (2011) has referred to as "filter bubbles," communities of likeminded individuals forming around opinions and beliefs concerning controversial or debatable topics.

With filters being ubiquitous, it is crucial to stress that the information we see rarely represents the whole picture. The perceived aura of objectivity that statistics emanate can be misleading, mainly because the data responsible for the calculation of ratios, probabilities, and proportions is always preselected according to a research question, filtered, and correlated according to specified parameters, and interpreted subjectively. Furthermore, the collection of data also intersects with critical problem areas such as ethics (both of data usage and collection), the verification of research results, ownership, storage, access, privacy, and the importance of context. This is especially relevant in the area of self-optimization that QS gadgets and apps are offering. In their introduction to *Quantified Selves and Statistical Bodies*, Pablo Abend and Mathias Fuchs argue for a greater focus on the physical aspects of body optimization. They claim that "the tracking and quantifying of bodily functions precedes the assumption of a body that can be changed and shaped in reconciliation with the results obtained from measurement" (2016: 11). Similar to Young and Lupton, they also point out that the truth promised by QS is conditional in the sense that it can only be attained by religiously comparing, interpreting, and acting based on the data (ibid: 12). The critical approaches presented above highlight that there are definite downsides to the euphoric point of view about self-tracking and self-optimization advocated by Wolf, Reeves, and companies producing QS gadgets. One, what precedes the idea of a freely modifiable and optimizable body is the belief in a body that is deficient by default. This ties in well with a neoliberal ideology that locates the responsibility for success or failure fully within the subject. It also explains, at least in part, why the growth of quantification and optimization regimes happens alongside that of normative policing of corporeality, such as body and fat shaming, and the increasing number of mental health issues that stem from individuals feeling their body is inappropriate. Two, the promised improvement can only be attained by using QS technology, which is problematic because access and affordability are factors that easily create a division based on class or income. Those who do not want to track themselves and be tracked or those who do not have the means to do so are left behind, and the kinds of improvements these devices suggest are of course dependent on their technological filters. As Deborah Lupton puts it, "Digital data about people's lives are also vital in their effects. [. . .] they have begun to play a significant role in influencing people's behaviours, sense of self, social relationships and, increasingly, their life chances and opportunities" (2016: 5).

Another problem of the 21st century "numerical self" (Young 2012: 29) lies in the gamification of tracking practices and the way tracking changes human agency. As stated earlier, developers and marketers are always trying to keep users engaged for as long as possible to increase the amount of data which can be collected, analyzed, correlated, and sold. Viewed in conjunction with the "nudge theory" that has become increasingly popular in behavioral economics, and whose pioneer, Richard Thaler, received the 2017 Nobel Prize in economics, it is thus not surprising that most apps nowadays feature game mechanics. The idea behind nudging is to make subtle suggestions to the user, encouraging them to act in a pre-determined way but without giving off the impression that this is an 'other-determined' behavior. Instead, the user should be given the impression that his/her behavior is the result of an independent decision and actions are done solely for their own benefit. By combining methods of nudging with gamification practices in self-tracking apps and devices, developers can thus increase users' willingness to optimize themselves by putting an emphasis on aspects such as playfulness, competition, and enjoyment rather than discipline and the fight against procrastination or laziness. While the inclusion of game mechanics can help subjects stay motivated and thus is not negative per se, its potential to foster addictive or compulsive behavior in users has to be taken into account.

This strategy ties in well with the emergence of what George Ritzer and Nathan Jurgenson have called "prosumer society" (2010: 17), a new state in the development of capitalism that started with the rise of fast-food restaurants in the 1950s but exponentially accelerated and evolved with the emergence of the internet, and especially those websites and services that influenced the term Web 2.0 (e.g. Facebook, Twitter, Google, YouTube etc.). Generally speaking, as the word itself suggests, the prosumer inhabits a hybrid position at the intersection of production and consumption (ibid: 18), meaning that he or she contributes to the production processes before paying to consume the resulting product or service. In the context of the Web 2.0, the most obvious application of this term can be seen with content creators on YouTube or influencers on Instagram, who both like, share, and comment on the content they encounter while also producing their own. Interestingly, Ritzer and Jurgenson do not consider the risk of exploitation of prosumers by traditional capitalist means very high. In fact, they claim that contemporary prosumers are actively resisting "the incursions of capitalism (e.g. efforts to gain greater control and greater profits)" (ibid: 21), adding that exploitation is unlikely to happen because the prosumers "seem to enjoy, even love, what they are doing and are willing to devote long hours to it for no pay" (ibid: 22). Considering the practices of quantification discussed here as well as the enthusiasm displayed by many users of QS technology, they appear to be correct. However, one could argue that Jurgenson and Ritzer underestimate the power of the algorithms to correlate and monetize data. Furthermore, their claim that exploitation does not exist if the subject enjoys the activity being exploited is too simplistic. For the question of exploitation it is irrelevant whether the subject enjoys the activity or not. This is especially relevant in the context of the Web 2.0 and its capabilities of monetizing user engagement and participation. It is no coincidence that the discourse on digital technologies is increasingly focused around concepts such as free or hidden labor and the exploitation of users and customers through algorithms, data collection, and data correlation.

Considering this in conjunction with the fact that individuals are both voluntarily and involuntarily tracked, it becomes increasingly important to take a critical stance towards not only gamification, but the practices of tracking and data collection as a whole. As Christopher Till (2014) argues, the digital economy is radically altering concepts of labor, compensation, and the relation of work and pleasure within contemporary neoliberal society. The perfect neoliberal subject is an entrepreneur and "attends to fashions, is focused on self-improvement, and purchases goods and services to achieve 'self-realization'" (Marwick 2013: 13). In an environment that is catered towards optimization and efficiency in all areas of life, users of tracking apps and devices are no longer just tracking themselves for their own sakes, but are actively generating vast amounts of valuable data. Thus, self-trackers occupy a prosumer position because they buy tracking devices and use health apps in order to optimize their health and performance. Simultaneously they are producing a digital resource that can and will be monetized and used to sell them products that are more catered to their preferences and individual habits. Most users are not aware of this, however, and the practices and mechanics of gamification contribute to the masking of the true value being extracted from the voluntary and involuntary tracking of digital activity. According to Till, a *Financial Times* study "found that the twenty most popular health and fitness apps share information with almost seventy different companies" (2014: 449). While many self-trackers do not consider the practice of tracking to be labor, Till argues that it is nevertheless vital that scholars and prosumers recognize "the commodification of exercise activity" (ibid: 451) and actively reflect on its consequences: "they are labour, because the corporations are treating them as such. Surplus value will be extracted from these activities by corporations, as if they were work; if we do not recognize it, then we cannot challenge it" (ibid: 452). He connects these kind of arguments to the concept of "immaterial labour," championed by Italian Marxist scholars like Christian Marazzi (2010), Paolo Virno (2006), and Maurizio Lazzarato (2006). They hold that the "like economy" in effect turns the users of social media into a collective of workers, whose individual mouse clicks and likes, when aggregated, "become valuable and productive for the corporations who have the means to exploit them financially" (Till 2013: 41). Along similar lines, scholars such as Tiziana Terranova and Trebor Scholz have proposed to view this as "free labour" (Terranova 2011: 46) because it is essentially unpaid. Gamification plays an important role in the masking of capitalist interests in these practices. Through the implementation of game mechanics, "corporations have successfully convinced users that it is leisure, not labour, through an erosion of the distinction between work and play" (Scholz 2011: 2).

As Till's examples show, there are definite and justifiable concerns about data storage, control, and privacy. Once an individual starts tracking him- or herself, possession of the data goes over to the company offering the service or gadget and can hardly be controlled from that point onward. The data produced by self-tracking is both highly individualized and personal, which is exactly why it is of immense commercial value. It is largely because of this value that many critics of QS and Big Data envision scenarios in which tracking is transformed from being about the body and the self into a "Technology of the Social," as Thomas Lemke (2011) puts it. In that context, tracking practices might become obligatory for everyone or happen passively whenever people use digital devices of any sort, which, needless to say, is problematic. This includes one of the biggest issues revolving around QS, which is that Big

Data technologies have become a means of widespread surveillance. Since almost every service, gadget, or app collects data on its users (e.g. personal health data, movement data from navigation apps, consumer data from online shopping, biometric data etc.), the idea of a transparent subject, with all its negative consequences for privacy, personal freedom, and self-directed agency, no longer belongs to a distant dystopian scenario.

In fact, Shoshana Zuboff (2019) claims that current developments in the fields of digital technology and infrastructure have led to the emergence of what she calls "surveillance capitalism." Zuboff notes that in the age of smart homes and the increasing interconnectivity of "smart" devices, capitalist exploitation has evolved and is now primarily based on the surveillance of customers. She locates the birthplace of this new form of capitalism at Google, but notes that other companies such as Amazon or Facebook have followed a similar path. In essence, "Surveillance capitalism claims human experience as free raw material for translation into behavioral data" (Zuboff 2019: 14), using the information collected to develop behavioral prediction models. Big Data technology and machine intelligence play a crucial role in this process, as "surveillance capitalists discovered that the most-predictive behavioral data come from intervening in the state of play in order to nudge, coax, tune, and herd behavior towards profitable outcomes" (ibid: 15). For Zuboff, this is an unprecedented development, as capitalists have hijacked the formerly positive and liberating aspects of digital connectivity to create a vampiric form of capitalism that "feeds on every aspect of every human's experience" (ibid: 16). Most interestingly, however, she argues that companies like Google are not interested in selling products to their users directly, but to mine their data and experience and sell it to a third party: "Surveillance capitalism's actual customers are the enterprises that trade in its markets for future behavior" (ibid: 17).

One final point that needs addressing here is the way our ongoing connection with digital technology changes the way knowledge is conceptualized and spread. According to Young, the increase in sophisticated and easy to handle soft- and hardware enables people to track pretty much anything they want as long as it is quantifiable and can be expressed and visualized numerically (ibid: 19), an assumption confirmed by apps such as Beeminder. Aside from subjects relying on data as objective knowledge about the world and their behavior, Young's observation echoes a broader development in the natural sciences in the 21st century. That is the belief in the mathematical calculation of the universe and in a resulting large-scale predictability. Klaus Mainzer (2014) points out that the way knowledge is generated in the 21st century largely depends on the use of algorithms and other Big Data techniques and practices. As a result of these developments, the value ascribed to the collection, generation, and subsequent correlation of data has increased exponentially. The inherent danger of relying too much on data, according to Mainzer, is that the supposed predictability and speed at which results can be achieved blurs the overall picture and threatens to make mathematical theory and laws increasingly unimportant. He argues that Big Data debates need to be connected to a historical foundation and theoretical background in order to properly evaluate limits and possibilities of a change in the epistemological concepts of our time. Critical approaches to the dominance of Big Data in epistemology, science, commerce, marketing, and politics frequently try to warn both scientists and the public about trusting the results of quantitative methods and statistics without further reflection.

Capitalist Dream, Individual Nightmare?

In the context of the increasing importance of quantified data and knowledge it is worthwhile to consider alternative sources of reflection, the generation and negotiation of knowledge, and experimentation. Although commentators located in the areas of science, technology, engineering, and mathematics, the so-called STEM disciplines, frequently dismiss the humanities for lacking empirical depth, literature nevertheless can make an important contribution in this debate on knowledge production. As Winfried Fluck and other commentators have demonstrated, literature does possess diagnostic capabilities and can serve as a space for experimentation in which potentialities can be played through, explored, and negotiated. In their capacity as the memory banks of a given culture, literary works thus are important storages of cultural, social, and aesthetic experiences and knowledge. In this context, I want to present some of the central points Eric Garcia and Gary Shteyngart make in their novels and demonstrate how they relate to quantification being used as a control mechanism and the biotechnological modification of the human body. Garcia's *Repossession Mambo* (2009) introduces us to a scenario in the not too distant future in which biomedical and technological advancements have made it possible for any organ in the human body to be replaced by an artificial – and usually enhanced – version. These so-called artiforgs enable users to lead a healthy and indefinite life because they regulate bodily functions and factors such as food intake or blood and oxygen levels, while being immune to diseases, tissue degradation, or age-related performance decrease. Formerly only available to the rich and wealthy, the Credit Union, the major creditor, "opened wide the jeweled gates of mechanical rejuvenation to the poor and downtrodden working classes" (Garcia 2009: 31), creating a scenario in which "only the very poor, or those who have abused their credit to the point of criminal activity are unable to secure loans for their artiforgs" (ibid: 189). The future portrayed here is posthuman (or rather transhuman) in the sense that having artificial implants is highly desirable, with people lining up in front of credit offices to apply for loans and subjects who are in possession of their own, fully natural human bodies, becoming the exception.[2] It thus depicts a future 'after' the traditional concept of what constitutes a human, in which the understanding of embodiment has changed because a central aspect of human existence, namely the processes of aging and death, have been removed. This is what conforms to the transhumanist ideal of transcending the limitations of the human body and achieving immortality. However, the protagonist credits the success and demand for artiforgs less to technological advancements than to expert marketing (ibid: 73), a fact exemplified by the presence of slogans like "*A Lifetime Can Be Yours*" (ibid: 61, original emphasis) or the Credit Union's advertisement spot "'What's New In You?'" featuring "three little multiethnic kids singing about their newly implanted artiforgs" (ibid: 201). It demonstrates the conscious effort on the side of capitalist corporations to create and control consumer demand, which in this case involves blurring the lines between the human, transhuman, and object. The human body is reconceptualized as fully modifiable, with hospitals resembling workshops more than actual medical facilities.[3] This is best exemplified by the case

---

2   To explain very briefly, critical posthumanism is a school of thought that engages critically with the legacy of Cartesian humanism and its idea that human subjects are universally rational and thus enjoy complete autonomy from their environment. Instead, posthumanism stresses the subject's embeddedness in a multitude of contexts, its dependence on the body and environment it inhabits, and the agency of nonhuman entities, whether those are objects, technology, or animals. For a more detailed explanation see Hayles (1999), Badmington (2003), and Herbrechter (2013). In contrast to this, transhumanism envisions the transcendence of the limiting boundaries of the human body. In this ideology, a posthuman is a subject that has evolved beyond original humanity, where 'post' refers to a stage 'after' the human. For an extended definition see Dinello (2005) and Bostrom (2012).

3   Envisioning the body as a machine in need of maintenance adds another level of meaning considering that Repo Men are a staple in the American credit system, where the

of Bonnie, who suffered from a rapidly progressing, aggressive form of cancer that caused her life to be "filled with trips to the hospital and supply houses, her natural organs replaced one by one with perfectly designed replicas, as good as or better than the originals... Bonnie was 74-percent artificial" (ibid: 219).

The consequences of this technology are far-reaching and have fundamentally transformed this fictional society according to a rational logic of quantification. In this scenario, the worth of an individual is only expressed in terms of calculations and numerical data, measured by factors such as capital owned, interest paid, wages earned, organs repossessed, and hours worked. Cultural capital is not worth anything, as media only serve as the long arm of corporate marketing departments intending to sell the dream of immortality. This seems to work well. As the protagonist points out, "I don't know a single person who's died of old age, unless you count living long enough to be killed as dying of old age" (ibid: 134), cutting straight to the heart of the paradoxical immortality depicted. While infinite life is a real possibility, people can only live forever as long as they are able to pay the loans and interest of the high-tech organs. Those who cannot will receive a visit from the Bio-Repo-Men, who are allowed to legally repossess the organs, usually leaving the subject dead in the process. These headhunters are not legally obligated to provide medical care or ensure medical assistance and follow a legal framework called "The Federal Artiforg Code" (ibid: 178) that regulates all interactions between "manufacturer, supply house, direct marketer, client, and organ" (ibid: 178) down to the minutest detail. The unnamed protagonist himself is a former Repo-Man who required an artificial heart after an accident and could no longer pay, making him transition from being the hunter to being prey. Garcia introduces a society in which the fusion between tracking technology, a logic of quantification, and a biomedical-commercial sector has created a situation of absolute control, where the bodies of individuals literally become assets. In what resembles the irresponsible loan and mortgage strategies on the housing market that dominated the US financial sector in the years leading to the 2008 global financial crisis, the credit institutes in *Repossession Mambo* gladly assist almost every citizen in taking out a loan for an organ. By doing so, citizens are embedded into a legally binding contract that subjects them to their creditor's control and goodwill. As the protagonist puts

---

practice of repossessing cars to reclaim debt from defaulted debtors is a standard procedure.

it, "The linchpin of the artiforg credit system is that all equity rides within the body itself. That way, when it comes time to foreclose, there's no way for the client to cut and run" (ibid: 65).

In order to ensure the continued functionality of this system, the government has developed and legalized an extensive arsenal of surveillance technology for the use of private firms and corporations such as the Credit Union, as the headhunters it employs are in no way associated with the police or any other representative of the executive branch. As part of the repossession process, the Repo-Men receive wanted posters including a photo and all kinds of statistical data on the debtor, including

> last known address, phone numbers, credit card statements, health records, hygiene habits, and shoe size of the wanted individual, as well as similar information about close friends and relatives. There is no privacy where the Union is concerned; the forms they make you sign in triplicate make that abundantly clear. (ibid: 78)

They furthermore carry scanners allowing them to examine all artiforgs in an area and see if their users are behind with their payments. Although there is mentioning of laws protecting the privacy of citizens, they are all catered to serve the interests of the artiforg companies or the Credit Union. When looking at the details of the loan deals, what becomes immediately clear is that the system works in a way that almost certainly ensures people stay encumbered. As the protagonist points out in one example, "the client had a credit rating of 84.4 when he applied for the thyroid – respectable in today's financial climate – and had been awarded the artiforg at an interest rate of 32.4 percent over a period of 120 months" (ibid: 181). Even without seeing the actual numbers it is clear that this loan is almost impossible to pay off without working permanently. The protagonist's heart, in contrast, cost a total of $183.000, causing him to face monthly payments of $3,815.62 (ibid: 188). In other words, a communion of state, financial sector, marketing, and medical-industrial sector exerts absolute control over its citizens. Everybody wishes to live indefinitely, which makes them desire the artiforgs whose accumulated debt then forces them to spend their prolonged lives working to pay them off. Garcia presents the dystopian version of a capitalist dream: the immortal and infinitely productive worker. This dream, the novel makes clear, is a nightmare for the working populace, and against the prospects of this kind of immortality, death appears like a better deal, as everyone involved with the artiforg business is essentially unfree, living under constant pressure and fear. It can also be read as an affirmation of aging as a symbol of inherent humanity and finitude. The negative outlook on immortality furthermore underlines the positive sides of being allowed to have a non-functioning or less-than-optimal human body.

A similar scenario is presented in Gary Shteyngart's *Super Sad True Love Story* (2010). By connecting biological aging processes with the replacement of print through digital media, the novel correlates the quantification of personal data with human agency and value. The novel's protagonist Lenny Abramov, a melancholic middle-aged Russian American, works as a "Life Lovers Outreach Coordinator (Grade G) of the Post-Human Services division of the Staatling-Wapachung Corporation" (Shteyngart 2010: 3), promoting a service which promises to prolong the life of people with the proper credit score indefinitely. Pitching their product to a potential customer, Lenny

> painted him a three-dimensional picture of millions of autonomous nanobots inside his well-preserved, squash-playing body, extracting nutrients, supplementing, delivering, playing with the building blocks, copying, manipulating, reprogramming, replacing blood, destroying harmful bacteria and viruses, monitoring and identifying pathogens, reversing soft-tissue destruction, preventing bacterial infection, repairing DNA. (ibid: 122)[4]

Similar to *Repossession Mambo*, this passage invokes an idea of the human subject whose embodiment is no longer an unchangeable and natural fact. The body instead is portrayed as a vehicle that can be repaired, modified, and preserved. The scenario is dominated by quantification in all areas of life and society. Lenny hopes to be accepted into the program and therefore conducts all necessary tests on himself as well. As he points out, even some of the wealthiest customers he deals with are "ITP, Impossible to Preserve" (ibid: 16), because they do not live a healthy lifestyle by for example counting calories, measuring fats and trans-fats or avoiding harmful substances. In other words, "You had to *prove* that you were worthy of cheating death at Post-Human Services. Like I said, only 18 percent of our applicants qualified

---

4   The language used by Lenny to convince potential customers mirrors that of the "äpparat"'s data profiles, as can be seen when comparing this passage to Lenny's profile: "LENNY ABRAMOV ZIP code 10002, New York, New York. Income averaged over five-year-span, $289,420, yuan-pegged, within top 19 percent of US income distribution. Current blood pressure 120 over 70. O-type blood. Thirty-nine years of age, lifespan estimated at eighty-three (47 percent lifespan elapsed; 53 percent remaining)" (88).

for our Product" (ibid: 151, original emphasis). The burden of proof includes regular fitness and stress tests, as well as measuring and publicly displaying a variety of biometric data. These practices of quantification are also reinforced on the corporate level, with repurposed train station schedule boards displaying employee names alongside the results of physical examinations, bio-data such as estrogen, testosterone, or triglyceride levels, and what is called "'mood + stress indicators,' which were always supposed to read 'positive/playful/ready to contribute'" (ibid: 56). In true neoliberal fashion, employees are told to resist committing "the Fallacy of Merely Existing. FME. There'll be plenty of time to ponder and write and act out later. Right now you've got to *sell to live*" (ibid: 65, original emphasis). It is therefore not surprising to see a fierce competition among employees, who can actually lower each other's evaluations through ratings. This results in a constant chase for high scores and ratings that recalls the competitiveness in many of the 'gamified' tracking apps that can already be observed today, with the major difference that these games have very real and potentially devastating consequences.

However, the quantification of the subject extends far beyond the confines of Lenny's workplace. Details such as credit rating, health records, and even sexual preferences are publically available and can be read by everyone in possession of an "äpparät," an absurd evolution of today's smartphone. This is representative of a knowledge discourse that favors quantifiable over qualitative information and in which a person's 'worth' is constantly evaluated. Following the quantified-self logic, observational procedures like 'measuring' and 'tracking' become every-day tools for understanding and 'mapping' the human body. The äpparät can also be read, as Regina Schober has argued, in the sense of Michel Foucault's concept of the apparatus, a device facilitating "the strategic formation of discourses, institutions, and laws that exert power over the individual and over knowledge" (365). As a technological extension of the human body in the sense of Marshall McLuhan, these devices are "reducing human perception exclusively to the binary information readable to the smart machine, [confining] both physical and emotional processes of human consciousness within the technological apparatus" (365). The äpparät thus is a representation of "the increasingly informational processes of knowledge production based on search engines" (365). However, the novel's critique lies not only in the way the logic of quantification is portrayed as reductionist in this context, but also in Lenny's eventual decision to abandon his dream of infinite life in favor of death and decay. All of this takes place against a backdrop of a US society and economy in decline, with the dollar as a stable international currency having been replaced by the Chinese Yuan. This is evident from the summary that Joshie, Lenny's boss at Post-Human Services, gives of the overall situation in the United States: "Forget the dollar. It's just a symptom. This country makes nothing. Our assets are worthless... Maybe the Chinese or the Singaporeans will buy us outright" (ibid: 64). This is what eventually happens towards the end of the novel, when a Chinese delegation arrives in New York to take over the country, proclaiming "Welcome to America 2.0: A GLOBAL Partnership THIS Is New York: Lifestyle Hub, Trophy City" (ibid: 320). In this context, the company's strategy to artificially limit access to its life-prolonging services in order to only attract the richest "High Net Worth Individuals" (ibid: 10) gains an additional meaning. Lenny's boss Joshie has fully incorporated a capitalist logic that equals the chance of survival with the amount of capital in an individual's possession, which also explains why he is selling a treatment that is still in development and whose functionality is not guaranteed.

To the extent that the novel portrays the possibilities of infinite life extension through technology, it depicts a scenario similar to *Repossession Mambo*. Shteyngart's novel offers a vision that, in spite of the explicit use of the term "Post-Human," corresponds more with transhumanist endeavours at transcending the limits of embodiment than with the redefinition of human agency that is commonly associated with the school of critical posthumanism. Joshie advises his employees who hope to become immortal to keep a diary. This archaic form of written self-tracking and self-reflection is supposed to help them stay in touch with their old selves, as the experience of immortality is predicted to change the structure of their consciousness altogether. Joshie's fantasies of infinite life are ironically the product of Golden Age science-fiction novels and *Isaac Asimov's Science Fiction Magazine* (Shteyngart 2010: 215), and his "Post-human philosophy" (ibid: 124) fuses an essentialist view of the human subject's rationality with a dose of neoliberal elitism and meritocratic thought. The emphasis on rationality also explains why the evaluation of potential candidates includes psychological elements. Lenny puts one of his potential customers, Barry, through tests such as "the willingness-to-persevere-in-difficult-conditions test," the "response-to-loss-of-child test," or the "Infinite Sadness Endurance Test" (ibid: 123), only to realize that Barry would not be admitted to the program because he cares too much about his children. In other words, the kind of people that Joshie deems worthy are individuals who completely lack empathy and emotions, instead possessing a cold rationality. Requiring candidates to behave this way thus contributes to them losing crucial aspects of what is commonly considered humanity. Joshie also believes that these wealthy, ultimately rational elites would, by virtue of their immortality, become the future leaders of (post-)humankind, which highlights the problematic dimension of transhumanist ideals, as a society defined by the absence of empathy would not be considered desirable by most people. The novel's critique of this ideology is further underlined by Lenny, whose love for the humanities, and especially his books, qualifies him as a perfect humanist, declaring "*I am going to die*" (ibid: 302, original emphasis). This proves to be the right decision when the life-prolonging procedures ultimately prove to be faulty, reducing Joshie, and presumably other clients, to drooling masses of muscle and flesh (ibid: 327), while Lenny remains healthy in his non-ideal but still fully human body.

From this it is clear that positions of either euphoria (e.g. Wolf, Reeves, advertising language) or skepticism vis-à-vis tracking and quantification are problematic. While QS technology, self-tracking, and Big Data can have a positive impact on cultural, social, political, and certainly individual dimensions of life, it is important to also reflect on possible issues that a logic of quantification can produce if it is combined with a repressive or otherwise problematic political ideology. Garcia's and Shteyngart's novels both offer a critical perspective on issues of biotechnology, market capitalism, and the quantification as well as commodification of the human body. In addition, one could consider both novels to represent aspects (or to address representative aspects) of the contemporary surveillance capitalism observed by Zuboff. Whether it is the talking credit poles and "äppäräts" in *Super Sad True Love Story* or the fusion of irresponsible finance companies, biotech firms, and marketers to create what amounts to a bizarre mixture of indentured servitude and enslavement in *Repossession Mambo*, both novels showcase elements of the instrumentalization of technology for capitalist means that Zuboff describes.

Furthermore, when taking into account global developments in the field of digital technology, biotechnology, Big Data, and surveillance, the dystopian scenarios presented by both novels appear to be closer to our reality than one would have anticipated a few years past. Cases of influence operations with the goal to sway elections are just one example of how digital and quantitative methods and technology can be used to exert control over individuals to achieve a certain predetermined goal. This also includes attempts by authoritarian regimes at using machine intelligence and other Big Data technologies to identify, track, and silence dissidents. One example with the potential to be an explosive and transformative social technology is the social credit system, slated to become mandatory for all of China in 2020. Although this deadline has approached already, there is little information about its implementation. Cities across the country have served as testing stages for pilot projects, even though there has been no official announcement about the final version of this system. Because information about the extent and exact rules of the social credit system is scarce, it is thus too early to properly evaluate its impact. And yet, in some pilot projects, users receive points for good behavior such as posting positive messages about the government, buying the 'correct' products, or adhering to the rules, while receiving a penalty for offenses such as jaywalking, criticizing the government, or even associating with people that have a low score. The system incentivizes behavior defined by the government as 'good' by offering various advantages to people with high scores, such as easier visa applications or better loan deals, while discouraging 'bad' behavior through a variety of disciplinary measures, such as reduced internet speed or not being allowed to enter certain areas.[5] As Genia Kostka notes in her study about the approval of social credit systems by Chinese citizens, "what the different SCS initiatives have in common is that, by setting up systems of benefits and sanctions, they aim to steer the behavior of individuals, businesses, and other organizations in China" (2019: 1566). Surprisingly, Kostka's survey found that 80 per cent of respondents strongly approve of social credit systems, "while just 1 per cent reported either strong or somewhat disapproval. To some extent, the high degree of approval of SCSs and the almost non-existent disapproval we found might reflect the nature of conducting a survey in an authoritarian setting" (ibid: 1573). It might also explain why the approval was strong even among younger people and older, wealthy, educated citizens. Overall, this shows how dangerous a quantitative knowledge system can be if it is paired with a repressive or authoritarian government.

---

5   The true extent, scope, and impact of social credit systems in China are hotly debated. An extended look at the trials can be found, for example, in Nicole Kobie's article in *WIRED*, "The Complicated Truth about China's Social Credit System." Scholars such as Law Researcher Jeremy Daum, on the other hand, disagree with the apocalyptic tenor found in most media reports. In an interview with Elizabeth Lynch, Daum argues that Western media are misconstruing the goal and extent of these systems, and that most accounts given in Western media are merely projections of Western fears and prejudices about China's policies.

To sum up, this analysis has shown the importance of a critical engagement with digital tracking technologies, the concept of the Quantified Self, and emerging forms of digital global capitalism. Both *Repossession Mambo* and *Super Sad True Love Story* act as second-order observation systems and provide explicit critiques of the 'datafication' of individual lives and agency. However, just as the epistemological outlook presented by QS advocates and tech companies appears to be overwhelmingly positive, fictional engagement with these topics appear to be mostly negative. So, while the potential for critical reflection and the highlighting and exploring of possibly dystopian scenarios needs to be acknowledged, the general tenor of negativity and critique makes it difficult to imagine what a positive depiction of digital tracking technology and biomedical practices might look like or if such an endeavor would be worthwhile. Considering that tech development and evolution of digital technology shows no signs of slowing down, with advancements in Artifical Intelligence and Robotics that could fundamentally change society on the horizon, there might be a necessity to find a middle ground capable of negotiating between techno-euphoria and techno-skepticism.

Works Cited

Abend, Pablo/Fuchs, Mathias (2016): "Introduction." In: *Digital Culture & Society* 2/1, pp. 5-21.
"About Us," 2019 (https://spirehealth.com/pages/about-us).
Amer, Karim/Noujaim, Jehane (2019): *The Great Hack*, Netflix, July 24, 2019.
Badmington, Neil (2003): "Theorizing Posthumanism." In: *Cultural Critique* 53/Winter, pp. 10-27.
"Beeminder – Engineer Yourself," 2019. (https://www.beeminder.com/).
Bostrom, Nick/More, Max/et. al (2018): "Transhumanist FAQ," (https://humanityplus.org/philosophy/transhumanist-faq/).
Bouk, Dan (2015): *How Our Days Became Numbered*, Chicago: University of Chicago Press.
Boyd, Danah/Crawford, Kate (2012): "Critical Questions for Big Data." In: *Information, Communication & Society* 15/5, pp. 662-279.
Chiang, Ted (2019): *Exhalation*, New York: Random House.
Dinello, Daniel (2005): *Technophobia!*, Texas: University of Texas Press.
Foucault, Michel (1995): *Discipline & Punish*, New York: Random House.

___ (1998): "Technologies of the Self." In: Luther H. Martin/Huck Gutman/Patrick H. Hutton, *Technologies of the Self: A Seminar with Michel Foucault*, Boston: University of Massachusetts Press, pp. 16-49.

Garcia, Eric (2009): *Repossession Mambo*, New York: Harper.

Hayles, Nancy Katherine (1999): *How We Became Posthuman*, Chicago: University of Chicago Press.

Herbrechter, Stefan (2013): *Posthumanism: A Critical Analysis*, London: Bloomsbury.

Keegan, Jon (2016): "Blue Feed, Red Feed." May 18 (http://graphics.wsj.com/blue-feed-red-feed/).

Kobie, Nicole (2019): "The Complicated Truth about China's Social Credit System." In: *WIRED* June 7 (https://www.wired.co.uk/article/china-social-credit-system-explained).

Kostka, Genia (2019): "China's Social Credit Systems and Public Opinion: Explaining High Levels of Approval." In: *New Media & Society* 21/7, pp. 1565-1593.

Lazzarato, Maurizio (2006): "Immaterial Labor." In: Paolo Virno/Michael Hardt (eds.), *Radical Thought in Italy: A Potential Politics*, London: University of Minnesota Press, pp. 132-146.

Lemke, Thomas (2011): "Beyond Foucault: From Biopolitics to the Government of Life." In: Ulrich Bröckling/Susanne Krasmann/Thomas Lemke (eds.), *Governmentality. Current Issues and Future Challenges*, New York: Routledge, pp. 165-184.

Lupton, Deborah (2016): *The Quantified Self: A Sociology of Self Tracking*, Cambridge: Polity Press.

Lynch, Elizabeth (2018): "What's the T on China's Social Credit System? Jeremy Daum Explains – Part 1 of 2" November 12 (https://chinalawandpolicy.com/2018/11/12/what-the-t-onchinas-social-credit-system-jeremy-daum-explains-part-1-of-2)

Mainzer, Klaus (2014): *Die Berechnung der Welt*, München: C.H. Beck.

Marazzi, Christian (2010): *The Violence of Financial Capitalism*, Bellinzona, Switzerland: Semiotext(e).

Marwick, Alice (2013): *Status Update: Celebrity, Publicity, and Branding in the Social Media Age*, New Haven: Yale University Press.

Pariser, Eli (2011): *The Filter Bubble: What the Internet is Hiding from You*, London: Penguin.

Reeves, Daniel (2011): "How To Do What You Want: Akrasia and Self-Binding." January 24 (https://blog.beeminder.com/akrasia/)

Rettberg, Jill Walker (2014): *Seeing Ourselves Through Technology*, New York: Palgrave Macmillan.

Ritzer, George/Jurgenson, Nathan (2010): "Production, Consumption, Prosumption." In: *Journal of Consumer Culture* 10/1, pp. 13-36.

Schober, Regina (2016): "Between Nostalgic Resistance and Critical Appropriation: Contemporary American Fiction on/of the Information Age and the Potentials of (Post)Humanist Narrative." In: *Amerikastudien/American Studies* 61/3, Heidelberg: Winter, pp. 359-379.

Scholz, Trebor (2011): "Why Does Digital Labor Matter Now?" In: Trebor Scholz (ed.), *Digital Labor: The Internet as Playground and Factory*, London: Routledge, pp. 1-9.

Shteyngart, Gary (2010): *Super Sad True Love Story*, London: Granta.

"Standard Beeminder Contract." (https://www.beeminder.com/contract).

Stephenson, Neal (2016): *Seveneves*, London: HarperCollins.

Terranova, Tiziana (2011): "Free Labor." In: Trebor Scholz (ed.), *Digital Labor: The Internet as Playground and Factory*, London: Routledge, pp. 33-57.

Till, Christopher (2013): "Architects of Time: Labouring on Digital Futures." In: *Thesis Eleven* 118/1, pp. 33-47.

___ (2014): "Exercise as Labour: Quantified Self and the Transformation of Exercise into Labour." In: *Societes* 4/3, pp. 446-462.

Virno, Paolo (2006): *Multitude: Between Innovation and Negation*, Los Angeles: Semiotext(e).

"Who We Are," 2019 (https://www.fitbit.com/about).

Wolf, Gary. "Quantified Self," (http://antephase.com/quantifiedself).

___ (2010): "The Quantified Self," September 27, (https://www.youtube.com/watch?v=OrAo8oBBFIo).

Young, Nora (2012): *The Virtual Self: How Our Digital Lives are Altering the World Around Us*, Toronto: McLelland & Stewart.

Zuboff, Shoshana (2019): *The Age of Surveillance Capitalism*, New York: Hachette.

Reconsidering Agency and Choice: The Office, the Wall, and the Tax Code (Herman Melville, "Bartleby" and David Foster Wallace, *The Pale King*)

Ulfried Reichardt

The present volume's title "Laboring Bodies and the Quantified Self" refers to the ways in which persons, and in particular their corporeality, are disciplined in and through processes of labor. The intersection of the economic sphere and subjective experience is pertinent here, and the ways in which bodies are shaped in this process. I will focus on two literary texts and interrogate how they fictionally analyze the relationship between labor and the self. I am primarily interested in investigating how work situations produce specific versions of the self, including physical selves, in the ways in which subjects are formed by their working conditions, and in how far they are themselves actively involved in it as free individuals. The focus will be on the 'corporate self', and the constellation I will investigate concerns persons working in organizations. Of course, the body ('corpus') and the corporation are closely related, linguistically as well as conceptually. Two frames of reference are of interest here – the intersection between organizations and individuality as an important, if often neglected dimension of posthumanism, that is, of the limitations of human agency and individual freedom, and secondly self-experience in the context of liberal humanism, and, moreover, of contemporary neoliberalism which economizes every aspect of life. The concepts of posthumanism and the basic ideas of liberalism create friction, because the notion of self-determination and the claim that human beings are to various degrees determined by other factors (bacteria, objects, tools, and also organizations) stand in stark contrast. I therefore want to discuss the linkage between the concept of free choice in the context of the concepts of (neo-)liberalism on the one hand, and individualism on the other by analyzing two major fictional texts that precisely negotiate this problematic, Herman Melville's "Bartleby, the Scrivener.

A Tale of Wall Street" (1853) and David Foster Wallace's *The Pale King* (2011). US American literary fiction has been highly perceptive in dealing with the contradictions arising from liberal social structures early on. Fiction can stage situations in which characters experience these conflicts and thus show them instead of just analyzing them in abstract ways.

At the beginning of the last century already, the philosopher Georg Simmel emphasized the close relationship between the money economy and quantification as an important dimension of modern culture. Calculating enables people to act individually by choosing between several options that can be observed and measured in the form of numbers, and thus to shape themselves. At the same time, however, this renders them, as Simmel remarks "cog[s] in an enormous organization of things and powers" (1964: 422). While the effect of pervasive quantification is one of the decisive dimensions of modern experience, I will primarily emphasize the texts' negotiation of the most important category of liberal humanism which is 'choice', the freedom to choose between alternatives and to shape one's own life.

Choice, of course, is intricately linked with the concept of will. Sharon Krause emphasizes: "Choosing is indeed one way that we exercise agency, and a society that restricted individual choices arbitrarily or too fully could not count as free" (2015: 3).[1] With regard to the work place, choice implies the liberty to enter into a work contract, a free decision which nevertheless binds the person subsequently to the rules of the organization she or he has entered. 'Contractuality' is one of the basic concepts of liberal democratic societies.[2] Seen from this perspective, the 'quantified self' is a special case of self-fashioning that involves involuntary labor (called 'prosumption', giving one's data

---

1   The theoretical context of my analysis is the critical reassessment of liberal humanism, which has come under attack from several directions. One study I find very helpful is Sharon Krause's *Freedom Beyond Sovereignty* which tries to rethink free actions and choice in the context of the obvious counterarguments that freedom has to be substantiated and relativized by reference to factors such as race, class, gender etc. Hers is a complex attempt to rescue liberalism from its detractors without naively falling back on obsolete positions. A further point of reference is Louis Dumont's notion of individualism as an ideology. Thomas Heller and David Wellbery as well as Armin Nassehi, among others, have emphasized that in spite of the theoretical deconstruction of the subject in poststructuralism, the individual continues to be the central figure in law, literature, popular culture, and society in general and thus still has to be studied.
2   Sir Henry Sumner Maine claimed that "the movement of the progressive societies has hitherto been a movement *from Status to Contract*" (1861: 141, original emphasis).

to the media corporations, mostly unknown or not explicitly at one's own free will) and working at achieving one's best self in order to be fit for the market (labor, marriage, social relations) (Danter/Reichardt/Schober 2016). Yet the degree to which 'selves' are shaped by concrete working conditions is even higher. Therefore, I choose critical fictional explorations of persons in offices as test cases to think about freedom and agency, limitations by the work contract, as well as the intersection of individuality and organizations, and US-American forms of (post-)individualistic personhood. The larger framework of my inquiry concerns major contours of the formation of subjectivity in US-American society, with a special look at the vicissitudes of individualism, as it has been characteristic of the United States. If US-American cultural history can be written as the history of an increasing movement of continuing individualization, as Winfried Fluck claims (2009: 60), then an urgent question is if this development can continue endlessly or if it might ultimately lead to an implosion and thus turn against itself. Will liberalism at some point tip over into illiberalism?

With respect to the current debate about posthumanism as an important facet of today's human condition, I want to suggest that it should not only focus on language, digitalization, biotechnology, and globalization, but also trace the contours of these developments regarding those economic dimensions which are related to the effects of organizations on individuals and their range of possible action. Self-determination has been the central concern of liberalism, starting with John Locke's concept of owning oneself (1980:19). Yet, in labor contracts, you bind your work force and thus your body deliberately for certain times to the rules and constraints of an abstract organization, such as a corporation, which then will dispose over somebody's time and body during the working hours. It is evident that work is a defining part of one's individuality and existential experience. Hence agency and labor are intricately intertwined, and thinking about the freedom to choose with regard to work is a good starting point for investigating the status of individual agency and biopolitics (Foucault) in modern societies. I argue that the fact that in a liberal democratic society persons may enter into contracts, at least potentially, at their own will, binds them in very different ways and more firmly than is the case with enforced work that can only be controlled by external force (Tocqueville 1988: 290). We are observing an internalized form of limited agency, the internalization of 'the corporation and its rules', if you wish. If you are part of the office and the office is part of you, rebelling against its impact is difficult in a way very different from external violence, such as the brutal violence in slavery or totalitarian societies.

I will historicize my analysis by going back to the early days of corporate life in the United States (cf. Newfield 1996). A crucial mid-19th century text in this context is Herman Melville's "Bartleby, the Scrivener," a story that has been interpreted in numerous ways, stretched into various directions of metaphysics. Yet, it has rarely been read with a focus on agency and choice in the context of Transcendentalism's radicalization of liberal humanism's notion of individual liberty in Ralph Waldo Emerson's concept of "self-reliance" (1841) and Henry David Thoreau's "civil disobedience" (1849). "Bartleby" will be juxtaposed with David Foster Wallace's unfinished novel *The Pale King*, which dramatizes work in a tax agency in contrast to the cultural stance of ironic indifference that for the author is symptomatic of postmodernism. The cultural context is what Wallace regards as the overextension of freedom and choices in the libertarian climate of the sixties counter-culture and the seventies entertainment culture. The juxtaposition of two texts that are historically more than one hundred and fifty years apart may be justified by the fact that criticism has often stressed the similarity of concerns, but more importantly, because Melville critically observes a cultural and social constellation in its early stage that has become even more problematic in today's neoliberal condition.

The main thesis of this essay is that both Melville and Wallace test the limits of freedom as the freedom of choice and the range of agency in working situations, and implicitly or explicitly argue that too much choice and versions of radical individualism may tip over into the complete loss of choice. I regard the authors as exponents of philosophical positions they take vis-à-vis concrete and specific political, social, and religious conditions. Both texts may be read as critiques of anti-conformist movements, Transcendentalism as well as mid-20th century counter-culture, assessments which nevertheless do not opt for conformity and conservatism either. This subject is particularly important at times when liberalism as the founding ideology of the West during the last two centuries has come under severe attack from the left and in particular from the populist right, paradoxically shortly after its final global victory had been declared at the turn to the present century.[3] The basic ideas

---

3   I am referring to the anti-liberal and authoritarian tendencies in populist movements in several states during the last years which explicitly attack the social and cultural ideas and achievements of liberalism, whereas the leftist, in US diction liberal groups attack the economic aspects of (neo-)liberalism. Theoretical posthumanism's main tar-

of liberalism have to be critically reassessed if they are to be defended against its detractors. Moreover, at a time when artificial intelligence and automation could pass a threshold beyond which human agency might actually become precarious, exploring the gray area between will and force is of the highest urgency. The counterfoil is totalitarianism, political and social as well as religious systems that order and punish without giving any rationally based reasons. The question, then, I am interested in, and the texts that I will analyze focus on is: where is the end of liberty in freedom, and where does an abundance of choices tip over into no longer having any choices?

"Bartleby, the Scrivener. A Tale of Wall Street": Choosing Not to Choose

Melville's "Bartleby" is one of the most important US-American texts for thinking about the contradictions of individualism in the context of political and economic liberalism. It was published at a time (1853) when the republic had been established long enough to appear stable as a political entity to most observers and its principles seemed unquestionable, if not to Melville, when democracy in the manner of Andrew Jackson had already deteriorated into mass democracy, when modern forms of capitalism, of the financial industry and of corporations were emerging in the US, and with these also the 'homo oeconomicus' as the dominant model of the individual. At the same time the counter tendency to market capitalism, constant competition, and its effects on the individual, as well as on the culture as a whole was already strong in its most articulated form in American Transcendentalism with its concepts of self-reliance, civil disobedience, and a romantic pantheistic conception of nature. Melville was critical of both sides of the individualist coin, and his "Bartleby" can be regarded as the most complex critique of extreme forms of American individualism of its time.

Bartleby arrives as a new clerk at the office of the lawyer-narrator. The story is set on Wall Street, and the whole action takes place within the confined space of the lawyer's office. There are two other workers, Turkey and Nippers, both of whom are described as physically impaired in different ways. The working conditions are not especially hard ("very dull, wearisome, and

---

get of critique is liberal humanism's tendency to set humans at the center of everything. There are, then, conflicting views of what exactly constitutes liberalism.

a lethargic affair" [1994: 2239]), yet the office work has severe effects on the employees' bodies, namely indigestion and extreme restlessness. While the lawyer can handle the irregularities of the two clerks' behavior, Bartleby completely stops working on the third day already. He remains a stranger, and the narrator does not know anything about his past or context.[4] Bartleby does not comply at all, even if he does not refuse to do the work outright. Body, working conditions, and work contract, as well as will and choice as a condition of freedom are intricately linked from the beginning. Soon Bartleby's only response to his employer's requests consists in uttering his famous formula "I would prefer not to," the lawyer's increasingly frantic, yet ineffective ways of attempting to handle the situation, and the denouement which is Bartleby's death in jail as an ultimate consequence. While the plot develops mainly by way of the (non-)interaction between employer and employee, we only get to know the lawyer's thoughts and motives. We cannot be certain if he is a reliable narrator – a lot of what he says is self-reflexive – whereas Bartleby remains a black box. The only external signs we get to know are his instances of passive resistance, crystalized in his formulaic sentence.

An obvious symbol is the wall – Wall Street, but also the surroundings of the office ("deficient in what landscape painters call 'life'" [1994: 2235]).[5] In particular, Bartleby is hidden by a wall from the lawyer, who can call him but does not have to see him. He is described in a way rendering him almost inhuman ("pallidly neat [...] incurably forlorn!" [ibid: 2238]). There is nothing "ordinarily human about him" (ibid: 2240). His lack of any social features excludes him from human society. The lawyer himself turns almost into "a pillar of salt" (ibid: 2240) – emphasizing their complementarity –, as Bartleby is determined "not to comply with [his] request – a request made according to common usage and common sense" (ibid: 2240). The lawyer immediately recognizes this behavior as "passive resistance" (ibid: 2242). The following exchange is therefore symptomatic: "I would prefer not to." "You *will* not?" "I *prefer* not" (ibid: 2243). In the lawyer's imagination, Bartleby seems to have

---

4   He is a "man without characteristics," as the title of Robert Musil's important novel (1930, 1933, 1941) has it.
5   Leo Marx argues that "The walls are the controlling symbols of the story [...]." He continues that "in fact it may be said that this is a parable of walls, the walls which hem in the meditative artist and for that matter every reflective man" (1974: 357). In his reading, the story is about Melville's situation as a failed professional writer at the time of composition.

merged with the surrounding walls – "behind his screen he must be standing in one of those dead-wall reveries of his" (ibid: 2246).

In contrast to narratives dealing with totalitarian regimes, here it is the mysterious protagonist himself, a subaltern person whose motivations, thoughts, and acts are inscrutable, yet whose firm will is explicitly foregrounded.[6] Melville's short story critically tests the concept of self-determination in the study of a character who is self-reliant to such a degree that he destroys himself in the act of radical self-determination. The critical target is Transcendentalism, in particular Emerson who articulated a position of almost unconditioned free agency, will, and self-creation as the ideal of the American person, but also the empirically existent American citizen as social individual who was analyzed by Alexis de Tocqueville in the 1830s. The second reference points to the social and political developments of increasing industrialization, professionalization, and functional differentiation of American society in the 19th century in the context of Jacksonian Democracy.

Both the concrete conditions of a modern liberal and emergent capitalist state as well as Romantic anti-conventional thought constitute the context of Bartleby's trajectory. Bartleby is the self-determined person with a vengeance, a man who resists the pressures of conformity to such a degree that he disappears. The idealist notion of self-reliance leads into an endless loop where freedom tips over into bondage, where choice tips over into the complete lack of choice. It is the liberal humanist tradition of self-determination that is fictionally tested in the lawyer's office on Wall Street in the early 1850s, pushing it to its limit point.

While Bartleby frequently says 'I', he never says 'No'. Being able to negate is one of the defining criteria of human language. "I would prefer not to," however, is not an outright refusal. Rather, Bartleby acts in the negative, yet does not explicitly refuse to act. If he spoke and thus entered the communicative exchange, this would imply a direct refusal, and if he answered 'no' it would as well. Yet by doing neither, he refuses to refuse and, therefore, to take any position at all, which, as the story elaborates, nevertheless is a position that does have ultimate consequences. Bartleby's non-responsive response could be regarded as an act of deferral or postponement. But as he repeats his formula serially, and as this is (almost) his only statement, the deferral turns back onto itself and cancels the implied temporalization. The subjunctive could be

---

6   Several critical texts discuss Melville as well as Wallace in comparison to Franz Kafka's bleak cosmos of what could be called "total institutions."

read as a sign of politeness. Yet, 'not to' leaves the act of what he prefers not to do dangling in the void, rendering the phrase even more vague and inconclusive. Ultimately, Bartleby chooses not to choose, and he makes this point very emphatically. His response is a strong form of passive resistance – the lawyer exclaims that "he burns to be rebelled against" (1994: 2243). While Paul Watzlawick, Janet H. Beavin, and Don D. Jackson state that "One cannot not communicate" (1976: 53), one also cannot not choose, as no choice is a choice as well.[7] Not participating in social exchanges, a stance that may be seen as a radically individualistic decision for freedom, nevertheless has severe effects on the person choosing to do so. He or she does not only attempt to get rid of coercion but also loses any support or sense of belonging. As Bartleby leaves the realm of actions, he cannot be coopted. Yet in order to fight conformism, he de-individualizes himself and no longer belongs to society. The fact that Bartleby serially repeats his non-committing sentence may be understood as a hint that language is 'always already' public and not a medium primarily within the reach of an individual's intentionality. There can be no private language, as Ludwig Wittgenstein states.

Other interpretations have argued that Bartleby's refusal is indeed rebellious. Gilles Deleuze interprets Bartleby's formula that is neither affirmation nor negation as a poetic deviation used to express something not to be said in standard language. He calls this pattern "the logic of negative preference, a negativism beyond every negation" (1979: 71). It denies any alternative and creates a void in language. Giorgio Agamben explains Bartleby's refusal with reference to philosophical Skepticism and claims that keeping all options open by not deciding is a position of strength ("epoché"): "The scribe who does not write (...) is perfect potentiality" (1999: 247). "To be able is *neither to posit nor to negate*" (ibid: 257).[8] That Bartleby's remaining in the state of the merely potential is the central point of the story is underlined by the fact that the lawyer reads "Edwards on the Will," and "Priestley on Necessity" (1994: 2252) to reposition himself conceptually on firm ground. In contrast to Agamben, however, I do not think that pure potentiality is possible for long. Rather, Bartleby's formula introduces a difference that makes a difference, as Gregory Bateson

---

7   Bartleby's response may be understood as a contemporary version of the classical Greek verb genus 'middle voice', which is located between active and passive and can still be observed in reflexive constructions today.
8   I suggest that Agamben is thinking of a society which allows total control over parts of its population, the *homo sacer* of Roman slavery or of the German camps, which, however, does not apply to Bartleby's situation.

has it.⁹ Paradoxes, oscillation, and suspension cannot endure, as time continues. His behavior has severe consequences, as the course of Melville's story shows.¹⁰

Gabriel Alkon's interpretation is closer to my own view when he regards the story as an attack on Emerson's optimism and questions Agamben's reading. He emphasizes that "In the story of Bartleby, Melville has prepared a message for Emerson: potentiality alone is powerless and hopeless" (210: 140). He argues that "Bartleby's will [...] is the will of the supposedly sovereign individual who is the necessary constituent of the sovereign market-state" (ibid: 137). Yet Bartleby is the *"reductio ad absurdum* of liberal ideology" (ibid: 140). Alkon summarizes: "Both Emerson and Agamben are attempting to think against the logic of sovereignty, from within that logic; and they are therefore attempting to think the impossible" (ibid: 141). In the character of Bartleby, Melville deconstructs the Romantic notion of resistance by not acting. Bartleby's will is the will of indirect negation, of the agency of not acting, which enacts an increasing process of depersonalization.

While Melville is arguing against Emerson, he simultaneously targets the alienated working situation of clerks in organizations, which they entered into, at least potentially, on their own free will. It is worth repeating that the story is set on Wall Street and that office life was a relatively recent urban phenomenon in the 1850s. The sociopolitical context is the liberal concept of contractualism, implying the freedom to enter into the contracted relationship. Tocqueville claimed with regard to the situation of American women in marriage that they are bound particularly tightly to the marriage contract as they enter into it on their own free will, not having been forced into the bond by their families (1988: 290). Similarly, Bartleby is not coerced into the working position. He could leave and is even challenged several times to do so. Nevertheless, the working situation is asymmetric; Bartleby is a subaltern and on the receiving side of orders. It is a capitalist organization in which Bartleby

---

9   The exact quote is: "In fact, what we mean by information – the elementary unit of information – is a difference which makes a difference, and it is able to make a difference because the neural pathways along which it travels and is continually transformed are themselves provided with energy" (1972: 465).
10 Thus Deleuze's claim as to Bartleby's messianic character does not seem plausible: "A schizophrenic vocation: even in his catatonic or anorexic state, Bartleby is not the patient, but the doctor of a sick America, the Medicine-Man, the new Christ or the brother to us all" (1974: 90).

prefers not to copy-read, a system that is also harshly criticized in the character of the lawyer.[11] As Jane Desmarais remarks, political readings locate "the story within the context of America's capitalist expansion. [...] 'Bartleby' is an allegory of modern America and the failure of democracy to preserve the individual's right and freedom to choose" (2001: 3-4).[12] Yet, she herself argues that "Bartleby's lifelessness is both the product and outcome of a sterile bureaucracy which as an external reality has little to do with the natural impulses and desires of the individual" (ibid: 4).

Summing up, Bartleby's passive resistance constitutes a strong version of nonconforming self-determination and can be read as the over-extension of Transcendentalism's call for radical self-reliance. It tips over into its opposite. Yet, as Franz Fanon writes with reference to Hegel's master-slave dialectic, only by an act of resistance can the slave come to a consciousness of himself (1994: 215). As Bartleby does not resist in any other way than refusing to act at all, there is no place for him to survive in society, and not even in prison.

The Pale King: Indifference, Attention, and the Necessity of Choice

"If anyone was going to become the Melville of the corporatised society, the post-natural environment, the pharmacologically altered human landscape we all now inhabit, [Wallace] was the one" (Lasdun 2011). David Foster Wallace's novel can productively be brought into a conversation with "Bartleby," as it focuses on choice as the central category of Americans' relationship with their society as well as in their daily life. Individualism as a dimension of liberal humanism is critically explored with a look at contemporary culture. Written about one hundred and fifty years later, the cultural and technological context has changed, of course, but the limits of freedom are still of central interest. Again, they are tested in an office; work and its existential meaning for

---

11 The story is highly complex and multi-faceted. Thus one could also legitimately argue, as some interpretations do, that Bartleby as a dependent laborer in capitalism does not have a choice other than working in this office or that factory. I, nevertheless, want to stress the self-determined act of not resisting.

12 Pointing to the concrete political context, Leo Marx writes that "The documents [Bartleby has to proofread] are mortgages and title-deeds, and they incorporate the official version of social (property) relations as they exist at the time" (1974: 361). "[F]rom Bartleby's point of view, Wall Street *was* America" (ibid: 369).

the individual are the focus. In his novels, Wallace struggled with the entertainment culture and the repressively tolerant society, in literary terms, postmodernism, he participated in himself. His dilemma was to fight a condition he was deeply immersed in and could not get beyond without falling back onto a previous conservative position which he also found problematic. His point of attack is the ironic stance of established postmodernism. Working towards what he called "new sincerity" meant finding new grounds for engagement beyond postmodernist irony, for existential meaning without falling prey to current ideologies and faiths.[13] While the novel remained unfinished, it is a thought-provoking attempt at thinking through some of the contradictions of American society and of individualism as an implicit or explicit ideology.

Let me take a statement by one of the characters who is speaking about "liberal individualism" as a starting point: "Corporations are getting better and better at seducing us into thinking the way they think [...] Wanting and having instead of thinking and making" (Wallace 2011: 132-33). The speaker criticizes a lack of communal responsibility which he diagnoses in the contemporary United States, attributes this attitude to the functioning of corporations – defined by Ambrose Bierce as "an ingenious device for obtaining individual profit without individual responsibility" (1993: 19), – and laments a shift from creation and production to consumption. The general thrust of Wallace's critique of US-American culture, then, concerns a lack of civic virtues and communal engagement as well as the dominance of the entertainment industry over individual creativity.

The Pale King has many characters make statements of social commentary that are more discursive than narrative and carry the novel's argument: "The sixties were America's starting to decline into decadence and selfish individualism – the Me generation" (2011: 134). "What my problem is is the way it seems that we as individual citizens have adopted a corporate attitude. That our ultimate obligation is to ourselves" (ibid: 139). Individualism as a grounding dimension of a society of free citizens is regarded as having turned into self-centered solipsism in Wallace's analysis, a danger Tocqueville already diagnosed in the early 19th century. In contrast to Melville's analysis, exagger-

---

13   What Wallace does not clearly reflect is that radical irony often leads to a tipping point where a person jumps into a belief system of certainty. Yet he explicitly refers to Søren Kierkegaard's notion of the jump into (meaning conferring) faith – which is logically paradoxical, as you can only know what comes beyond after you have jumped, but then different rules apply, as Kierkegaard argued against Leibniz.

ated individualism here is chastised as rather trivial egotism. The individual in Wallace's view has become self-centered rather than self-reliant in the Emersonian sense. The organization staged and interrogated in *The Pale King* is the Tax Agency (IRS) in Peoira, Illinois, at the beginning of the 21st century, and the focus is on work in an office there. Both Melville's lawyer's office and the IRS are intricately linked with American social and political values, as the law is present in every niche of public and private life in the US. The tax code, which is the legal basis and reference of the work done at the IRS, is an important interface between the individual and the state for American citizens. It is here that responsibility, loyalty, and the egotism of the individual might clash: "given that the federal tax system still proceeds largely on voluntary compliance, the psychology of the Service's relation to taxpayers is complex" (ibid: 243). Therefore, "If you know the position a person takes on taxes, you can determine [his] whole philosophy" (ibid: 84). According to Wallace, an individual's relationship to the state, and moreover to the collective, can best be observed in his or her morals regarding paying taxes. While taxes seem to be among the topics least suitable to novelistic treatment, Wallace regards this social practice as being symptomatic of American society in general. He presents it in order to probe Americans' collective spirit on the one hand, and working conditions in the IRS as a test case for self-discipline as opposed to ironic indifference, paying attention to boring tasks which are nevertheless important for the existence of the state and society on the other. He stages different aspects of work in these offices to question agency within closely circumscribed boundaries which he contrasts with the endlessly open choices postmodern consumerism seems to offer. Acting in a sincere way for him is functioning within a manageable and clearly bounded context. Similarly to Bartleby, the working conditions are not physically severe, but almost unbearable because of extreme monotony. We observe laboring bodies and minds going through extremely repetitive motions. These do not affect the body directly, like severe working conditions in a factory, yet the doubling of a high level of concentration and an even higher level of extreme repetitiveness of tasks that do not challenge the office worker cognitively, affect him or her in ways that involve self-aggression and even an existential *horror vacui*.

A central character in the novel, Chris Fogle, symbolizes what Wallace satirizes as a postmodern attitude, as he constantly watches TV and shows a non-committal indifference towards everything. In college he "was a total conformist to the late seventies standards of so-called nonconformity" (ibid: 166). Fogle is presented by Wallace to critically stage the dangers and paradoxes of non-conformism spilling over into a consumer attitude coopted and controlled by the entertainment industry (cf. Frank 1997). He becomes aware of his ironic, yet also nihilist passivity when he unexpectedly finds himself in the Advanced Tax lecture course of a Jesuit substitute lecturer. He realizes that "It had something to do with paying attention and the ability to choose what I paid attention to, and to be aware of that choice, the fact that it's a choice" (Wallace 2011: 189). Moreover, "part of what was so galvanizing was the substitute's diagnosis of the world and reality as already essentially penetrated and formed, [...] and that now a meaningful choice lay in herding, corralling, and organizing that torrential flow of info" (ibid: 242). The American Dream of an ever-possible new beginning is deconstructed as an illusion. There are no longer any open frontiers left, or as Melville wrote, there is no new world, as this is the new world already.[14]

Fogle realizes that indifference and boredom had been the main coordinates of his life so far. He did not experience coercion or external pressure but rather too much freedom which left him without any compass to navigate on the ocean of options to choose from. The pattern of his behavior resonates with Georg Simmel's analysis of the blasé attitude as the response he observed in people living in the new metropoles around the turn of the last century (1964: 413). Fogle suspects that rather than having been hypercool, he may actually have been "the worst kind of nihilist [...] My essential response to everything was 'Whatever'" (Wallace 2011: 154). David J. Michael comments that "This is almost certainly an allusion to Melville's 'Bartleby the Scrivener'" (2012: 50). Fogle's reflections may be read as Wallace's assessment of postmodernism's stance of "anything goes":

> That I drifted and quit because nothing meant anything, no one choice was really better [...] I was free to choose 'whatever' because it didn't really matter. But this, too, was because of something I chose [...] If I wanted to matter – even just to myself – I would have to be less free, by deciding to choose in some kind of definite way. (Wallace 2011: 225-26)

The overabundance of choices is seen as the main hindrance to meaningful commitment. The lecturer is the first genuine authority figure Fogle ever meets. He explains "commitment as the loss of options [...] the death of childhood's limitless possibility, of the flatter of choice without duress" (ibid: 230)

---

14   In Clarel he wrote: "Columbus ended earth's romance: / No New World to mankind remains!" (1991: 461).

and emphasizes that "Enduring tedium over real time in a confined space is what real courage is" (ibid: 231). Accepting boredom is a reversal of mindless distraction and may set creative energies free.[15] It is, of course, no coincidence that he is a Jesuit; the implicit reference is to the Jesuits' militant religious decisionism.

A central topic of the novel is the experience of boredom and its relation to the capacity of paying attention, as opposed to be endlessly diverted by a multiplicity of ever-new information, a topic certainly relevant in today's world of social media as well. Yet the costs of paying attention are high: "Lock a fellow in a windowless room to perform rote tasks just tricky enough to make him have to think, but still rote, tasks involving numbers that connected to nothing he'd ever see or care about, a stack of tasks that never went down, and nail a clock to the wall where he can see it, and just leave the man there to his mind's own devices" (ibid: 381). The numbers and quantities the office workers have to handle seem to be completely separated from their own experience and lifeworld, thus leaving them suspended in a complete void. Numbers as media for navigating reality may be helpful but can also be completely alienating. Here they are deprived of any meaning and tend to lose any semantic value for the clerks. While such a predicament looks like torture, the novel reevaluates the experience by quoting "Kierkegaard's *Strange that boredom, in itself so staid and solid, should have such power to set in motion*" (ibid: 387). Michael points out that "The condition that Wallace diagnoses is best thought of as cultural acedia […] his generation needed to grow up […] But the view of adulthood that comes through in […] *The Pale King*, is ambivalent, both gesturing towards the adult responsibility while recoiling in terror at the boredom that attends it" (2012: 47). The ambivalence is not dissolved, and might be one reason why the novel remained unfinished.

Does the novel completely endorse the critique of a postmodern cultural attitude, or is Fogle's moment of insight itself presented from an ironic distance? The lecturer is described in rather unbecoming ways; he "wore an archaically conservative dark gray suit whose boxy look might have been actual flannel" (Wallace 2011: 217). Is he the typical 1950s "Man in the Gray Flannel Suit"?[16] The novel stresses how much Fogle is impressed by the Jesuit teacher,

---

15 Thomas Pynchon's original title for *Gravity's Rainbow* was *Mindless Pleasures*!
16 Cf. *The Man in the Gray Flannel Suit* (1956). Film, directed by Nunnally Johnson, based on the novel by Sloan Wilson (1955).

but it also ridicules him in his description. Moreover, Fogle's father is retrospectively praised for his secondary virtues, in particular his discipline, yet he is also ironized in the description of his family life and through an absurd death. Wallace's considerations in his often-quoted commencement speech at Kenyon College 2005 certainly highlight commitment as the panacea for escaping culturally induced solipsism (Wallace 2009). However, one could argue that the juxtaposition of discursive, almost essayistic passages, and narrative in a postmodernist manner, including sometimes almost surrealistic fictional situations, can be taken as a symptom of the ambivalence Wallace shows towards his critique of attitudes and aesthetics he in many ways shares. Thus, Wallace advocates a less self-centered attitude, yet satirizes it at the same time in *The Pale King*.

What are the consequences for our analysis of individualism and liberalism, laboring bodies, and organizations? *The Pale King* criticizes self-centered non-conformism and chastises the US-American entertainment culture for offering an overabundance of choices free of consequences. These choices, however, are no longer the ones political liberalism envisioned and leveled against limitations through orders and coercion by powerful authorities, but rather neoliberalism's consumer choices. Too many choices lead to no choice at all, or, as Fogle puts it, "whatever" (Wallace 2011: 154, 225). The solution to focus on any commitment to escape boredom in most cases leads to more boredom in the office, at least in the novel. Wallace's search for a "new sincerity" (cf. Kelly 2010), through which he hoped to escape the limits of postmodernism's irony, resonates with notions of a fixed, pre-structured framework of values, such as existed in hierarchically ordered societies, for which the Jesuit could be an appropriate metaphor. It was precisely against such inflexible values systems with their strong emphasis on 'honor' based on social stratification in contrast to individual 'dignity', against which the bourgeoisie rebelled by emphasizing authenticity as counter strategy (Trilling 1973). Yet Wallace himself does not give up irony as an aesthetic position, nor does his criticism leave individualism as implicit presupposition behind. The critique of non-conformism and the striving for attentiveness are still attempts at improving the characters' individual lives and provoking individual creativity, and they are presented as persons without communal links. Alkon's criticism of Emerson and Agamben might apply here as well, namely that they "are attempting to think against the logic of sovereignty, from within that logic; and they are therefore attempting to think the impossible" (210: 141). I want to suggest, somewhat provocatively, that Melville already analyzed what Wallace attempted to understand.

To conclude, Melville and Wallace explore, deconstruct, yet implicitly themselves presuppose the US-American individualist *apriori*, an epistemological individualism that is as often implied and unacknowledged as the modern, historically evolved self-identity and its premises. An important result of my investigation is that the critique of liberal humanism here, and most of the time, itself depends on the premises of liberal humanism. While Melville diagnoses the possible *aporias* of an overextended individualism without pointing to any alternative, Wallace explicitly criticizes ironic self-centeredness as a dimension of postmodern culture and searches for alternatives, yet does not positively endorse more communal arrangements. Office, organization, and corporation intersect in working situations with personhood, bodies, and the individual in complex ways that can be analyzed as posthumanist in the sense that any notion of autonomy and self-reliance is severely put into question. Posthumanism, then, is just a recent formulation of a condition that has existed for a long time, has been observed before in literature and theory, and stands in stark contrast to excessively optimistic US-American self-descriptions. To paraphrase Karl Marx, history is made by humans but not under conditions they chose themselves (1952: 151).[17] The laboring body is one of the decisive sites where the struggles and tension between social structure, will, and the self are fought and experienced.

Works Cited

Agamben, Giorgio (1999): "Bartleby, or Contingency." In: *Potentialities: Collected Essays in Philosophy*, Stanford, CA: Stanford UP, 243-271.

Alkon, Gabriel (2010): "Freedom and Integral Will: The Abandonment of Sovereign Power in Emerson, Melville, and Agamben." In: *Telos* 152 (Fall): 127-44.

Bateson, Gregory (1972): *Steps to an Ecology of the Mind*, Chicago: University of Chicago Press.

---

17   "Die Menschen machen ihre eigene Geschichte, aber sie machen sie nicht aus freien Stücken, nicht unter selbstgewählten, sondern unter unmittelbar vorgefundenen, gegebenen und überlieferten Umständen."

Bierce, Ambrose (1993 [1911]): *The Devil's Dictionary*, New York: Dover Publications.

Danter, Stefan/Reichardt, Ulfried/Schober, Regina (2016): "Theorizing the Quantified Self: Self-Knowledge and Posthumanist Agency in Contemporary US-American Literature." In: *Digital Culture & Society* 2.1, Pablo Abend/Matthias Fuchs (eds.), Special Issue "Quantified Selves and Statistical Bodies," pp. 53-70.

Deleuze, Gilles (1979): "Bartleby; or the Formula." In: *Essays Critical and Clinical*, trans. Daniel W. Smith/Michael A. Greco, Minneapolis: U of Minnesota P, pp. 68-90.

Desmarais, Jane (2001): "Anorexic and Passive Resistance: A Literary Case Study." In: *Soundings: A Journal of Politics and Culture* 18, pp. 82-93. Online.

Dumont, Louis (1983): *Essais sur l'individualisme: Une perspective anthropologique sur l'idéologie moderne*, Paris: Éditions du Seuil.

Emerson, Ralph Waldo (1994): "Self-Reliance." In: *The Norton Anthology of American Literature*. Fourth Edition, Volume 1, New York, London: W. W. Norton, pp. 1045-1062.

Fanon, Franz (1994 [1952]): *Black Skin, White Masks: The Experience of a Black Man in a White World*, trans. Charles Lam Markmann, New York Grove Press.

Fluck, Winfried (2009): "The Humanities in the Age of Expressive Individualism and Cultural Radicalism." In: Laura Bieger/Johannes Völz (eds.), *Romance with America? Essays on Culture, Literature, and American Studies*, Heidelberg: Winter, pp. 49-68.

Foucault, Michel (2008): *The Birth of Biopolitics: Lecture at the College de France, 1978-79*, Michel Senellart (ed.), trans. Graham Burchell. Houndsmille: Palgrave Macmillan.

Frank, Thomas (1997): *The Conquest of Cool: Business Culture, Counterculture, and The Rise of Hip Consumerism*, Chicago, IL: U of Chicago P.

Heller, Thomas C./ Wellbery, David E. (1986): "Introduction." In: Thomas C. Heller/Morton Sosna/David E. Wellbery (eds.), *Reconstructing Individualism: Autonomy, Individuality, and the Self in Western Thought*, Stanford, CA: Stanford UP, pp. 1-15.

Kelly, Adam (2010): "David Foster Wallace and the New Sincerity in American Fiction." In: David Hering, (ed.), *Consider David Foster Wallace: Critical Essays*, Sideshow Media Group Press, 131-46.

Krause, Sharon, R. (2015): *Freedom Beyond Sovereignty: Reconstructing Liberal Individualism*, Chicago: U of Chicago P.

Lasdun, James (2011): "The Pale King by David Foster Wallace – Review," *The Guardian*, 16 April, 2011. Online.

Locke, John (1980 [1690]): *Second Treatise of Government*, C. B. Macpherson (ed. and introd.), Indianapolis: Hackett.

Maine, Sir Henry Sumner (1986 [1861]): *Ancient Law: Its Connection with the Early History of Society and Its Relation to Modern Ideas*, 10th ed., reprint, New York: Dorset.

Marx, Karl (1852): "Der achtzehnte Brumaire des Louis Bonaparte." In: *MEW* Bd. 8.

Marx, Leo (1974): "Melville's Parable of the Walls." In: Paul Gerhard Buchloh/Hartmut Krüger (eds.), *Herman Melville*, Darmstadt: Wissenschaftliche Buchgesellschaft.

Melville, Herman (1994): "Bartleby, the Scrivener. A Story of Wall-Street." In: *The Norton Anthology of American Literature*, Fourth Edition, Volume 1, New York, London: W. W. Norton, pp. 2234-2258.

___ (1991 [1876]): *Clarel: A Poem and Pilgrimage in the Holy Land*, Evanston and Chicago: Northwestern UP & Newberry Library, 4.21.

Michael, David J. (2012): "Pale King or Noonday's Demon? Acedia, The Pale King, and David Foster Wallace's Moral Vision," Master's Thesis in Literature, Culture, and Media, Centre for Languages and Literature, Lund University. Online.

Nassehi, Armin (2012): "The Person as an Effect of Communication." In: Sabine Maasen/ Barbara Sutter (eds.), *On Willing Selves: Neoliberal Politics vis-à-vis the Neuroscientific Challenge*, Houndsmills: Palgrave Macmillan, pp. 100-20.

Newfield, Christopher (1996): *The Emerson Effect: Individualism and Submission in America*, Chicago: U of Chicago P.

Reichardt, Ulfried (2018): "Self-Observation in the Digital Age: The Quantified Self. Neoliberalism, and the Paradoxes of Contemporary Individualism." In: *Amerikastudien/American Studies* 63.1, pp. 99-117.

Simmel, Georg (1964 [1903]): "The Metropolis and Mental Life." In: Kurt H. Wolff (trans., ed. and introd.), *The Sociology of Georg Simmel*, New York: Free Press, pp. 409-24.

The Man in the Gray Flannel Suit (1956), Nunnally Johnson (dir.), based on the novel by Sloan Wilson (1955). Film.

Thoreau, Henry David (1994): "Resistance to Civil Government." *The Norton Anthology of American Literature*, Fourth Edition, Volume 1, New York, London: W. W. Norton, pp.1704-1719.

Tocqueville, Alexis de (1988 [1835/40]): *Democracy in America*, Cumberland House, Hertfordshire: Wordsworth.

Trachtenberg, Alan (2007 [1982]): *The Incorporation of America: Culture and Society in the Gilded Age*, New York: Hill and Wang.

Trilling, Lionel (1973): *Sincerity and Authenticity*. The Charles Eliot Norton Lectures, Cambridge, MA: Harvard UP.

Wallace, David Foster (2011): *The Pale King*. London, New York, et al.: Penguin.

___ (2009): *This Is Water: Some Thoughts, Delivered on a Significant Occasion, about Living a Compassionate Life*, New York: Little, Brown and Company (Kenyon College Commencement Speech).

Watzlawick, Paul/Beavin, Janet H./Jackson, Don D. (1967): *Pragmatics of Human Communication: A Study of Interactional Patterns, Pathologies, and Paradoxes*, New York: W. W. Norton.

"To Be Reckoned in the Gross": Corporate Storytelling and Quantified Selves in Joshua Ferris's *Then We Came to the End*

Stefanie Mueller

"Ten Things We Know to be True": Corporate Storytelling in the Information Age

When we look at the development of corporate culture in the United States in the course of the 20th century, one of its most striking aspects is the growing importance of stories. This seems almost self-evident on the level of brands and consumer goods. Obviously, we may say, advertising has seen the value in selling us not just individual products but entire brands, creating positive brand identities that can outlast companies long after the (however substantial) material basis for such stories has vanished. It is less self-evident, perhaps, on the level of financial management, where business administrators deal with "forecasted revenues, operating income, and cash flows" – in other words, with numbers which are often considered as the opposite of stories (Damodaran 2017: 1). However, as corporate finance specialist Aswath Damodaran has admitted, "one of the most important lessons I have learned is that a valuation that is not backed up by a story is both soulless and untrustworthy" (ibid: vii). Likewise, stories and storytelling have become a central tool on the level of internal management: with the decentralization of corporate management, stories – in the shape of corporate philosophies, for example – serve the goals of horizontal management by building loyalty among employees and making the abstract corporate entity knowable for its members as well as for affiliates. In other words, they foster a sense of *individual* identification with the company, despite the fact that such corporate management actually aims at employees *en masse*. Therefore, when we consider this increasing importance of stories alongside numbers for the management (and ultimately maintenance) of corporate capitalism, it becomes clear how central an analysis of corporate stories and of the identities and practices that they shape is to our understanding of the corporate workplace in the information age.

If we look for an example of the type of stories US American corporations like to tell today, we can turn to Google, a company who is familiar to many internet users and whose search engine has become a central gateway to information and knowledge on the web. Google's corporate philosophy is commonly known under its motto "Don't be evil," but the official title reads "Ten things we know to be true": "We first wrote these '10 things' when Google was just a few years old. From time to time we revisit this list to see if it still holds true. We hope it does – and you can hold us to that." In effect, this list comprises the core values of Google's corporate philosophy. The image (or brand) that emerges from the list highlights a youthful company culture ("9. You can be serious without a suit") that is user-oriented ("1. Focus on the user and all else will follow"), dedicated not only to democratic ideals ("4. Democracy on the web works," and "8. The need for information crosses all borders") but to business ethics as well ("6. You can make money without doing evil"). What is more, its shifting use of first person plural and second person singular ('we' and 'you') in its corporate philosophy contributes to the impression that not only the corporation and its employees can strive to excel ("10. Great just isn't good enough"), but that, somehow, we as users can (and perhaps should), too.

That corporate mission statements contain "virtues that [stand] apart from purely business values" is not a new phenomenon, of course (Marchand 2001: 2). As historian Roland Marchand has shown, the rise of corporate storytelling and brand-management was a response to the "crisis of legitimation" that large industrial corporations experienced at the beginning of the 20th century and which was a consequence of the sheer size of those organizations (ibid). The complexity and power of such corporations suggested to the public that they were wielding an influence and taking over positions that were traditionally reserved for institutions (the family, the church, the school). To justify this place in US society, corporations had to model themselves after these institutions and had to, in Marchand's words, "ris[e] above mere commercialism and remov[e] the taint of selfishness" and began to tell stories of public service and American values (ibid).[1] In the 21st

---

[1] Marchand describes a focus on "small-town" American and "[a] contrived sentimentalism" by the end of World War II (2001: 5).

century, furthermore, storytelling and branding used such values strategically, serving to maintain and improve coherence within the organization as well as customer loyalty to the organization. While customers seek unique experiences through products, employees seek stories that they can identify with and that give them meaning.[2]

Therefore, the first person plural in which such corporate mission statements are written and which orient the narratives seek to create coherence and consent.[3] They seek to present a unified and committed company, both to internal and external audiences, which is expressed, for example, in the tidiness and orderliness of the list itself: "Ten things we know to be true." However, the shifting pronouns of Google's corporate philosophy have yet another effect, because the corporate *we* and *you* of Google appear to not only be speaking to the company and its employees but also to the users reading the list. Such shifting of pronouns suggests that under the neoliberal regime of the 21st century, corporations are enticing us to become more like them, to become our best selves. "You can make money without doing evil." In fact, novels such as Dave Eggers's 2013 *The Circle* explore the extent to which the corporate voice has become a Siren: how corporate culture can be seductive and how we may desire to emulate the corporate entity and become a member of it. Joshua Ferris's earlier novel *Then We Came to the End* (2007) also explores the lure of the "corporate we," but to a drastically different effect. Instead of a seductive glossy surface, Ferris's novel presents us with the corporate body as "a collection of messy human beings" (Ferris qtd. in Clare 2014: 191). In the process, Ferris certainly puts the dread back into being part of an organization.

Written almost entirely in the first person plural, what Ferris has called the "corporate we" in an interview, the novel follows the fate of an office of copywriters at a Chicago advertising company in the months leading up to 9/11 and therefore also during a period that is known as the end of the dotcom bubble

---

2   As Fog et al. put it, "Employees increasingly demand that their employer has values that they themselves can identify and feel comfortable with. We would rather earn slightly less and feel good about what we do for a living. It needs to make sense as part of the bigger picture" (2010: 23).

3   In *Narrative and Numbers*, Aswath Damodaran admits that it is the first time that he chooses to write a business guide in the first person singular. While this is obviously a different genre, the reason he gives is instructive: "Rather than use the royal 'we' and force you, as readers, to adopt my stories, I felt it would be much more honest (and more fun) to let you pick apart my stories and disagree with them" (2017: viii).

(ibid). Therefore, the company is going through layoffs. "We were fractious and overpaid," it begins. "Our mornings lacked promise" (Ferris 2007: 3). By focusing on an advertising company, Ferris takes his readers into the heart of corporate story-spinning. Advertising is an occupation that is often deemed part of the creative economy, but here it emerges as dull and grotesquely removed from reality. In general, the novel's capitalist critique is not subtle, such as in its equation of corporate capitalism to cancer. Yet, its value lies in how it explores the employees' experience of being reduced to numbers, to productive (or rather unproductive) bodies, and thus, "to be reckoned in the gross," as the novel's epitaph by Ralph Waldo Emerson puts it.

In fact, *Then We Came to the End* has been called "a prime example of the office novel" and "reflects the nature of employment in the information age" (Russell 2018: 319-320). While it does not reckon with the impact of social media in the same way as Eggers's *The Circle* does, it does, for instance, explore fully the experience of working under heightened conditions of sociability and connectivity. Unlike novels that focus more on the changes in the workplace, which were brought on by social media and new digital technology, the intention of *Then We Came to the End* is to tell the story of our changing relation to work, in an age in which the latter is not only becoming increasingly immaterial, but also increasingly dominated by the twin imperatives of innovation and creativity. Moreover, it contributes to our inquiry into the relationship between the quantified self and laboring bodies by approaching this relationship metaphorically and aesthetically. Metaphorically, in that it explores a situation in which the employees are reduced to numbers, because the decision to let employees go is based on their economic potential as well as their cost for the company; aesthetically, in that the novel explores this experience of being "reckoned in the gross" through a specific narrative mode, the "corporate we."

In the pages that follow, I take a closer look at the quantified selves of the creative economy in *Then We Came to the End*. I am particularly interested in how Ferris conveys the experience of being quantified, of being economically, socially, and narratively "reckoned in the gross." In addition, I want to show to what effect Ferris uses the narrative voice of corporate storytelling, which is inarguably one of the genre's most conspicuous characteristics. While it has been said that literature can offer alternative epistemologies and counter models,[4] I argue that Ferris' novel may be offering an alternative, but one

---

4 See, for example, Danter et al. 2016: 64.

that remains firmly within the neoliberal imaginary. By showing how *Then We Came to the End* fits into an older tradition of anti-corporate and anti-collective rhetoric, I argue that, while the novel may be criticizing labor and selfhood under corporate capitalism, it effectively praises labor and selfhood under entrepreneurial capitalism.

We-narration and Immaterial Labor in the Corporate Cubicle

In its depiction of the office's work, the novel evokes many of the well-worn tropes, even stereotypes, about the creative economy. These range from the high value that is placed on lifestyle and lifestyle attributes, such as employees keeping a surfboard desk, a bike, and a gumball machine in their offices; to the company's quiet condoning of quirks and regressive, juvenile activities, such as swivel chair races; and to the pampering of employees with perks, such as flowers, free bagels, and company logo polo shirts. "We worked in the creative department developing ads and we considered our ad work creative" (Ferris 2007: 27). However, most of this creativity draws on an increasingly "loose" way of playing with words, such as when they are asked to update the package design for chocolate cookies and one of the copywriters simply invents an ingredient (ibid: 329).[5]

> The trick was to play loose with words. [...] When we said, 'Don't miss out on these great savings!' we really meant we gotta unload these fuckers fast. [...] Words and meanings were almost always at odds with us. We knew it, you knew it, they knew it, we all knew it. The only words that ever meant a goddamn were, 'We're really sorry about this, but we're going to have to let you go.' (ibid: 329)

Increasingly, however, this "loose" way of playing with words is shown to influence the employees' perception of themselves and their environment, such as when the gossip they tell one another becomes ever more outrageous and elaborate. In fact, it appears that their grip on reality itself – being able to distinguish between what is real and what is not, or what is appropriate and what is not – becomes tenuous.

Since it is grotesquely far removed from real world concerns, the novel suggests that their work is not only immaterial but also essentially pointless,

---

5   Cf. Ferris 2007: 48-49.

and the number of characters suffering from physical and mental illnesses attests to its destructive import. While it may sound innocent and has been considered funny, the majority of the copywriters put more energy into avoiding work than actually doing it.[6] Benny Shassburger, for example, promises one of the building's security guards to teach him how to use Photoshop, but the promise turns out to be a scheme that will allow Benny to spend an entire day at the office and actually finish his assignment without ever touching the computer himself. More serious is the case of Carl Garbedian, who begins to steal a coworker's medication and is admitted to a hospital for "toxic poisoning" (ibid: 144). Finally, there is Lynn Mason, one of the company's partners and the head of the creative department. Lynn is presented as a sympathetic character, one of the few who maintain moral standards and show basic human kindness towards others. But she is also presented as childless and as falling for the wrong type of man, a female Robinson Crusoe with a capitalist work ethic and a cat named "Friday," who eventually succumbs to capitalism's malign influence: Lynn is first diagnosed with breast cancer and finally dies of ovarian cancer (ibid: 197).

The equation of (corporate) capitalism to cancer is also manifest in the pro-bono project that the department is asked to take on at the beginning of the novel. Not only a near-impossible project, it is also symbolic of the kind of loss of reality described earlier.

> 'Think of it as an awareness campaign, okay? Only you're not making the target audience aware of anything, you're just making them laugh.' When that still made little sense, he added, 'Okay, if we're selling something, we're selling comfort and hope to the cancer patient through the power of laughter. How's that?' (ibid: 176)

Of course, there is absolutely nothing funny about cancer, and the assignment's origins are dubious to begin with. As one of the characters observes, "The point I'm trying to make [...] is that there is really very little humor in a diagnosis of cancer. And what humor there is, is humorous only in the context of a whole lot of sadness. Now, how can we be expected to do that with a stock photo and a ten-word headline?" (ibid: 184). The point that the novel is trying to make, however, is that this is precisely what the corporate spin doctors of

---

6   Alison Russell has called the novel "comic but also heartbreaking," and, with reference to Benny Shassburger, comments on how Ferris puts his characters in "ludicrous situations" (2018: 319, 321).

advertising companies constantly do: promote the benefits and the products of a system whose ideal of a happy harmony between supply and demand has become malignant and cancerous. Originating in the organic metaphors that have become standard in depictions of capitalism – such as *the evolution of companies*, the *corporate life cycle*, or *the company DNA* – the novel thus expresses its critique of (corporate) capitalism as a systemic disease of contemporary US culture.[7] Yet, the main line of criticism that the novel hurls at corporate capitalism is demonstrated by its presentation of the office team and the use of we-narration.

A conspicuous feature of the workplace described in the novel is the atmosphere of rumors and even paranoia. When their colleague Tom Mota has been let go, for example, his antagonistic behavior and his e-mail messages begin to spark the suspicion that Tom may return to the office in some threatening way. This, of course, proves true to some extent, as Tom does indeed return to the office carrying a paintball gun, which his panicked colleagues mistake for a deadly weapon. The novel suggests that, to some degree, this atmosphere is fostered by not knowing who would be let go next: "We hated not knowing who was next to walk Spanish down the hall. How would our bills get paid? And where would we find new work?" (ibid: 160). But, ultimately, this problem of not knowing is attached more generally to the company itself: "We were deeply concerned about who was next, and what criteria for dismissal the partners were operating under" (ibid: 91). In the end, however, it becomes evident that the criteria for dismissal are based on the employees' productivity and therefore their economic value for the company.

It is in this shift from their imagined value as creative individuals to their economic value as mere employees that their experience of quantification for the "corporate we" begins to unfold: "We were corporate citizens, buttressed by advanced degrees and padded by corporate fat. We were above the fickle market forces of overproduction and mismanaged inventory. What we didn't consider was that in a downturn, *we* were the mismanaged inventory [...]" (ibid: 19). The novel's epigraph by Emerson alludes to this experience: "Is it not the chief disgrace in the world, not to be a unit; – not to be reckoned one character; – [...] but to be reckoned in the gross, in the hundred, or the thousand, of the party, the section, to which we belong ... [?]". The term "inventory"

---

7   Richard Powers' *Gain* (1998) is the canonical example of a text in which the organicist rhetoric of economics is taken at face value and serves as the basis for a novel that juxtaposes the story of a female cancer patient with a corporation.

is charged even further as some employees begin to rearrange or even steal pieces of actual inventory and come to realize that the company keeps track of its property: "'They know everything! They knew everything we'd taken!'" (ibid: 32, italics in the original). Bereft of their value as individuals, they experience reification as they are abstracted into numbers on a corporate spreadsheet, numbers that can be less relevant than bookshelves and swivel chairs.

The group's overall response to this experience, which forms a large part of the novel's story, has sometimes been described as humorous, and may indeed have been perceived as such given that the book was a success.[8] Yet, a closer look at the group's responses suggest a different reading. Far from good-natured pranks, many of their actions are thoughtless, cruel, and sometimes even reprehensible. When their colleague Carl has been admitted to a hospital for depression and toxic poisoning, the group shows little sympathy:

> 'How are you feeling?' Carl had several big white pillows behind him and he was hooked up to an IV. 'Everything looks double,' he replied, 'and red.'
> We found that exceedingly hard to respond to. Everything looks double and red? Oh, well, that will go away, Carl. That's just a temporary side effect of *permanent brain damage*. (ibid: 145, emphasis in the original)

This sarcastic response to their sick coworker is yet outmatched by their behavior towards another colleague, whose child had been murdered and who, after her return to work, continues to show signs of deep grieving. After she is discovered at a McDonald's during her lunch break, where she quietly sits in the children's pool of plastic balls, remembering her daughter, her coworkers begin to stalk her. "Over the course of the next few weeks, practically everyone made it over to the McDonald's. [...] You see, everyone was talking about it. It wasn't something you could afford to miss. You *had* to go" (ibid: 131, emphasis in the original). Importantly, such episodes and incidents of cruelty are not presented as exceptions, but as the norm, and occur within a larger context of aggression, sexism, and casual racism.

Ferris's novel seeks to convey the powerful pull of the majoritarian perspective and how it subsumes even those characters who occasionally show kindness by employing a collective narrator or we-narration. In this way, he also succeeds in formally expressing the experience of being "reckoned in the

---

[8] As Ralph Clare notes, the book did well with readers in the US and was nominated for a National Book Award (2014: 190).

gross," of being de-individualized and considered a mass by a capitalist organization. In general, such we-narration is rarely sustained throughout an entire text and instead "tend[s] to be intermittent" (Fludernik 2017: 141); it is also more prevalent in factual than in fictional narratives.[9] Following the works of Alan Palmer and Monika Fludernik, we can also distinguish between inclusive and exclusive we-narrators, according to whether or not the addressee is included in the narration, and we can pay special attention to the relationship (and its development over time) between the collective narrator and individuals and/or subgroups.

Regarding the latter, a closer look at *Then We Came to the End* suggests that despite its consistent use and overall discursive dominance, the "corporate we" in Ferris's novel does not actually represent a unified group. Instead, the narrator appears to acknowledge the existence of subgroups. For example, in the following passage, the narrator acknowledges differences of gender and sexuality within the group explaining, "some of us had a hard time finding boyfriends. Some of us had a hard time fucking our wives" (Ferris 2007: 8). Likewise, in certain scenes, individual characters will be singled out and speak directly and immediately for themselves, whereas the we-narrator's words are reported.

> [W]e asked Yop what he was still doing here.
> 'I don't know,' he said. 'I can't go home, not yet. It doesn't feel right.'
> But should you really be *here?* we asked him. In Lynn's office?
> (ibid: 43, emphasis in the original)

In such scenes, the we-narration appears not only colloquial but even oral, such as through the use of italics that convey a conversational inflection ("But should you really be *here?*"). Yet, it also appears very much oriented by emotions, such as curiosity, fear, and resentment. In fact, one of the most divisive factors in the groups' daily routines is the competition among themselves and the feelings of jealousy. In a particularly crass example, a colleague displays initiative by presenting an idea for an ad campaign during the first project meeting and therefore way before the rest of the team had had a chance. "We looked at her with our chins floating in our coffee cups. Hold up! we wanted to shout. You can't have concepts. We haven't even double met yet!" (ibid: 109).

---

9   Ed Park's novel *Personal Days* (2008) is another example of we-narration and is often analyzed alongside *Then We Came to the End*. See, for example, Clare 2014.

Rather than a cooperative spirit that would also allow the group to develop collective agency beyond the short-term impulses of pranks, the group is driven by the "desire [...] to inspire jealousy, to defeat all the rest" (ibid). Accordingly, once they have all been fired and have started working at different companies, they lose touch.

The consistent use of the collective mode nonetheless evokes a distinct, recognizable voice, one that is recognizable because it is consistently aggressive, petty, and conceited: "We alone had perspective" (ibid: 115). In one particular exchange in which Lynn Mason tries to identify the individuals that have harassed a coworker, Benny Shassburger blames it on a *corps d'esprit* or *zeitgeist*.

> 'Give me a name, Benny,' she said. Benny deflected her request. 'It wasn't any one person, I don't think,' he said. 'It was more of like a zeitgeist.' [...] 'All due respect, Benny, [...] [i]f you have a name for me of who's responsible for this, I'd like you to say it.' 'I don't have a name for you,' he said. 'It was just something going around, a lot of people were talking about it. It was a joke, I thought.' 'Sounds like you must have a whole bunch of names for me, then,' replied Lynn. 'Yeah, but not one specific name,' said Benny. (ibid: 132)

Based on this and similar passages, scholars like Lisa Siraganian or Ralph Clare have argued that the novel does indeed try to convey the existence of a separate corporate entity, one that is more than the sum of its parts, a phrase most often used to explain the notion of a corporate legal person being separate from its agents and shareholders. For Clare, in particular, it is the novel's ending that most strongly indicates that, "contra Ferris, individuals (if we can still call them that) do *not* embody the corporation; *the corporation embodies them*" (2014: 191, emphasis in the original). Therefore, when the novel comes to a close, and one by one, all former employees have left, the narrator is still present to observe, "We were the only two left. Just the two of us, you and me" (Ferris 2007: 385).

The closing lines suggest that the implied reader has been part of the narration all along – and why shouldn't she/he/they be? Earlier in the novel, the narrator rhetorically asks, "there are, what, a hundred and fifty million of us in the workplace?" (ibid: 159). This is clearly more than the group of individual characters working for the advertising company and closer to what we could call US America's white-collar workforce. Even the distinction between "marketeers" and consumers appears to collapse eventually: "Our souls were as screwy and in need of guidance as all the rest. What were we but sheep like them? We *were* them. We were all *we* – whereas for so long we had believed ourselves to be just a bit above the others" (ibid: 234-235, emphasis in the original). Therefore, rather than the voice of a particular corporate body, the collective narrator appears to represent the spirit of those who are reckoned in the gross on a daily basis: "fractious and overpaid," it is the spirit of what David Riesman called "the lonely crowd" in 1950 and what Alexis de Tocqueville described as the "tyranny of the majority" in 1835 (2003: 292).

Corporate Stories Then and Now

As far apart as these two dates and authors may appear, if we want to understand *Then We Came to the End* and its representation of the "corporate we" and the workplace in the information age, we need to analyze the novel in the cultural tradition on which it draws. There is the more recent literary and social context of the postwar rise of corporate capitalism and consumer culture, of course, which scholars have previously noted.[10] But there is also an older cultural context, dating back to at least the early 19th century, in which corporate organization was already perceived as a threat to US individualism. Ferris's novel ultimately invests not only in the more recent strain but also revives that older tradition, with ambiguous results. On the one hand, the novel effectively criticizes corporate capitalism and in particular its de-individualizing tendencies; on the other, its only alternatives to corporate collectivization are entrepreneurialism and possessive individualism, which are alternatives (if we may call them so) that remain firmly rooted within the neoliberal imaginary.

The title of Ferris's novel is taken from the first line of Don DeLillo's *Americana* (1971), a novel that critically examines corporate business, consumer culture, and the advertising industry in the US in the 1970s. Nevertheless, *Then We Came to the End* is also a spiritual heir to the 1950s and 1960s and to the glory days of advertising which individual characters almost nostalgically allude to.[11] "'What has happened to America,'" the character Tom Mota asks his

---

10 Almost all interpretations of the novel mention this connection. See, for example, Clare 2014, Russell 2018, Siraganian 2017.
11 For another example of nostalgic returns to this period, we could turn to the American drama series *Mad Men*, which ran from 2007 to 2015. See, for example, Mueller 2014.

colleagues one day during lunch, during which he alone orders a martini, and elaborates,

> 'that the two-martini lunch has been replaced by this, this...' He gazed at us with disdainful shakes of his bulldog's head. '... this boothful of pansies, all dressed up in your khakis and sipping the same iced tea? Huh?' he said. 'What has happened?' He genuinely wanted to know. 'Didn't General Motors,' he continued lifting the new martini in the air delicately, so as not to spill, 'IBM, and Madison Avenue establish postwar American might upon the two-martini lunch?' (Ferris 2007: 116)

The flipside of this nostalgia, for an age in which ad-men decided the fate of the US economy over cocktails during lunch, is the novel's simultaneous investment in the period's anxieties over the corporate threat to American individualism. Sociological texts from the period such as David Riesman's *The Lonely Crowd* (1950) and William H. Whyte's *The Organization Man* (1956) claimed that corporate organization was to blame for rising conformity and diminishing individualism in middle class society.

From a literary perspective, *Then We Came to the End* also pays tribute to one of the best-known 20th century US "office novels," Sloane Wilson's *The Man in the Gray Flannel Suit* (1955). Wilson's novel tells the story of Tom Rath, who applies for a job at a public broadcasting corporation after his return from the Korean War. Tom has a young family to support, as well as an illegitimate child to think of, and hence, decides to join the corporate rat race, the competition for success within the organization. In the course of the novel, Tom begins to realize that such success means *selling out*: selling one's personality and thus authenticity to the corporation.[12] In the end, Tom is saved by real estate as an inheritance allows him to cut back hours and spend more time with his family. The characters that most clearly mirror Tom Rath in *Then We Came to the End* are Tom Mota and Carl Garbedian. The nostalgic Tom Mota takes the inverse route of Wilson's protagonist and leaves the corporate organization for the military (where he is ironically killed by "friendly fire"). Carl, on the other hand, retreats to suburbia and experiences the kind of regeneration that both novels show as only possible if based on older capitalist models.

This anxiety over individualism, moreover, was both gender-specific and race-oriented. It was white middle class men who felt threatened by the corporate reorganization of the workplace and "the looming threat or promise

---

12   See Russell 2018 and Siraganian 2017.

of social equality, whether personified in the black man, the immigrant, the New Woman, or the youngster bent on rising to the top" (Leverenz 2003: 1). In his study of the culture of early corporate America – the period from Reconstruction to World War I – David Leverenz has shown how "paternalism [as] a normative management style" defined the practice of the nation state as well as of corporate America and negotiated between the promise of social mobility and the desire to control the work force (ibid). "The rise of corporate and professional work threatened traditional norms of fatherhood and honor, two linked ideologies that for centuries had emboldened and constrained men's behavior" (ibid: 5). More recently, scholars working on emotions and capitalism have made a related argument, suggesting that the importance of social skills (empathy, communication, etc.) in corporate capitalism has contributed to "the process of redefining masculinity inside the workplace" (Illouz 2007: 15).[13]

That such redefinitions can rouse specific anxieties becomes evident in the following examples from *Then We Came to the End*. For instance, when Tom Mota insults his coworkers by using a homophobic slur because they no longer practice workplace rituals that were coded heterosexual and masculine; or when Lynn Mason, who is as far as we know the company's only female partner, succumbs to cancer of the reproductive organs after she is shown to have committed herself single-mindedly to success in the corporate rat race. Finally, it is also apparent when the "corporate we" casually considers whether they hated their ambitious colleague Karen "not because she was Korean but because she was a woman with strong opinions in a male-dominated world," only to eventually shrug the question off because "[o]ur diversity pretty much guaranteed it was a combination [of many reasons]" (Ferris 2007: 111, 113).[14]

---

13   Of course, Ferris's novel can also be read in the context of post-9/11 culture in the US. For example, Susan Faludi has argued that the trauma of the attack provoked a reflexive return to mythologized gender roles that allowed men to feel as powerful protectors but required women to retreat to the role of frail mothers and wives. Some of the novel's resentment towards women, as expressed in the examples below but also through not one but two characters who hate their wives and bond over this hatred (Tom and Carl), may also, to some extent, originate in this more recent socio-cultural development.

14   Few scholars have commented on this aspect of Ferris's work. Yet, Ruth Maxey writes, "Despite Ferris's longstanding personal awareness of being 'a white man in a white man's world' (qtd. in Fassler n. pag.) along with the concomitant political advantages and creative disadvantages of this position, there remains an uncomfortable relationship with racial difference and racialized language across his fiction" (2016: 211).

In this way, Ferris's novel takes part in a cultural tradition that not only associates corporate capitalism with the diminishment of individualism but also with the dethroning of white, heterosexual masculinity. In other words, the novel suggests that what gets lost in numbers is not only the individual but the white male possessive individual. However, *Then We Came to the End* presents one individual who appears to withstand the pull of the corporate collective, namely Joe Pope, a mid-level manager who reports directly to Lynn Mason. In the course of the novel, Joe becomes the target of increasingly serious pranks or rather workplace bullying. What raises the ire of the "corporate we" is the fact that Joe refuses to participate in office gossip and even small talk. "His inscrutability created a pervasive uneasiness. Why did he have to be such a dull mystery?" (ibid: 69). While his name suggests a holier-than-thou attitude that is explicitly criticized by one of the characters ("you sound like an elitist," ibid: 254), such implicit and explicit criticism of Joe Pope's position is literary lampshading. Ultimately, he is clearly portrayed as a sympathetic character because he acts rationally: he reflects on his words and deeds, and, in his interactions with his coworkers, he tries "to deal with each of [them] on an individual basis" (ibid: 134). Even more significantly, he reveals a formative experience from his high school days that supports the novel's depiction of collectives as negative.

In the second half of the novel, we learn that Joe Pope separates himself from the "corporate we" (and in fact, has a voice of his own like Lynn Mason) because of his memories of participating in the beating of a fellow student. Joe remembers how he joined a "clique in high school" that one day decided to punish a fellow student for what they considered a transgression of their code of conduct (ibid: 258). While he did not actively join the violence, Joe acknowledged that he did not help either but simply "watched." "Eventually they left him for his parents to find in the backyard – *we* left him, I mean. I ran away with everybody else" (ibid: 260, emphasis in the original). Ultimately, Joe's confession of his past experience with "mob" violence is presented as a crucial insight into the willpower necessary to resist the power of collectives in general (ibid: 253): "I went to college. I never joined a fraternity. [...] But I tell you what else I never did. I never joined that loose association of counter-fraternities, either. That was every bit as much of a club. [...] Joining the club, losing control. Losing my convictions" (ibid: 261). Moreover, through these themes of mob violence and the de-individualization experienced by joining cliques and clubs, the novel in fact alludes to US-American fears of corporate and collective bodies that have their origins in republican ideology and the Atlantic world of the 18th century.

The novel's epigraph by Emerson and the frequent allusions to and quotes from Henry David Thoreau and Walt Whitman obviously serve to evoke American Transcendentalism as a philosophy of self-reliance and radical individualism.[15] Yet, at the same time, it connects the book to a historical moment in which the power of groups and their place in a republic was very much a topic of public debate. Take Tocqueville's observations of US culture and society in the 1830s and 1840s, for example. A central theme in Tocqueville's commentary on American democracy is the significance of clubs and voluntary associations. This 'associational revolution', as historians have called it, served to fill the absence of a monetary elite in a society that rejected aristocracies, and it included clubs just as much as it did corporations. Incorporation allowed private citizens to pool their resources and build bridges and toll roads as well as to found and manage schools, hospitals, and so forth.

However, while there were clear benefits to associations, Tocqueville also famously warned of the threat of conformity in a democracy and what he called "the tyranny of the majority." Similarly, anti-corporate rhetoric, such as that employed against rechartering the Second Bank of the US in the 1830s, ultimately drew on an 18th century imaginary, in which the building of colonies and republics required the management and control of a heterogenous and unruly labor force: "the many-headed hydra[,] an antithetical symbol of disorder and resistance, a powerful threat to the building of state, empire, and capitalism" (Linebaugh & Rediker 2012: 2). This threat was a constant one in a democratic republic, of course. It comes as no surprise, therefore, when the most militant individualist in *Then We Came to the End*, Tom Mota alludes to the fears of decline and corruption that are so central to the republican tradition: "one thing [Tom] wrote I will never forget. I still have the letter. He called this country the best republic that ever began to fade" (Ferris 2007: 381). Not only does Ferris update and integrate this tradition into his novel's critique of corporate capitalism and culture in the 21st century, but he also uses its complimentary narrative of Romantic individualism to present a counter narrative.

---

15   However, as Christopher Newfield (1996) has shown, Emerson's philosophy is much more corporate than scholars in the 20th century have allowed it to be.

Individualism Reloaded: Emerson and Entrepreneurial Capitalism

Through its allusions to earlier 20th century "office novels" and postwar culture, as well as to the republican dread of unruly masses, the novel suggests that being reckoned in the gross and being quantified entails a diminishment and even loss of individuality that is detrimental to society. It ties this experience to the organization that has become a central institution in the lives of "a hundred and fifty million [...] in the workplace," the corporation (ibid: 159), but it also offers what appears to be a counter narrative. Guided by the "in-house Emerson scholar" Tom Mota, Carl Garbedian overcomes his depression long enough to decide to leave the company voluntarily and to return to nature: from the immaterial labor of the advertising agency, Carl moves on to the material labor of a landscape gardening firm (ibid: 341). The novel's closing pages present a physically fit and happy Carl, who has not only left the advertising agency but also the corporate collective and has thereby found peace of mind. But, like Sloan Wilson's protagonist in *The Man in the Gray Flannel Suit*, it is ultimately property and (self-)ownership, the pillars of liberal individualism, that save Carl.

The subplot of Carl Garbedian's survival and rebirth is particularly noteworthy because, at the end of the novel, Carl is the only employee who has left the company voluntarily. As mentioned earlier, Carl is a deeply depressed copywriter who, as the we-narrator puts it, initially "had a gut like the male equivalent of a second trimester. He wore off-brand, too-tight jeans and generic tennis shoes, which, to us, conveyed the extent to which he'd given up" (ibid: 59). He also has an increasingly strained relationship with his wife Marilynn, a successful doctor, from whom he tries to hide his depression. After his attempt to self-medicate and his subsequent hospitalization, however, Carl begins to read Emerson and even begins to seriously consider Tom Mota's offhand suggestion to open a "landscaping business" together (ibid: 306). While Tom goes to jail, Carl does in fact end up opening the company, and when the office members reunite a final time at the end of the novel, it turns out that Carl is more than moderately successful:

> Carl told us the details of his landscaping company, Garbedian and Son, a modest outfit. 'Come on, be honest,' Marilynn [his wife] said. She turned to Hank. 'It's a phenomenon, is what it is.' 'Is that true, Carl?' asked Hank. We all urged Carl to tell us more. Finally he admitted, 'We work in twenty suburbs.' We thought, Holy shit! Twenty suburbs? The guy must be raking it in.

[...] He was smiling and nodding and he had his arm around Marilynn as if landscaping had changed his life. (ibid: 375)

And, of course, the suggestion is that landscaping has indeed changed his life. The new Carl is described as happy, healthy, and mindful:

[Carl] was hardly recognizable. His gut was gone and he was tan as an almond. He was wearing a dark blue linen blazer with an open-collared shirt and he'd done something with his hair. His legs crossed, he was focused on Hank with great curiosity, perfectly still, listening. (ibid: 372)

His ability to listen and to focus, as well as his self-possession stand in stark contrast to the gossipy, frazzled "corporate we," as do more generally, his health and his contentment. It seems, then, that leaving the corporate workplace and the immaterial labor of the quantified selves in favor for material and creative in nature has brought out Carl's best self.

In his analysis of *Then We Came to the End*, Ralph Clare has suggested that the novel ultimately presents Joe Pope as the ideal alternative to the quantified selves of the "corporate we." In *Then We Came to the End*, "the Emersonian individual need not abandon his white-collar roots [...] because, apparently, the office worker – more specifically the committed corporate ladder climber like Joe Pope – *is* the neo-Emersonian self-made man" (2014: 190). Yet, whereas Joe Pope simply disappears into the anonymity of the corporate organization, Carl's example is clearly in line with the novel's previous celebration of both the Emersonian self-reliance, its critique of the immaterial labor, and the loose way of playing with words, required of the employees at the agency. By contrast, Carl's new job is intensely material (he works outside and with natural materials) and hence, by the standards of the novel, intensely real. His physical health and fitness have improved significantly (rather than worsened) through his new job, and his relationship to his wife has markedly improved as well.

However, on closer inspection, Carl's counter narrative of neo-Emersonian self-reliance may be an alternative to the subject positions available within *corporate* capitalism but not within capitalism as such. What is Carl but the creative, energetic individual at the center of entrepreneurial capitalism? In his study *The Invention of Creativity*, Andreas Reckwitz (2017) has shown that the Romantic ideal of self and labor is already part of the myth of creativity by way of the contributions of the 'Arts and Crafts' movement. Reckwitz explains that the Arts and Crafts movement presented an attempt to resist the hegemony of industrial mass production at the end of the 19th century by insisting on the dissolution of the difference between work and art. It did so by returning to the concept of traditional craftsmanship, essentially elevating it to a form of art, i.e., aestheticized labor with an emphasis on what individuals create with the labor of their hands, as well as on the materiality of the objects thus created, and on the equality of maker and user. In this sense, therefore, the Arts and Crafts movement incorporates the ideals of self, nature, and individualism that Emersonian Transcendentalism has come to represent. But, as such, as Reckwitz points out, it also becomes part of Joseph Schumpeter's and Werner Sombart's ideal of the innovative entrepreneur.

This resolution of Carl's dilemma is consistent with the novel's prior critique of life and work under corporate capitalism.[16] Throughout, it portrays corporations as sites of quantification or rather collectivization that offer only subject positions determined by standards of productivity. Employing the "corporate we" as narrative instance, the novel questions the idea that a corporate organization can serve as an institution: either as a place for values *and* business, or a place for community. However, what is significant is that the novel does not actually question the ideal of the productive self, which is still at the center of the quantified self in the 21th century.[17] Instead, it evokes an older model of proprietary capitalism in Carl, the founder of a landscaping enterprise called Garbedian and Son, thereby alluding to one of the most powerful institutions serving the rise of capitalism, the patriarchal family. Through the novel's allusions to postwar American culture, its use of the first person plural, which is so characteristic of corporate communications, and finally through its presentation of Carl's happiness, as based on owning property and quite literally self-possessive individualism, the novel criticizes corporate capitalism, but it does not ultimately question the capitalist system and the economization of the subjects within it. At the center of Ferris's corporate story, we still find the productive self, though one that owns itself.

---

16   Consider Tom Mota who may leave the corporation (though involuntarily) but only to join yet another, though public, organization, the army. Not incidentally, Tom is killed by "friendly fire," which is to say, by the members of his organization.

17   "Related to the notion of 'possessive individualism', as already drawn out by John Locke (Macpherson 1962), the quantified self is deeply engrained in US-American self-definition" (Danter et al. 2016: 55).

Works Cited

Clare, Ralph (2014): *Fictions Inc.: The Corporation in Postmodern Fiction, Film, and Popular Culture*, New Brunswick: Rutgers University Press.

Damodaran, Aswath (2017): *Narrative and Numbers: The Value of Stories in Business*, New York: Columbia University Press.

Danter, Stefan/Reichardt, Ulfried/Schober, Regina (2016): "Theorising the Quantified Self and Posthumanist Agency: Self-Knowledge and Posthumanist Agency in Contemporary US-American Literature." In: *Digital Culture and Society* 2/1, pp. 53-67.

DeLillo, Don (1971): *Americana*, Boston: Houghton Mifflin.

de Tocqueville, Alexis (2003): *Democracy in America and Two Essays on America*, New York: Penguin Random House.

Eggers, Dave (2013): *The Circle*, New York: Penguin Random House.

Faludi, Susan (2007): *The Terror Dream: Fear and Fantasy in Post 9/11 America*, New York: Metropolitan Books.

Ferris, Joshua (2007): *Then We Came to the End*, Boston: Little, Brown and Company.

Fludernik, Monika (2017): "The Many in Action and Thought: Towards a Poetics of the Collective in Narrative." In: *Narrative* 25/2, pp. 139-163.

Fog, Klaus/Budtz, Christian/Yakaboylu, Baris (2005): *Storytelling – Branding in Practice*, Berlin/Heidelberg: Springer.

Illouz, Eva (2007): *Cold Intimacies: The Making of Emotional Capitalism*, Cambridge: Polity Press.

Leverenz, David (2003): *Paternalism Incorporated: Fables of American Fatherhood, 1865-1940*, Ithaca: Cornell University Press.

Macpherson, C. B. (1962): *The Political Economy of Possessive Individualism*, London: Oxford University Press.

Marchand, Roland (2001): *Creating the Corporate Soul: The Rise of Public Relations and Corporate Imagery in American Big Business*, Berkeley: University of California Press.

Maxey, Ruth (2016): "National Stories and Narrative Voice in the Fiction of Joshua Ferris." In: *Critique: Studies in Contemporary Fiction* 57/2, pp. 208-216.

Mueller, Stefanie (2014): "'A Man is Whatever Room He's In' – Identity, Home, and Nostalgia in AMC's Mad Men." In: Caroline Rosenthal/Stefanie Schäfer (eds.), *Fake Identity? The Impostor Narrative in North American Culture*, Frankfurt am Main: Campus, pp. 192-209.

Newfield, Christopher (1996): *The Emerson Effect: Individualism and Submission in America*, Chicago: University of Chicago Press.

Palmer, Alan (2010): *Social Minds in the Novel*, Columbus: Ohio State University Press.

Park, Ed (2008): *Personal Days*, New York: Penguin Random House.

Powers, Richard (1998): *Gain*, New York: Farrar, Straus and Giroux.

Reckwitz, Andreas (2017): *The Invention of Creativity*, Cambridge, UK: Polity.

Rediker, Marcus/Linebaugh, Peter (2012): *The Many-Headed Hydra: Sailors, Slaves, Commoners, and the Hidden History of the Revolutionary Atlantic*, London/New York: Verso.

Riesman, David/Glazer, Nathan/Denney, Reuel (1950): *The Lonely Crowd: A Study of the Changing American Character*, New Haven: Yale University Press.

Russell, Alison (2018): "The One and the Many: Joshua Ferris's Then We Came to the End." In: *Critique: Studies in Contemporary Fiction* 59, pp. 319-331.

Siraganian, Lisa (2015): "Theorizing Corporate Intentionality in Contemporary American Fiction." In: *Law & Literature* 27/1, pp. 99-123.

"Ten Things We Know to be True," In: Google. Web. 15 July 2019. https://www.google.com/about/philosophy.html.

Whyte, William H. (1956): *The Organization Man*, New York: Simon & Schuster.

Wilson, Sloan (2002 [1955]): *The Man in the Gray Flannel Suit*, Boston: Da Capo Press.

Racialized Self-Improvement: Advice in Black and White Self-Help of the Interwar Years

Kristina Graaff

Self-help can be described as a standardized and rule-governed knowledge formation that offers instructions on how to draw upon one's resources to improve oneself. It exists in oral and written forms, among them speeches, lectures, sermons, radio shows, guides, autobiographies, and newspaper columns. In its focus on self-reliance, personal reinvention, progress, and navigation of new environments, self-help gained particular traction in America, shifting over time – in content and form – in line with the social, political, and economic conditions of different eras (Currell 2006a: 133). In the 17th century, the Puritans practiced self-examination as a way to measure their religious purity and striving towards salvation (Starker 2002: 14). In the 18th century, figures like Benjamin Franklin contributed to self-help's secularization (ibid). Franklin's autobiography (1791), in which he offered a list of virtues and used charts to trace his own achievements, marked a pivotal point in the history of self-help. By introducing ways in which virtues could be rationalized and transformed into measurable tools for mental and behavioral modification, it provided parameters for the quantification and optimization of the self and thereby paved the way for modern self-help cultures. For much of the 19th century, self-help promoted predominantly Victorian values such as industriousness, self-denial, modesty, and Christian living as ethical principles for the conduct of life (Lamb-Shapiro 2014: 18-19, 48-49). By the middle of the century, also Black self-help practices, which for quite some time had a vitally important function on a lived and practical level in enslaved communities and among freedwomen and -men, began to trickle into print culture through abolitionist literature, advocating the imperatives of emancipation, literacy, and comprehensive education. After the Civil War, Black reformist authors began to publish guidebooks that "highlighted which modes of etiquette and behavior would help former slaves navigate freedom's byways" (Mitchell 2004: 116). Thus, on its way to becoming a mass-mediated culture distributed on a national scale, self-help developed and differentiated alongside the "formation of new social structures [that required] new social strictures" (Currell 2006a: 133).

With the emergence of the New Thought Movement, many self-help cultures gained a spiritual tendency and shifted towards instructions on mental healing and the development of individual intuition and personal skills (Moskowitz 2001: 20-21). Progressively, self-denial turned towards self-actualization; hard work towards self-development; and frugality towards efficiency. At the end of the 19th century, Victorian virtues had gradually given way to modern values. With capitalist expansion, self-help provided more and more instructions on how to adapt to the market place. Values such as work and diligence were now increasingly linked to the gaining of material wealth (Currell 2006a: 133, 138; Susman 2003: 275). By the early 20th century, advice had turned into a mass demand and self-help – now a market in itself – became part of a growing mass culture.

As I argue, the interwar years are a particularly relevant time to investigate self-help as a modern tool for quantifying and optimizing the self. It was during this period that self-help turned into a fully commodified and institutionalized mass medium. For the first time produced in a professional way, by experts and for profit, it reached an audience of millions. Interwar self-help was simultaneously shaped by and helped to navigate the profound societal transformations that were taking place at the time and that required human adjustment on a vast scale. Among them were automated mass production, made possible by the assembly line, as well the growth of the service industry that demanded adjustment to new modes of labor. Additionally, urbanization led to shifting forms of personal interaction and navigation of space, while waves of migration and immigration brought newcomers to urban centers that were looking for guidance. Finally, massive wage cuts and unemployment during the Great Depression created a climate of deep precariousness and insecurity. As an affordable consumer product that reached a broad audience and that offered normative do's and don'ts, self-help of the interwar years thus mediated a sense of predictability and carried the promise of reducing risk during unstable times (Currell 2006a: 136). That self-help of the interwar period gave the impression of being able to manage insecurity was inextricably connected to its popularized use of new scientific assessment tools (Currell 2006a: 133, 135; Susman 2003: 158). Advice cultures of the 1920s and '30s thus adopted concepts and quantification methods that had recently been introduced especially by disciplines like psychology, medicine, and sociology and transformed them into easily accessible 'how-to' formulas. Interwar self-help thus popularized instruments used to measure, categorize, and hierarchize human bodies and to establish new standards in the process and thereby contributed to the era's craze for quantifying and optimizing the nation's population according to new norms. As I assert, self-help's action-orientated rhetoric produces performative narratives that have the potential to function as a catalyst to introduce and consolidate new normative standards.

While most self-help sources share stylistic devices and ideologies of improvement, progress, and growth, they nevertheless differ depending on the addressed target groups and their respective class, gender, and racial positionalities. Taking into account that interwar's social realities varied tremendously for differently racialized populations, I will conduct a close reading of two prominent forms of self-help that were primarily addressed at African American and white mass audiences. The first source is the advice column "The Way to Health," which was published in the Black newspaper *The Chicago Defender* from 1913 to 1937. The second is Dale Carnegie's bestselling self-help book *How to Win Friends and Influence People*, which was published in 1936. In my analysis, I will place a particular focus on how the optimization advice that the different sources provide intend to standardize subjects in relation to shifting modern labor demands. While indicative of the audiences' specific needs, the two self-help sources by no means exhaust the wide range of interwar advice cultures available at the time.[1]

Conceptualizing Self-Help: Governmentality and Critical Race and Dis/ability Studies

My close readings are centrally informed by two theoretical frameworks: Michel Foucault's concept of governmentality and approaches from Critical Race and Dis/ability Studies. In his earlier work, Foucault had strongly

---

1 Other bestselling self-help books of the interwar years include Walter B. Pitkin's *Life Begins at Forty* (1932), *Live Alone and Like It* (1936) by Marjorie Hillis, Napoleon Hill's *Think and Grow Rich* (1937) as well as Dorothea Brande's *Wake Up and Live!* (1936). Among the era's prominent advice columns are "Mental Hygiene in the Home" published in *Ladies Home Journal* (1930-32), "Afro Health Talk" published in the newspaper *Baltimore Afro-American* (1937-42) as well as *The Pittsburg Courier*'s "Friendly Advice to Girls" (1927-36).

stressed processes of discipline and the domination of subjects as "docile bodies" (1995: 135). In his later work, however, he became more interested in how subjects constitute themselves between coercion and practices of self-formation. To investigate that contact point, Foucault introduced the concepts of "technologies of power" and "technologies of the self" (1988: 18). As he states, technologies of power "determine the conduct of individuals and submit them to certain ends or domination, [what is taking place is] an objectivizing of the subject" (ibid). The technologies of the self, on the other hand, "permit individuals to effect by their own means or with the help of others a certain number of operations on their own bodies and souls, thoughts, conduct [...] so as to transform themselves [...] in order to attain a certain state of happiness, [...] wisdom, [and] perfection [...]" (ibid). It is the connection between these two technologies that Foucault conceptualizes as governmentality (ibid: 19).

As I argue, governmentality is a fruitful concept for the analysis of advice cultures because self-help can be examined as representing this very contact point. Advice usually provides instructions for individual optimization ("technologies of the self") while simultaneously prescribing formulas for the standardization of a larger population body ("technologies of power"). Drawing upon governmentality thus allows to show how self-help functions simultaneously on a micro and macro level and permanently negotiates standardization and individualization. Governmentality also illustrates the entanglement of power relations and, applied to self-help, the complexity with which authoritative instructions are embodied and enacted. As Foucault puts it, power is not "pure violence" but "a subtle integration of coercion-technologies and self-technologies" (1993: 204). In the same way, power is not simply exerted top-down within self-help. Instead, advice sources provide universalized best-practices that subjects are expected to implement individually and voluntarily into the various spheres of their lives. More precisely, advice circulates power in the form of 'expert knowledge' in a decentralized manner between the advisor and the advised, relying on authority and trust. Communicated from the perspective of a self-declared 'trustworthy expert', self-help advice shifts the authority of the advisor to the advised to take control of themselves. Trusting the advisor that they can trust themselves, advice seekers draw upon their own resources for improvement and successful self-management. Since self-help addresses individuals as parts of a larger social entity – either by inviting them to adjust to new standards and norms, to successfully 'master' others, or to improve the destiny of one's community – it exemplifies the conceptualization of power as "a productive network which runs through the whole social body" (Foucault 1977: 119).

Secondly, my analysis of self-help draws upon a theoretical framework that combines approaches from Dis/ability Studies and Critical Race Theory – to address, among other aspects, the racialization of ability and the ableism inherent to processes of racialization. It is for several reasons that I connect my analysis of self-help to the notions of dis/ability and race. On one level, I assume that self-help as such is inherently ableist as it presupposes unlimited human resources and aims at the continuous optimization of bodies and minds. On another level, I argue that especially self-help of the interwar years – relying on the newly invented quantification tools – circulated instruments to determine who was (not) considered able-bodied and able-minded and thereby inscribed new standards of (un)acceptable behavior. The ways in which self-help contributed to the formation of dis/ability standards were not only informed by class and gender politics, but also centrally driven by racialization.

Further, Dis/ability Studies frame dis/ability as a social construct and process that changes over time. When examining self-help for its construction of ableist norms, dis/ability can thus function as a "tool of cultural diagnosis" (Snyder and Mitchell 2005: 12) that allows to trace histories of normalization along the shifting lines of race, gender, and class (Annamma, Connor, and Ferri 2013: 10; Thomson 1996: 9, 135). Contextualizing dis/ability historically also reveals how definitions of in/capacity are closely related to an era's economic regime, especially to the labor market (Erevelles 2014: n.p.; Snyder and Mitchell 2005: 15, 69). During the 1920s and '30s and its introduction of automated mass production, new disability categories flourished because "an increasing value [...] [was] placed upon bodily homogeneity [...] and the workplace standardization of capacities" (Snyder and Mitchell 2005: 23). This reveals how classifying, pathologizing, and managing human differences is not only inextricably connected to modern capitalism, but intrinsic to modernity as such (ibid: 4-5).

Medical Advice in the *Chicago Defender*: Dr. Wilberforce Williams's "The Way to Health"

During the interwar years, newspapers were the most important channel to circulate self-help advice to African American mass audiences. *The Chicago De-*

fender, which had been founded in 1905, was the most widely distributed Black newspaper of the time with a print run of over 230.000 copies per week, and an estimated readership of four to five individuals per copy (Currell 2006b: 44f.).[2] It addressed not only those who had recently migrated to urban areas. Distributed deep into the South, it also actively supported the Great Migration, through articles that detailed the violence under Jim Crow as well as job advertisements that touted the good wages of factory work and success stories of those who had gone up north (Jones Ross and McKerns 2004: 56, 60; Michaeli 2016: 61–79). In fact, the newspaper's call for migration itself can be understood as a form of self-help that contributed massively to the movement of populations and shifting demographics from rural to urban areas.

The Defender provided advice in numerous ways, including editorials, articles, and aphorisms that communicated practice-oriented 'how to' messages. The most explicit source of self-help during the interwar period, however, were its advice columns, which usually ran weekly, at times over decades. Among the paper's longest-running columns was "The Way to Health. Talk on the Preventive Measures, First Aid Remedies, Hygienics and Sanitation" by the Black physician Dr. A. Wilberforce Williams, which appeared weekly between the years 1913 and 1937. The column encapsulates how the era's self-help advice functioned as a tool for quantifying and optimizing the self. Williams, who was specialized in internal medicine, was the first Black doctor to maintain a newspaper health column ("Dr. Williams, Pioneer Medical Columnist, Dies," 1940: 1-2). Born to modest circumstances in Louisiana in 1865 and having worked his way up to medical school at Northwestern University (Mather 2010: 284), he embodied self-help's spirit of social as well as spatial mobility. As a reformer of the Progressive Era, Williams used his column to practice 'racial uplift' – an ideology according to which Black elites were expected to support less advantaged members of the community in their presumed necessity for improvement by mediating specific behavioral scripts which carried the promise of racial inclusion and equality (Gaines 1996: xiv). Shared by other so-called 'race leaders' – including W.E.B. Du Bois and Booker T. Washington – 'racial uplift' was not only based on intra-racial distinctions drawn along class lines and tied collective betterment to the adjustment of 'the masses', it

---

2   Other prominent African American newspapers at the time included New York's *Amsterdam News*, the *Pittsburgh Courier*, the *Baltimore Afro-American*, and the *Atlanta Constitution*.

also inextricably connected 'uplifting' education with self-help and self-optimization.

Published over a period of 24 years, "The Way to Health" varyingly consists of letters by readers with health-related inquiries and Williams's responses as well as input on medical issues selected by the columnist. The column's overall aim is to advise readers on how to maintain the strength of their individual bodies and how to contribute to a communal and national body by adjusting their behavior to modern medical standards of reproduction, hygiene, and disease prevention. Williams's instructions are inextricably connected to the era's economic regime, in particular the recently introduced mode of automated mass production. The columnist thus addresses his readers first and foremost as workers who participate in the Fordist labor market. To emphasize this point, Williams repeatedly draws an analogy between the human body and the machine:

> In order to be up to the highest point of efficiency, it is necessary that [...] [t]he human machine must be laid up once in a while for repairs just as any other machinery. This is best done by not waiting until the machine begins to knock and rattle and skip [...] but at the first instance of any irregularity of function, [...] [or better even] before there is any impairment [...], the wise individual will go and have himself examined by his physician, who [...] is his machinist, and ascertain [...] any likelihood of his becoming unfit. (January 19, 1918: 12)

Comparing the human 'machine' to a factory machine functions as a vehicle to instill new forms of (self-)monitoring in the subject. Carried out on the level of both self-observation and of seeking professional medical assessment, the analogy links "technologies of the self" with those of power, the latter allowing for the tracking of a population's health on a larger scale. Driven by the aim to maintain an able-bodied workforce that meets the demands of automated mass production, Williams's advice seeks to convince his readers of the necessity of preventive health care. As he suggests, just like factory machines are in need of routine inspections to ensure their ongoing output, the body requires regular health checks to maintain its smooth running. According to his instructions, human bodies are to be subjected to the same rationalization processes that are deployed in the factories to produce standardized goods. The analogy thus serves as a device to introduce new tools of quantification for the assessment and management of bodies in terms of their functionality, endurance, and efficiency. How such efficiency is achieved is outlined in a step-by-step manner that combines mental focus, behavioral habit formation, and repetition – common pillars of self-formation that can already be found in Benjamin Franklin's self-tracing charts (Franklin 1987a: 95–97). As Williams claims,

> Efficiency is developed largely through the application of concentration, industry and training. [...] concentrate your attention upon any particular object of purpose to the exclusion of everything else [...]. you must train your mind. [....] the mind will obey if it is properly trained. [...] by repeated orders to your mind you have made it obey [...]. [...] And the more you have practiced this the easier your lessons become [...]. (August 20, 1921: 16)

In his emphasis on mental focus, power of thought, as well as repetitive and diligent training towards self-modification, Williams connects Victorian self-help values with advice traditions of the New Thought movement – stripped off their spiritual dimensions – and adjusts them to a Fordist regime whose production processes demand human capacity for mental concentration, industriousness, and repetition. With this, Williams not only 'updates' previous self-help traditions to meet the standards of the time, he also links his racial uplift advice to a white-authored self-help tradition, a fact that also finds expression in the column's title, "The Way to Health" – an obvious reference to Benjamin Franklin's essay "The Way to Wealth" (1987b [1758]), which endorses values of industry, diligence, patience, and self-reliance.

Williams is aware of how the labor market determines the laborers' abilities. As he observes: "If you are strong, robust, healthy, the market is willing to pay you a fair wage for a day's labor" (August 4, 1923: 12). However, "the world is not looking for, nor employing [...] weak, sickly, emaciated individuals" (August 20, 1921: 16). His statement not only speaks to the "binary coding system into which all human beings could be slotted: 'normal' and 'defective', [...] 'fit' and 'unfit'" (Snyder and Mitchell 2005: 79), which was institutionalized during the interwar years via newly invented scientific measurement tools. It also exemplifies how bodily standards are determined and perpetuated by the economy, an observation shared by dis/ability scholar Robert McRuer who states that "Hard bosses and exploitative conditions helped to secure both able-bodied identities and the sense that such identities needed to be (re)produced for the future" (McRuer 2006: 94). In his column, Williams heavily relies on the distinction between ability and disability, both to mark the effects of racial oppression as well as to invoke agency in his readers. To encapsulate the immobilizing effects of racial inequality, Williams refers to African Americans as "the race [that has] suffered many disabilities" (May 4, 1935: 24). While disability is referred to here in a figurative sense to stress how racial inequalities disable upward mobility, the column also reflects that racial discrimination causes actual impairment – a fact also stressed by Critical Race and Disability Studies that investigate how "harsh living conditions of poverty [...] [and] exploitative social relations of production and consumption [...] produce, propagate, and proliferate [...] preventable illnesses that result in disabilities" (Erevelles 2014: 4). When addressing such disabilities, however, Williams follows the common self-help approach that places the responsibility for maintaining bodily and mental functionality on the individual. Those who become disabled due to preventable diseases, such as tuberculosis or syphilis, or who infect others are addressed as "careless" (October 6, 1917: 12) or "a disgrace" (April 14, 1923: 12). Williams's ableism not only reflects the era's preoccupation with fitness, efficiency, and functionality; it also illustrates efforts to distance specifically African Americans from being associated with the notion of disability which he frames as an obstacle to achieving full citizenship rights.

His attempts to steer readers away from medical folk practices are equally motivated by the aim to achieve full acceptance and inclusion into American society. Numerous of his columns are dedicated to explaining that adjustment to current times requires to abstain from "ignorant [...] [and] superstitious" forms of self-medication that have no place "in this 20th century of marked increase in education and intelligence," among which he includes "quack doctors" as well as "charms, potions, powders, and other silly remedies" (September 10, 1927: 2). Instead, Williams seeks to install trust for the medical tools that follow the latest scientific insights on treatment and disease prevention and which he portrays as "accurate," "systematic," and "reliable" (November 25, 1916: 12). Providing detailed advice on what organs are in need of regular 'inspection' (from liver, heart, and kidneys to sexual organs) and what symptoms are indicative of what illness, Williams places an emphasis on introducing what he refers to as "modern" self-assessment tools. His advice reflects an interwar trend that displayed an increasing trust in the "systematic and supposedly scientific methods of measuring" (Susman 2003: 158) and the "prospect of control" that this knowledge seems to entail (ibid: 116). However, Williams's pleas to let go of traditional healing practices are also motivated by the need to challenge stereotypes of African Americans as "culturally backwards" (Sherman 2014: 228), illustrating again how a large part of his advice is concerned with countering white supremacist ideologies.

Williams's uplift advice, however, is not only aimed at adjusting to the changing demands of the labor market and at "struggling to break free of falsified white images" (Gaines 1996: 9). It also intends to instruct his audience on how to relate to their bodies as belonging to themselves. Hence, he calls upon his readers to not "overlook and neglect ourselves" (June 13, 1914: 8), but to invest "in the care, in the conservation, in the upkeep of [your bodies]" (May 22, 1920: 16). To gain the "ability to properly care for your body" (August 4, 1923: 12) is thus presented as an existential form of self-care that increases self-determination and with that self-ownership. Here, self-help advice turns into an instrument for claiming the self, both against a past of enslavement, where self-ownership, and as part of that self-care, were denied, as well as against interwar's immediate conditions that still did not extend full citizenship rights to Black Americans.

Throughout his column, Williams addresses self-care not only as a duty to oneself, but also to one's partner, family, a larger Black community, and the nation as a whole. This interrelationship finds most visible expression in Williams's engagement with eugenic ideologies which had "seeped into politics, permeated social science and medicine, shaped public policy and aesthetic theory, influenced national literature, [and] affected popular culture" during the interwar years (English 2004: 1). Without doubt the most radical form of body politics, the belief that populations can be governed via controlled reproduction is most obvious in Williams's marriage advice. As he suggests, only those free of conditions such as epilepsy, tuberculosis, and what he refers to as "feeblemindedness, insanity and many neurotic states" (February 16, 1935: 12) should have children, and he endorses state marriage laws that require medical records showing that the contracting parties are free from these conditions (October 25, 1913: 4; April 11, 1925: 12).[3] By deracializing 'disability' as a condition that can be found in all human populations, Williams shifts the distinction between differently racialized groups to a distinction between 'abled' and 'disabled' bodies. Ability is thus turned into a cross-racial tool of inclusion as it is undergirded by the promise that 'fit' Black subjects (who follow the instructions of individual and institutional medical assessment) will be incorporated into the larger national body. In his focus on diagnosing in/capacities, Williams not only follows the quantifying trend of the time

---

3   In 1913, 35 states had implemented such marriage laws ("State Laws Regulating Marriage of the Unfit" 1913). Other laws that set rules for marriage – such as miscegenation laws – are not addressed in Williams's column.

but also supports interwar's discourses of (self-)management and (self-)control. In his promotion of marriage and reproduction as self-help strategies of social change, Williams imposes a particular responsibility on women to abstain from marrying "unfit partners" or bearing children if they are not in the "possession of a state of good health" (February 2, 1935: 12). Abundant scripts prescribe how women should maintain their bodies as healthy vessels for the production of future generations. They entail thorough examinations of "teeth," "tonsils," "eyesight," "hearing," "kidney," "liver," and "heart" (ibid), and Williams instructs that all adjustable "defects [are to be] corrected on accounts of pregnancy" (ibid). Women are thus placed under particular scrutiny for assessing and optimizing their health status as their individual conditions are tied to the destiny of a larger population body.

Framed by eugenic ideologies and under the headline of 'health', his column exerts gender-specific forms of governing through reproduction-related advice. "Way to Health" thus exemplifies how interwar eugenics functioned as a governing tool that communicated adjustment to specific standards by tying individual behavior back to the destiny of an entire community. While instructions on how to diagnose and treat diseases and whom to marry rely on "technologies of the self" that individuals exert "on their own bodies" (Foucault 1988:18), Williams also emphasizes the biopolitical "duty" (May 31, 1924: 14) of each individual to contribute to the resilience of the Black population at large. As his column communicates, self-quantification and self-modification are a prerequisite to both collective belonging and change. Oscillating between a personal and collective address, Williams's instructions simultaneously function as "technologies of the self" and "technologies of power." In fact, his column illustrates the complexity of governing structures that are characterized by "a subtle integration of coercion-technologies and self-technologies" (Foucault 1993: 204). While uplift can be described as a top-down form of education, Williams's advice nevertheless rests on the assumption that subjects implement the conveyed best practices individually and voluntarily into their daily lives. Adjustment to prescribed standards is thus supposed to take place in form of a governing process in which behavioral imperatives are translated into independently embodied behavior.

Adopting an ideology that is racist in origin and transforming it into a tool to achieve racial equality by using it to generate an allegedly more resilient Black population encapsulates what Shantella Sherman describes as "the schizophrenic nature" of Black eugenics (2014: 112). However, Williams's column also illustrates that African Americans were not simply "objects of white eugenic fears, theories and practices" (Sherman 2014: 28) but acted as "active agents" that appropriated and modified mainstream eugenic discourses to their own ends. In this way, the column speaks to the need of having to come up with any possible instrument to produce "normalizing counter-discourses that humanized the race" (Mitchell 2004: 123). "Way to Health" thus testifies to the life-sustaining purposes that self-help still served for African American audiences during the interwar period. It is driven by an urgency to counter the "searing firestorm of racist claims that escalated lynching and rationalized disfranchisement and segregation" (Mitchell 2004: 123). Existential in core because often about ensuring sheer survival, Black self-help relied on any possible tool to make a step towards securing safer lives.

Dale Carnegie: *How to Win Friends and Influence People*

Another prominent source of self-help during the interwar years – primarily addressed at a white mass audience – was Dale Carnegie's *How to Win Friends and Influence People*. Published in 1936, it was the most widely sold self-help guide of the Great Depression, remaining on the national bestseller list over two consecutive years (Korda 2001: 71-72). Still in print, it has sold over 30 million copies worldwide to this day (Watts 2013: 3) and is listed by the Library of Congress among the "Books That Shaped America" ("Library of Congress" 2013). The guide's success during the Great Depression can be explained by its focus on personal reinvention and retrieval of individual resources. It promised change "during a period of fear that the wheels of progress and advancement had come to a halt" (Currell 2006a: 137). Implying "that 'recovery' was only possible by improving personal efficiency and streamlining oneself for new market conditions" (ibid), an approach that – similar to today's neoliberal agendas – places the responsibilities for institutional shortcomings on the shoulders of individuals, Carnegie's self-help book stressed agency in an era of financial precariousness which had left many readers feeling powerless. With its hands-on instructions on how to modify oneself in order to gain influence, prestige, and recognition, *How to Win Friends* entailed the promise of salvation to overcome stagnating times via self-improvement. Carnegie himself can be considered a prime example of personal reinvention. In contrast to Williams's linear professional career, Carnegie redefined his public persona numerous times before turning into a successful self-help author. After failed attempts to succeed as a salesman, actor, and novelist (Watts 2013: 90, 98, 186), he began teaching classes on public speaking and self-presentation at a New York YMCA, and it was out of his lecture material that he eventually published *How to Win Friends* (ibid: 105, 112, 121).

Emerging from his courses that particularly attracted "entrepreneurs, businessmen, shopkeepers, salesmen, middle managers, white-collar executives, professional men" (ibid: 1), *How to Win Friends* addresses a similar – predominantly white and male – audience. Reflecting the realities of a gendered and racialized economy that primarily enabled white men to access the emerging bureaucratic corporations, Carnegie's guide participated in processes of in- and exclusion by conveying self-improvement skills as gender- and race-specific.

How to Win Friends is a manual on how to adapt to modern capitalism, especially to positions in the service sector and middle management that require the careful navigation of personal interactions, often across social hierarchies. The guide's overall aim is to control situations and master others with the intent to optimize human interactions and make particularly business exchanges more smooth, efficient, and, hence, profitable. Carnegie's main principles to achieve such frictionless and rewarding encounters include "Don't criticize, condemn or complain" (2010: 50), "Remember [...] a person's name" (ibid: 112), "Be a good listener. Encourage others to talk about themselves" (ibid), avoid any argument (ibid: 122), and "Make the other person feel important – and do it sincerely" (ibid: 112). While the principles are addressed at individual readers, guiding them on how to effect behavioral change "on their own [...] conduct" (Foucault 1988: 18), they simultaneously submit the individual "to certain ends" (ibid) by suggesting to adjust to newly established norms of corporate interaction. Intertwining management *by* and *of* the subject, Carnegie's imperatives function as a governing device that has the potential to standardize human encounters and make them more predictable. His guide thus illustrates how interwar streamlining took place not only via assembly line production that standardized products and manual labor modes, but how it also informed the era's managerial economy.

In line with the era's preoccupation with scientific quantification, Carnegie deploys various devices to rationalize his principles. Aside from claiming that his book is rooted in decades of "research," including the examination of "countless biographies, trying to ascertain how the great leaders of all ages had dealt with people" (xvi), he popularizes psychological approaches and techniques. Blending Sigmund Freud's concept of the 'unconscious', Alfred Adler's 'empathy', and B.F. Skinner's 'operant conditioning' and interspersing them with the stories of successful business tycoons, including Charles Schwab, Andrew Carnegie, and John D. Rockefeller, as well as personal eyewitness accounts of successful change, his guide appears to be backed up by quantifiable 'formulas'.

Via these popularized tools Carnegie intends to achieve profound behavioral modification in his readers, a formation of "new habits" from the ground up (xxiii). Admitting that it is initially "difficult to apply these suggestions all the time" (ibid), he provides abundant self-monitoring strategies to ensure the principles' implementation and eventual embodiment. What he suggests as an efficient strategy is to "Offer your spouse, your child or some business associate a dime or a dollar every time he or she catches you violating a certain principle. Make a lively game out of mastering these rules" (ibid). By tying the behavioral recoding to a monetary incentive, Carnegie hints at the long-term material success that the new habit formation promises. Including not only business partners, but also friends, and family members in the monitoring process, the new behavior extends into all spheres of life and places all interactions under a profit motive. It links technologies of self-control with technologies that allow for the management of others, be it professional or intimate partners.

Especially facial expressions are monetized. Most valuable to Carnegie is thus "a real smile, a heartwarming smile, a smile that comes from within, the kind of smile that will bring a good price in the market place" (ibid: 67). He provides abundant examples of how a smile can improve business. It can calm down unsatisfied customers, create a positive office atmosphere and thereby more efficient workers, and express a personal interest in each customer who then develops greater "loyalty to your company" (ibid: 61). The sociologist Eva Illouz describes this mutual relationship – the emotionalization of economics and the economization of emotions – succinctly with the term "emotional capitalism" (2008: 60), in which "emotions have become entities to be evaluated, inspected, discussed, bargained, quantified, and commodified" (Illouz 2007: 109). Framed as a quantifiable entity, emotions are measured, rationalized, and instrumentalized for commercial purposes. Carnegie's guide makes clear that being able to show a 'genuine' and profitable smile at any occasion is hard-earned. It can be described as "emotional self-control" (Illouz 2007: 4) that is in itself a form of labor: "You don't feel like smiling? Then what? [...] force yourself to smile. If you are alone, force yourself to whistle or hum a tune or sing. Act as if you were already happy, and that will tend to make you happy" (Carnegie 2010: 70).

Aimed at a self-determined reconfiguration of the individual, *How to Win Friends* epitomizes a major shift in the formation of the self from 'character' to 'personality' that was first conceptualized by Warren Susman (2003) and subsequently elaborated on by other scholars. The shift emanates from a 19th century self that was primarily conceptualized in terms of a "holistic notion of character" (Illouz 2007: 80) that adhered to an "internalized morality of self-control" (Lears 2000: n.p.) and was formed around Victorian values of *"duty,* [...] *work,* [...], *honor, reputation,* [...] *manners,* [and] *integrity"* (Susman 2003: 273-274, original emphasis). Focused inward, it was considered "less given to a context-dependent manipulation" (Illouz 2007: 80). With the birth of corporate consumer capitalism, however, the self began to be increasingly constructed in terms of a 'personality' that revolved around "personal needs and interests" with the effect that "The vision of self-sacrifice began to yield to that of self-realization" (Susman 2003: 276). A strong personality was associated with attributes like *"fascinating, stunning,* [...] *magnetic,* [...] *masterful, creative, dominant,* [and] *forceful"* (ibid: 277, original emphasis). Oriented outwards, it "became something to be assembled and manipulated for the sake of impression-making and impression management" (Illouz 2007: 79). With its instructions on how to turn oneself into an optimistic, confident, and captivating persona, *How to Win Friends* illustrates vividly the shift to the perception of a self that could be molded and performed at one's own will. Although Carnegie presents this advice as universal, it is in fact applicable only to a particular professional segment of interwar society, given that managerial and middle-management positions were in the majority held by whites. Whereas Carnegie's readership was intended to be trained for positions of authority, Williams's advice had to be directed at the much more existential concerns of achieving racial equality and full access to citizenship rights, for which attributes like magnetism and creativity were less useful. Instead, Williams's advice adhered to values such as industriousness, frugality, cleanliness, dignity, and respectability, that are rather associated with 'character', illustrating how the shift from the formation of self in terms of 'character' to that of a 'personality' was not a uniform process, but inextricably connected to one's racial and thereby economic positionality. For Blacks, character formation however did not exclude the necessity to perform. On the contrary, the ability to immediately adjust one's self-presentation to changing situations was a crucial skill for navigating mainstream society and interracial encounters during the interwar years. Nevertheless, this type of – at times life-sustaining – performance differed from the one addressed by Carnegie, according to which individuals construct and perform a certain personality primarily for monetary gain.

Carnegie's self-help approach also differs from Williams's in the way in which it addresses structural conditions in relation to his readers' agency. Making happiness in business and in the home the overall aim of his advice – an abstract promise that is not further specified in *How to Win Friends* – Carnegie states: "Everybody in the world is seeking happiness – and there is one sure way to find it. That is by controlling your thoughts. Happiness doesn't depend on outward conditions. It depends on inner conditions" (71). Clearly continuing the tradition of the New Thought movement, whose followers believed that the human mind can control realities and actions through inner visualization (e.g. Trine 1897; Wattles 1910), Carnegie's statement testifies to a position of unacknowledged privilege by suggesting that it is up to each individual to decide if it will be impacted by outside forces.

How to Win Friends is thus rooted in a broad understanding of ableism which asserts that all individuals – no matter what gender, class, or racial positionalities – have identical opportunities to draw upon their capacities and freely perform mental and bodily optimization. Marketed as a guide that provides universally applicable formulas, it not only masks its actual target audience, but – opposite to Williams – also denies the existence of structural forces beyond one's control, including that of racial oppression and misogyny. As a result, failing to improve and optimize oneself is always attributed to the individual, never to societal limits.

To enforce this point, Carnegie cites William James, stating that "Compared to what we ought to be, we are only half awake. We are making use of only a small part of our physical and mental resources. [...] the human individual thus lives far within his limits. He possesses powers of various sorts which he habitually fails to use" (xix). Again excluding the existence of structural impediments that potentially counter one's unhindered development, the sole purpose of Carnegie's guide book is to "help you discover, develop and profit by those dormant and unused assets" (xix). In line with corporate consumer capitalism that hinges on assumptions of continuous profit via exploration of inexhaustible resources, ability is seen as limitless, all it requires is the right method and mindset to tease it out.

Interwar Self-Help: A Testament to Racial Inequality

Way to Health and *How to Win Friends* share several characteristics. Both are catered to a large target group and are driven by a belief in self-optimization and social mobility; both place a particular trust on modern quantification tools to assess and monitor the self and root their instructions in scientific approaches that are popularized and made accessible to a mass audience; and both are inextricably connected to the interwar economy, aiming at the readers' adjustment to the new work modes and at expanding their labor capacity. In their specific rhetorical form, which is common to self-help, the two advice sources are effective tools to initiate new behavioral standards. Using imperative directives, step-by-step formulas, exemplary case studies, and reiterations, they are inherently action-orientated. By pointing towards a better future – characterized either by racial equality, a healthy condition, a solid personality, or increased profit – both forms of self-help envision improved states of being to encourage adjustive behavior. Pairing practice-oriented instructions with future orientation, they function as performative devices that serve as a catalyst to set impulses for action and new practices. Both also share a governing function. By addressing their audiences simultaneously on a personal and on a larger population level, *Way to Health* as well as *How to Win Friends* aim at the individual internalization of prescribed norms and mediate standards of ablebodiedness and ablemindedness revolving around efficiency. While the two advice sources provide individual tools of self-quantification, they simultaneously seek to adjust their audiences to a larger collective, inviting their readers to identify as respectable citizens, healthy manual laborers, or profit-generating members of the managerial class. This invitation to belong goes hand in hand with the exclusion of those who are viewed as unable to adjust themselves to the respective group's norms and standards.

Given that the addressed audiences occupy varying positions in the era's economic regime and are faced with distinct conditions for achieving improvement and change, the advice provided by the two self-help sources also differs substantially. The unequal preconditions for self-help have already been pointed out by Frederick Douglass in one of his most popular speeches, "Self-Made Men" from 1872, in which he calls for a leveling of the playing field from which self-help could then evolve on equal terms. He explicitly points out the privilege – that remains completely naturalized in Carnegie's guide – when stating that "it is not fair play to start [Black subjects] out in life from nothing and with nothing, while others start with the advantage of a thousand years behind them" (ibid: 16). As Williams's column illustrates, half a century after Douglass's speech, self-help addressed at Black audiences is still preoccupied with providing advice on how to gain racial equality. Whereas Carnegie's guide is aimed at developing abilities that promise more profitable business exchanges, Williams's advice is centrally concerned with proving ability as such and disassociating oneself from what is perceived as 'disability'. *The Way to Health* is thus driven by the need to counter damaging images, while *How to Win Friends* is not concerned with functioning as such a corrective and instead focuses on individual improvement. In contrast to Carnegie, who presents his advice as universally applicable, using a seemingly all-inclusive "we," Williams clearly marks his speaker position as a Black man addressing members of the Black community. Not in the position to omit the fact that his readers' conditions and needs are impacted by racial inequality, Williams's advice has to emphasize agency with the aim to achieve full citizenship rights, which are considered a given in Carnegie's guide. While *How to Win Friends* focuses on the individual without having to necessarily invoke a community as a cohesive or empowering force, the racial uplift advice in *The Way to Health* is based on intra-communal responsibilities. As a result, the processes of quantification communicated in both self-help examples – including self-observation, self-assessment, and personal reinvention through the embodiment of new performative practices – differ.

The two self-help sources thus testify to the profoundly different life realities of its audiences – affecting social, political, and economic participation. However, despite their differences, they also indicate how self-help of the 1920s and '30s can be considered as a 'behavioral trendsetter' that communicated many expectations that drive US society to this day. Adjusting oneself to market demands, framing one's body as an asset, and practicing self-care as a duty of citizenship, while placing various spheres of life under a profit principle were not only ideologies that began to be implemented during the interwar period; they are also driving neoliberal society of this day.

Works Cited

Annamma, Subini/Connor, David Ferri, Beth (2013): "Dis/Ability Critical Race Studies (DisCrit): Theorizing at the Intersections of Race and Dis/Ability." In: *Race Ethnicity and Education* 16/1, pp. 1-31.

Brande, Dorothea (1969 [1936]): *Wake Up and Live!*, New York: Cornerstone Library.

Carnegie, Dale (2010 [1936]): *How to Win Friends and Influence People*, New York: Pocket Books.

Currell, Sue (2006a): "Depression and Recovery: Self-Help and America in the 1930s." In: David Bell/Joanne Hollows (eds.), *Historicizing Lifestyle, Mediating Taste, Consumption and Identity from the 1900 to 1970s*, Hampshire / Burlington: Ashgate Publishing, pp. 131-44.

___ (2006b): "Eugenic Decline and Recovery in Self-Improvement Literature of the Thirties." In: Sue Currell/Christina Cogdell (eds.), *Popular Eugenics: National Efficiency and American Mass Culture in the 1930s*, Athens, Ohio: Ohio University Press, pp. 44-69.

Douglass, Frederick (2019 [1872]): "Self-Made Men." Address before the Students of the Indian Industrial School at Carlisle, PA. The Frederick Douglass Papers at the Library of Congress. Folder 1 of 16. Web. 26 July 2019.

"Dr. Williams, Pioneer Medical Columnist, Dies." (1940). In: *The Chicago Defender*, March 2, pp. 1–2.

English, Daylanne (2004): *Unnatural Selections: Eugenics in American Modernism and the Harlem Renaissance*, Chapel Hill: University of North Carolina Press.

Erevelles, Nirmala (2014): "Thinking with Disability Studies." In: *Disability Studies Quarterly* 34/2.

Foucault, Michel (1977): *Power/Knowledge: Selected Interviews & Other Writings 1972-1977*, New York: Pantheon Books.

___ (1988): "Technologies of the Self." In: Luther Martin/Huck Gutman/Patrick Hutton (eds.), *Technologies of the Self: A Seminar with Michel Foucault*, Amherst: The University of Massachusetts Press, pp. 16–49.

___ (1993): "About the Beginning of the Hermeneutics of the Self: Two Lectures at Dartmouth." In: *Political Theory* 21/2, pp.198–227.

___ (1995): *Discipline & Punish: The Birth of the Prison*, New York: Vintage Books.

Franklin, Benjamin (1987a [1791]): "The Autobiography of Benjamin Franklin." In: Kenneth Silverman (ed.), *Benjamin Franklin: The Autobiography and Other Writings*, New York: Penguin Books, pp. 3-197.

___ (1987b [1758]): "The Way to Wealth." In: Kenneth Silverman (ed.), *Benjamin Franklin: The Autobiography and Other Writings*, New York: Penguin Books, pp. 215-225.

Gaines, Kevin (1996): *Uplifting the Race: Black Leadership, Politics, and Culture in the Twentieth Century*, Chapel Hill: The University of North Carolina Press.

Hill, Napoleon (2005 [1937]): *Think and Grow Rich*, New York: Tarcher/Penguin.

Hillis, Marjorie. (2008 [1936]): *Live Alone and Like It*, New York: Hachette.
Illouz, Eva (2007): *Cold Intimacies: The Making of Emotional Capitalism*, Cambridge: Polity.
___ (2008): *Saving the Modern Soul: Therapy, Emotions, and the Culture of Self-Help*, Berkeley: University of California Press.
Jones Ross, Felecia/McKerns, Joseph (2004): "Depression in 'The Promised Land': The Chicago Defender Discourages Migration, 1929-1940." In: *American Journalism* 21/1, pp. 55–73.
Korda, Michael (2001): *Making the List: A Cultural History of the American Bestseller 1900-1999*, New York: Barnes & Noble Books.
Lamb-Shapiro, Jessica (2014): *Promise Land: My Journey through America's Self-Help Culture*, New York: Simon & Schuster.
Lears, T. J. Jackson (2000 [1983]): "From Salvation to Self-Realization: Advertising and the Therapeutic Roots of the Consumer Culture, 1880-1930." In: *Advertising & Society Review* 1/1.
"Library of Congress: Books That Shaped America," January 22, 2013 (https://www.loc.gov/item/prn-13-005/).
Mather, Frank Lincoln. (2010 [1915]): *Who's Who of the Colored Race: A General Biographical Dictionary of Men and Women of African Descent*, Vol. 1, Chicago: Kessinger Publishing.
McRuer, Robert (2006): *Crip Theory: Cultural Signs of Queerness and Disability*, New York: NYU Press.
Michaeli, Ethan (2016): *The Defender: How the Legendary Black Newspaper Changed America*, Boston: Houghton Mifflin Harcourt.
Mitchell, Michele (2004): *Righteous Propagation: African Americans and the Politics of Racial Destiny after Reconstruction*, Chapel Hill: The University of North Carolina Press.
Moskowitz, Eva (2001): *In Therapy We Trust. America's Obsession with Self-Fulfillment*, Baltimore: The Johns Hopkins University Press.
Pitkin, Walter B. (1932): *Life Begins at Forty*, New York/London: Whittlesey House/McGraw Hill Book Company.
Sherman, Shantella (2014): *In Search of Purity: Popular Eugenics and Racial Uplift Among New Negroes 1915-1935*, PhD diss, University of Nebraska-Lincoln.
Snyder, Sharon/ Mitchell, David (2005): *Cultural Locations of Disability*, Chicago: The University of Chicago Press.
Starker, Steven (2002): *Oracle at the Supermarket: The American Preoccupation with Self-Help Books*, Piscataway, NJ: Transaction.

"State Laws Regulating Marriage of the Unfit." (1913). In: *Journal of the American Institute of Criminal Law and Criminology* 4/3, pp. 423–25.

Susman, Warren (2003 [1973]): *Culture as History: The Transformation of American Society in the Twentieth Century*, Washington: Smithsonian Institution Press.

Thomson, Rosemarie Garland (1996): *Extraordinary Bodies: Figuring Physical Disability in American Culture and Literature*, New York: Columbia University Press.

Trine, Ralph Waldo (1897): *In Tune with the Infinite or, Fullness of Peace Power and Plenty*. New York: Thomas Y Crowell & Company.

Wattles, Wallace (2018 [1910]): *The Science of Getting Rich*. Scotts Valley, CA: CreateSpace Independent Publishing Platform.

Watts, Steven (2013): *Self-Help Messiah: Dale Carnegie and Success in Modern America*, New York: Other Press.

The Solipsism of the Quantified Self: Working Bodies in David Foster Wallace's Body of Work

Dominik Steinhilber

The Quantified Self movement exemplifies a biocapitalist ontology of the self, because measuring the body in its quantifiable, objective dimension always explicitly or implicitly serves an optimization of the *laboring* body for economic ends. Stimulated by late 20th century developments in biotechnology that open up and facilitate the idea of a 'quality of life' "defined within, and measured by, any number of rating scales" (Rose 2001: 10), biocapitalism expands the neoliberal project of self-optimization and individual responsibility to bodily functions, situating and reproducing the pathologies of capitalism in the 'bio-material' of the body (Kunow 2015: 52). Although projects of self-quantification, from Puritan self-scrutiny to Benjamin Franklin's enlightened journal keeping, have a long history comorbid with American capitalism and individualism (Danter/Reichardt/Schober 2016: 57), current advances in widespread digitization have intensified, accelerated, and made universally feasible and economically exploitable the quantification of the self. The Quantified Self movement, promoting "Self-Knowledge Through Numbers" (Quantified Self Homepage), equates the subject with the body. This 'self-design', fusing self-knowledge and self-optimization while locating selfhood entirely in bodily biomaterial, is exclusively understood as the improvement of the value of the body. Thus, as Danter, Reichardt, and Schober remark, drawing on Nora Young, "The main difference to Franklin's approach is that today the goal is not virtue or morality, but bodily improvement and self-fashioning" (2016: 58). While earlier forms of self-quantification strove for self-perfection oriented toward a metaphysical telos in God, virtue, and moral values, (bio)capitalist self-quantification elides the transcendental, focusing on economic value.

David Foster Wallace's writing is heavily invested in negotiating conceptions of selfhood and embodiment in a contemporary neoliberal America. In this essay, his novel *Infinite Jest*,[1] published in 1996, will be examined with regard to the ways in which it negotiates the intersection of body, work, and selfhood. *IJ*, in particular with regard to its cast of young tennis professionals, can be read as a fictional negotiation of aspects of the quantified self, as it reflects on the interdependence of self-optimization through self-quantification and neoliberal ideals of individualism and competition. Moreover, it comments on the detrimental effects such self-objectifying, economy-driven forms of subjectivity might have on the formation of stable and meaningful selfhood and the working body. Neoliberal self-quantification, to Wallace, is an effect of capitalism's appropriation of a postmodern attitude. What Fredric Jameson calls "the cultural logic of late capitalism" (1991) has become an internal, almost naturalized dimension of the cultural discourse of the US American society his novels depict. This cultural logic projects the postmodernist equation of representation and reality onto the body and the self. As a consequence, Wallace seems to argue, individuals tend to become solipsistic; meaningful selfhood becomes problematic and the laboring body is experienced as highly fragmented. Solipsism, Wallace writes in his unfinished last novel, *The Pale King*, is "The assumption that [...] you are the world" (2012a: 516), adding that this is the "disease of consumer capitalism" (ibid.). As a tentative solution to this postmodern solipsism, Wallace proposes a reconceptualization of human interaction from materialistically conceived "bod[ies] in commerce with bodies" (2006: 160) to a public and mutual form of communication. Wallace uses later Wittgenstein's ordinary language philosophy as a model to reconceive intersubjective exchange as the reciprocal interaction between subjects that have bodies but are not equated to their bodies. While the atomistic philosophy of Wittgenstein's early *Tractatus Logico-Philosophicus*, which Wallace regards as underlying the neoliberal worldview, leads to solipsism, Wittgenstein's later *Philosophical Investigations* oppose this 'private language use' by defining meaning as conventional language usage. In *IJ*, this 'therapy' of solipsism is exemplarily played out in the opposition between the tennis philosophies of the 'Wittgensteinian coach' Schtitt, an analogy for public language games, and the new, neoliberal regime of the Ennet Tennis Academy. In conceiving the literary work as work, Wallace's fiction, by repeatedly drawing attention to the reader's and the author's body, promotes an alternative to the solipsizing privacy of neoliberal abstraction outlined in a dialogic author-reader relationship that breaks with the poststructuralist

---

1   Henceforth abbreviated as *IJ*.

notion of the 'death of the author'. Literary work is thereby not only an object of economic value but also becomes a communication about the subject of moral value.

Since this essay involves a number of conceptual leaps that are the result of Wallace's equation of economic concepts and language philosophy, a quick overview of the argument seems necessary. I will analyze Wallace's interrogation of selfhood and the body within biocapitalism in five steps: (1) The self-objectifying practices in tennis presented in the novel can be viewed as a reflection on biocapitalist work and self-quantification; (2) Wallace presents biocapitalism as the economic expression of a generalized ironic attitude toward existence in American society that has absorbed postmodernism and poststructuralism into its cultural discourse; (3) the novel frames its reigning neoliberal tennis philosophy as what Wittgenstein would call a private language use. Such a view of the world and language leads into solipsism; (4) Coach Schtitt's philosophy of tennis counters neoliberal competition and self-objectification in the same way Wittgenstein's *Philosophical Investigations* refute the atomism of the *Tractatus* he later dismisses as an impossible private language use;[2] and (5) I will apply this Wittgensteinian framework to the overall novel and its author-reader relationship, presenting Wallace's alternative to biocapitalism/poststructuralism by offering a reconceptualization of the self, work, and the body. Throughout this essay, relevant concepts of Wittgensteinian philosophy will be briefly explained.

Self-Quantification and Objectification in *IJ*'s Entertainment Industry

Although *IJ* was written at the very brink of our current digital era, it can nevertheless be read as a highly complex and critical reflection on the issues of digitization and (bio)capitalism that gave rise to the economy-driven concept of the quantified self. The novel's critique of neoliberal self-optimization becomes particularly apparent in the ways in which tennis as sport and

---

2 As Wallace refers to Wittgenstein's shift from the *Tractatus* to *Philosophical Investigations* as an "infanticide-by-bludgeon" (2012b: 108), he seems to share the schizophrenic view of Wittgenstein with earlier Wittgenstein scholarship that strictly distinguishes between an early and a late Wittgenstein, a distinction that is so extreme as to view Wittgenstein as in fact two authors. For the sake of tracing Wallace's argument, this by now revised distinction is nevertheless applied in this essay.

as discipline are presented. Students at the Ennet Tennis Academy (E.T.A.), one major setting of the novel's meandering plots, are prepared for a professional career in big league sports events which the novel significantly refers to as "the Show" (2006: 111). The term implies that these events accentuate the players as objects to be looked at. Within the paradigm of professional tennis, laboring bodies are regarded as commercially exploitable goods. As the "Show" promises *"appearance* fees, match-highlights in *video* mags, action *photos* in glossy print-mags" (ibid., emphasis mine) to the young career tennis players, the body as spectacle becomes a source of value rather than a means to the end of playing. Tennis as a game that provides bodies to be looked at to an entertainment-hungry US-American society is thereby transformed from a playful and non-productive activity into a form of labor. Students' bodies are redefined as commodities that are 'sold' on the biocapitalist marketplace of spectation.

"Work at E.T.A.," Jeffrey Severs remarks, "is really working out, that ritual of postmodern gym culture and body perfection that defined the 1980s-2000s US zeitgeist in which Wallace wrote" (2017: 99). Consequently, E.T.A., preparing its students for the "Show," teaches its young tennis players to identify their selves with their bodies. Dominated by a philosophy of competitive US individualism and "mechanistic materialism" (Burn 2004: 45), students at E.T.A. are seen as "grim machines" (2006: 438) whose training is supposed to "sink and soak into the hardware, the C.P.S.[cyber-physical-system]" (ibid: 117). The young athletes thus become, and are invited to view themselves as, "robotic" (ibid: 694), their minds and selves indistinguishable from a computer's "motherboard" (ibid: 118) into which tennis movements are programmed. Within this materialist configuration, students' success is attributed to their being "pure force" (ibid: 682), material objects in a game of tennis that is conceived of as "body in commerce with bodies" (ibid: 160).

The occurrence or "nonoccurrence" (ibid: 686) of the self on the court is thus reduced to "certain figures" (ibid) in measurable statistics. Objectifying the self, E.T.A. reduces its students to a set of bodily statistics. An athlete's entire performance is analyzed as atomistic, objectively trackable data resulting in statistics that converge in a "ranking" (ibid: 151). Knowing their selves "entirely in relation to one another" (ibid: 112), students at E.T.A. identify their selfhood with this ranking, literally forming a quantified, numerical self that leads to exchanges such as "'Hey there, how are you?' 'Number eight this week, is how I am'" (ibid: 693). The self in this capitalist worldview is understood as a set of numbers. The individual's experience of selfhood is logically correlated with its measurable outward performance. In the materialist philosophy of E.T.A., numbers that represent the body's actions are seen as identical to the self. The subject is thereby treated as, and becomes, an object.

Solipsism and The Cultural Logic of Late (Bio-)Capitalism

Such an economy-driven conception of the self as a quantifiable object radically isolates the subject. *IJ* links its depiction of biocapitalist self-objectification to its analysis of an alienating postmodern irony[3] which has become the "cultural norm" (Wallace 1993: 184) for US society. Postmodernism has been absorbed into America's cultural discourse and thereby internalized physically as well, thus drastically manifesting, so to speak, the cultural logic of late *bio*capitalism. Accordingly, society in *IJ* equates representation with reality, exchange value with use value, and the object body and the statistics it generates with the self. Quantitative methods of self-discovery can be understood as a capitalist reduction of the self and other to objects and their economic value. Interiority becomes an abstraction that can be described, yet from which the individual is detached in this climate of ironic self-objectification. Hence, the novel's protagonist and prodigal tennis player Hal increasingly "find[s] terms like *joie* and *value* to be like so many variables in rarified equations" (2006: 694, original emphasis).

As can be seen in "the Show," the novel's culture is described as an 'image culture' addicted to objectifying spectation in its equation of representation and reality. Seen from within a Wittgensteinian perspective, *IJ* identifies this postmodernist "machine language" (ibid) of competitive US individualism as solipsizing private language use. Private language use views words as "logical picture[s]" (Wittgenstein 2001: 4.03) of objective facts. Grammar and world are regarded as sharing the same logical pattern and therefore as running parallel to each other. Since a private language user has only access to these

---

3   Wallace's critique of irony is directed at this generalized ironic attitude toward existence, not at verbal irony in the sense of a rhetorical figure. While verbal irony produces a positive affirmation of meaning and value, *Infinite Jest* is predominantly concerned with opposing "an all-negating ironic attitude" (den Dulk 2012: 326). To Wallace, such a generalized abstraction is an effect of neoliberalism that leads to solipsism and self-centeredness. Unless otherwise specified, my use of the term irony in this essay refers to this existential irony.

pictures, the speaker is completely isolated from the external world: *"The limits of my language* mean the limits of my world" (ibid.: 5.6, original emphasis). Pushed to its logical conclusion, this view results in solipsism. The private language user construes the world entirely from their language. However, they lack any criterion of correctness with which to validate the forged connection: "whatever is going to seem right to me is right. And that only means that here we can't talk about 'right'" (Wittgenstein 1986: §258). An infinite regress of justifying what such a solipsist calls 'the self' ensues. Trapped within their own language, a private language user not only treats their own interiority as just another external object onto which they attach a nametag. In addition, the other also becomes an object. Since someone like this can neither communicate subjective experience, per definition an experience that is not the other's, nor perceive the other's interior, they would render their own and the other's selfhood as an object and be radically isolated. As much as the private language user treats their interior experiences as objects of which they are the sole owner, so does the other become a robotic construct of the solipsist's mind. Postmodern US individualism in Wallace's reading condemns the individual to such an isolating, private language use.

Such private language use, which reduces the world to objective facts, results "in the objectification of other subjects, creating a rigid hierarchical structure with the 'I' as elevated center" (van Ewijk 2009: 139). As Ewijk remarks, *IJ*'s US culture of late capitalist individualism is "trying to assimilate [the other] to the needs of the self" (ibid.: 138). The other thereby loses "every aspect of his or her 'otherness'" (ibid.) when it is approached as an object to be used. The individual is turned into "a prisoner of its own totalizing tendency" (ibid.).

The Solipsizing "Work" of Tennis in Biocapitalism

The specific style of tennis played at E.T.A. treats the players and their opponents alike as material objects and thus serves as Wallace's main metaphor for the language use in neoliberal times. The self is conceived as a "C.P.S." (2006: 117), a cyber-physical system that exists on two planes of reality, physical reality and the virtual reality of "machine-language" (ibid: 117). E.T.A., significantly "a private school" (ibid: 754), promotes a view on language, self, body, and world that resembles the mimetic word-object relation as outlined in Wittgenstein's *Tractatus*. It can thus be seen as what later Wittgenstein would dismiss as a private language use. Digitization and neoliberalism endorse such a language use that objectifies the self. Behavior, abstracted into the virtual reality of statistics, is materialistically equated to the self in E.T.A.'s "stats-tracking" (ibid: 82) form of tennis. As Burn notes, E.T.A.'s neoliberal regime "seeks to reduce the complexity of open systems to the simplistic workings of a closed system" (2004: 42).

E.T.A.'s tennis, "a deliberately *individual* sport" (Wallace 2006: 83, emphasis mine), is a microcosm of the American neoliberal culture of individualism, based, as the German senior tennis instructor Schtitt[4] remarks, on the "myth of competition" (ibid: 80). American society only cares about "The happy pleasure of the person alone" (ibid: 83). Such self-centered privacy, however, renders the individual "[l]onely" (ibid). It conceives of the "other guy" (ibid) as an opponent, an object solely to be assimilated into the "multiform cravings of the individual appetitive will" (ibid: 82) and thereby negates the other's 'otherness' in pursuit of the "illusion of autonomy" (Hayles 1999: 678). Such a subject cannot tolerate another subject beside itself. The other is assimilated to one's own self as it is perceived as one's own linguistic construct. This avoidance of a "confrontation with interconnection" (ibid.: 685) is an attempt to eliminate the other from communication that isolates the individual in radical solitude.

The students at E.T.A. "gauging their whole worth by their place in an ordinal ranking" (Wallace 2006: 693) conceive of their selfhood, understood as economical value, "entirely in relation to one another" (ibid: 112). Within this narcissistic attitude, the other is reduced to the needs of the self and perceived solely in relation to the self as object (van Ewijk 2009: 139). In Wallace's first novel *The Broom of the System*, the entrepreneurial "genetic-engineering giant" (1997: 149) Norman Bombardini approaches the problem of subject formation from a similar cultural logic. He seeks to "maximize Self by eating himself to infinite size" (Boswell 2003: 54). His infatuation with the protagonist Lenore leads up to his attempt "to eat her," to absorb the other into his own body/self. In *IJ*, such self-centered attempts at self-discovery are represented through E.T.A.'s ranking system, which objectifies both self and other and places them in direct competition for selfhood. By climbing the ladder of rankings, the individual expands the self through an assimilation of those who stand below it.

---

4   A stand-in for the later Wittgenstein who has practically been replaced by the postmodern materialism of the tennis academy under a new headmaster.

'Pointing at' the self as if it were an object leads into an infinite regress of (self-) justification, as it fails to "establish an association between the word and the thing" (Wittgenstein 1986: §6). Such a definition of the self does not exist outside of language but merely functions within a linguistic utterance. Self-knowledge through introspection implies "regarding thoughts and feelings as objects that we somehow have in possession, and, subsequently, of regarding gaining self-knowledge as observing (and thus knowing) these objects 'in' ourselves" (den Dulk 2015: 148). As Hacker writes, "there is indeed such a thing as self-knowledge and self-consciousness; but it does not consist in an array of reports and descriptions of one's sensations, perceptions, thoughts, and feelings" (1990: 60). The 'picture-theory' of language as a mimetic, pictorial representation of the world which the E.T.A. system tries to establish correlates bodily behavior and that which is embodied. E.T.A.'s practice of representing the player's self by a number ultimately leads to the tennis academy's "carrot-and-stick philosophies" (Wallace 2006: 693) that represent the infinite regress of self-justification such a position leads into.

Attempting to create a meaning for the self by preserving their ranking, E.T.A. students soon discover that "achievement doesn't automatically confer meaning or joy on one's existence" (ibid). Radically abstracting the world in its equation of self and body, the E.T.A. system turns students into detached ironists for whom "The world becomes a map of the world" (ibid). While younger students who "still worship the carrot" (ibid) by pursuing a 'completion' of the self in climbing the ladder of rankings are said to be comparatively happy, carrot-worship being "a lucky way to live. Even though it's temporary" (ibid), older students at E.T.A. have grown aware of the ever-deferred nature of the "carrot" and therefore move from a motivation of 'having' to a compulsive 'want' (ibid: 694). Their "standing entirely in relation to one another" (ibid: 112) through their rankings is thus understood as a Derridean différance, as meaning emerges uncontrollably in an endless interplay of signifiers. However, as the novel notes, both views are "just the inverse of the same delusion" (ibid: 694). They lead to solipsism since language that is merely self-referential cannot establish a stable and meaningful selfhood. Linguistic atomism, as described in Wittgenstein's *Tractatus* as well as deconstruction, are thus two sides of the same coin, as both rely on (the illusion of) a direct link between language and reality. In both cases, language, and by analogy the player's self in tennis, is seen as trying to acquire meaning "by referring (or *trying* to refer) to something outside itself" (den Dulk 2015: 138). This leads to the players' inability to "put into words (give reality to) [...] their selves" (ibid.: 146). The

Other in a 'tennis-*jeu*' is thus assigned the role of an object against which the self defines itself. As meaning, and therefore also the meaning of the self, is continually deferred, this results in a compulsive state of *"want"* (Wallace 2006: 694), typical of consumer culture. The logic of capitalist exploitation of the (other's) body for one's own self-definition creates an instable self. The students' selves become empty constructs captivated in "a kind of radical abstracting of everything, a hollowing out of stuff that used to have affective content" (ibid: 693). Self-knowledge through numbers, i.e., biocapitalist self-design as object, must reduce that which makes us human to abstract ideas. The postmodern logic of *IJ*'s society allows for "denotation but not connotation" (ibid).

The Subject's Deforming Digitization of the Body

This reduction of players' selves to abstract numbers produces grotesquely fragmented laboring bodies. As Severs remarks on the distinctive imbalance of the fragmented bodies described in the novel, "Wallace's expressionist idiom, inspired by Kafka, uses bodily deformity to vivify inward states: imbalance and leglessness are not realistic symptoms of psychology so much as a cultivated language for the psyche all its own" (2017: 96). However, bodily deformity, rather than just entirely a literary expressionist description of the character's inside, is presented as an effect of the cultural logic prevalent in the novel.

Biocapitalist politics are represented by way of a grotesque realism. As Bakhtin remarks, "a [grotesque] body [...] is never clearly differentiated from the world but is transferred, merged, and fused with it. [...] It acquires cosmic dimensions, while the cosmos acquires a bodily nature" (1984: 339). The grotesque body in *IJ* relates biocapitalist politics to human anatomy. Students at E.T.A. are thus described as "bodies hastily assembled from different bodies' parts" (Wallace 2006: 100). The materialistically rationalized training at E.T.A. encourages players to "carry a tennis-ball around in [their] stick-hand, squeezing it over and over [...] until [...] [their] right forearm is three times the size of [their] left and [their] arm looks from across a court like a gorilla's arm [...] pasted on the body of a child" (ibid: 173).

The body here manifests the capitalist language of digital doublings. With the world becoming a map of the world, the self-objectification that prepares E.T.A. students for their work in the entertainment industry not only defers the self. The language of the self's reduction to and fragmentation into the atomic facts of the body also manifests itself in a fragmentation and deformation of the body. The grotesque deformation of the players' bodies thus does not merely represent an inward state but manifests biocapitalist language use.

Notably, the detrimental effects of this capitalist logic of the body do not only affect the producers, the laboring bodies and quantified selves of the novel's young tennis players. 'Digit-ization', an understanding of the self as abstract digits, also deforms the consumers of entertainment. In fact, the solipsist double bind *Infinite Jest*'s image culture poses makes the digitized solipsist both producer and consumer of objectified body data. They are both alienated from the other and the self. The individual objectifies and absorbs the other in pursuit of totality and stable selfhood, being incapable of accepting the reality of the other as anything but 'use' for the self (subjective solipsism). At the same time, the (objectified) self is defined by the other, lacking centrality and coherence (objective solipsism).

Thus, toward the end of the novel, a terrorist group catches hold of the lethally entertaining 'Infinite Jest', kidnapping "field-test *Subjects*" (ibid: 727, emphasis mine) to digitally measure the film's "motivational range" (ibid):

> For inquiry into the degree of motivation the cartridge will induce, M. Broullime had rolled himself blindfolded into the room of storage holding an orthopedic saw and informed the Subject of the test that, as of beginning now, each subsequent reviewing of the Entertainment now would have the price of one digit from the Subject's extremities. [...] Broullime's explanation to Fortier was that thus a matrix could be created to compute the statistical relation between (n) the number of times the Subject replayed the Entertainment and (t) the amount of time he took to decide and remove a digit for each subsequent (n+1) viewing. The goal was to confirm with statistical assurance the Subject's desire for viewing and reviewing as incapable of satiation. There could be no index of diminishing satisfaction as in the econometrics of normal U.S.A. commodities. For the samizdat Entertainment's allure to be macropolitically lethal, the ninth digit of extremities had to come off as quickly and willingly as the second. (ibid)

As can be seen in this macabrely digital method of measuring subjective experience, the subject in the context of "econometrics" (ibid) is reduced to its body. With the logic of supply and demand projected onto the body, a "self-obliterating logic in the micro-economics of consumer high-tech" (ibid: 145) expands to the sphere of embodiment. The consumer of "the Entertainment," "the Subject" (literally) deconstructs the body in pursuit of solipsist self-forgetting. Digitization thus gains a double meaning. On the one hand, it describes a "digital doubling of the world" (Nassehi 2019: 135, my translation). Philosophical deconstruction becomes an increasingly naturalized mode of experiencing the world. On the other hand, digitization here describes a literal translation of interior processes into digits, material reality: the digits the test-subjects are willing to cut off, physically deconstructing themselves. Wallace implies that both forms of digitization and deconstruction are related, as the deconstructed body manifests the deconstructionist language. Digitization affects self and body alike. This digitization turns the consumer of objects into a 'prosumer': spectation generates data to be used by *IJ*'s terrorist group. "The Entertainment," so compelling it eradicates the self by turning viewers into catatonic, empty shells, also endangers the wholeness of the body. Wallace thereby relates the biocapitalist phenomenon of 'prosumption' to language. As the novel argues, a neoliberal, materialist, and therein ultimately solipsizing perspective on the subject as being the body disfigures the body of producer and consumer alike. The effects of objectification of subjects are the same on both ends of the entertainment industry.

Being a Body vs Having a Body

IJ offers a tentative solution to self-objectification by way of an ethical application of the later Wittgenstein's public language game philosophy.[5] Schtitt's theory of tennis that conceives of tennis as a public language game that derives its meaning from the reciprocal interaction of subjects according to a community's conventions, serves as a therapy to solipsism. The (laboring) body thereby undergoes a reconceptualization from being equated to the meaning of the self to the self being viewed as manifest in, yet not equal to, the body. Stable and meaningful selfhood can only occur in a communal

---

5   Wallace (mis)reads the shift in Wittgenstein's thinking from the atomism of the *Tractatus* to the ordinary language philosophy of his *Philosophical Investigations* as ethically motivated. Wallace therefore views the institution of public language games as a therapy for solipsizing private language use and thus as a moral, rather than logical, imperative.

interplay between subjects rather than the "body in commerce with bodies" (Wallace 2006: 160).

While the tennis taught by the statisticians at E.T.A. resembles a Derridean *jeu* in which the meaning of the self is continually deferred, Schtitt represents a therapeutic version of tennis in the form of a Wittgensteinian public language game. Alluding to both Derrida and Wittgenstein who refer to language as a game (jeu/Spiel), tennis in *IJ* appears as an analogy for either a solipsizing endeavor linked to neoliberalism or a communitarian public language game. The attempt to reduce the meaning of a word like 'the self' to an irreducible structure like the statistics of the body leads into an infinite regress. Wittgenstein, however, shows that such an essential meaning is irrelevant for the meaningful functioning of language. For Wittgenstein, a word's meaning is its usage in a specific context according to a community's rules and conventions (Wittgenstein 1986: §43). The 'real tennis' of Schtitt accordingly aims at a reconfiguration of the relationship between self and other by foregrounding the interconnection between players. In Schtitt's version of tennis, players are called to "sacrifice the hot narrow imperatives of the Self – [...] the individual appetitive will – to [...] a team [...] and a set of delimiting rules" (Wallace 2006: 83). This form of tennis gives the self "the chance to play" (ibid: 84) meaningfully within the conventions and intersubjective reciprocity of a community.

Schtitt thus views tennis not as a competition between opposing bodies but views the other as offering the "*occasion* for meeting the self" (ibid: 84, original emphasis). The meaning of the self is thus not derived from its (continually deferred) connection to the world as object but from the sanctioning function of a community that watches over usage's abidance by its rules and conventions. If self and other are treated as potential equals, the other is afforded with an 'otherness' that allows it to function as a dialogic partner. It becomes an other subject rather than an object. Self-knowledge neither derives from self-centered introspection nor from a competitive absorption of the other as an objectified opponent into the "multiform cravings of the individual appetitive will" (ibid: 82). Rather, the presence of the other as subject provides the individual with the opportunity "to transcend the self in imagination and execution" (ibid: 84) and to "[d]isappear inside the game" (ibid). Thus, meaningful self-knowledge is gained through the individual's "turning to his connection to the world" (den Dulk 2015: 148) and interacting with an other subject in "this infinite system of decisions and angles and lines" (Wallace 2006: 84).

Schtitt therefore opposes E.T.A.'s objectification of self and other, teaching his students that "You are not arms" (ibid: 461). From a Wittgensteinian perspective, self and body are not identical. As Hacker remarks with regard to Wittgenstein's conception of the body, while "the utterances [...] of human beings are *also* forms of behaviour, they are uses of language too – and they are not *about* behaviour" (1990: 242, original emphasis). Wittgenstein thus repudiates "the Cartesian and behaviourist conceptions of body and behaviour, as well as the Cartesian picture of the mind" (ibid.: 251). Rather, what communicates meaningfully according to communal conventions is the 'I' in the language game. It manifests itself in the body's behavior, but is not to be equated with it.

Schtitt's public language game opposes E.T.A.'s materialist identification of body and selfhood and demands of his students to "[o]ccur" in the "game's two heads' one world" (Wallace 2006: 461). While the body and its behavior cannot be eliminated from the game of tennis, it cannot be equated with the player's occurrence in the game, their self, either. As Hacker summarizes the later Wittgenstein's position, "if people's expressions of pain were not integrated into more general patterns of pain behaviour, their words would be meaningless" (1990: 242). Tennis provides a 'vocabulary' of movements to expand the "containing boundaries" of a game that is solely "bounded by the talent and imagination of self and opponent" (Wallace 2006: 82). Athletic prowess thereby expands the subject's repertoire of moves and responses to express itself (its self) in dialogue with the other, yet the body and its behavior is not what we mean when we speak about the subject. Meaningful selfhood can only be achieved if the player can abstain from the totalizing tendencies of a neoliberal individualism that conceives of the game as a semi-solipsist competition.

Schtitt's communal tennis does not oppose the optimization of the body and rankings based in statistics but uses "the rankings to help you determine where you are, not who you are" (ibid: 175). The work of the body in this communal, reciprocal approach to the game is to provide the subject with a vocabulary of tennis moves used to interact with the other player. Stable and meaningful selfhood, the novel shows, can only be achieved within such a reciprocal dialogue between subjects that *have* bodies that manifest self-expression but *are not* the self. Self-knowledge is not a matter of self-reflexive introspection, of viewing the self as an object that can be measured and quantified into digits. The self exists in and through a dialogue with a discrete other within the intersubjective reciprocity of a community.

Reading as Work of the Body

Wallace's therapy of postmodern solipsism extends the intratextual portrayal of Schtitt's Wittgensteinian theory of tennis to the literary work itself, understood as both a form of labor and a communication between coequal partners in the production of meaning. Wallace would therefore characterize the reader in poststructuralist theory as a prosumer: the meaning of a text is produced by the reader as she reads/consumes it. Constructing an analogy between tennis and the literary work, both being regarded as forms of labor in the entertainment industry, Wallace's fiction on the other hand stylizes itself as a 'public language game' between author and reader. The reader is thus provided with a coequal counterpart in the production of meaning. Reading can cease to be a self-reflexive, isolated activity and turn into ethically meaningful communication. The book is no longer merely an object of value 'prosumed' by the reader, but a reciprocal conversation about the subject of values. Highlighting the materiality of the work, as literature is a medium the reader (and the author) have to put physical work into, Wallace stages the author-reader relationship by emphasizing the laboring body. His fiction thus breaks with the poststructuralist concept of the "death of the author" in order to reestablish author and reader as embodied subjects capable of sincere and therapeutically effective communication. Such a reconfiguration of author and reader, however, does not entail a regression to biographical reading. While the conception of the author as historical entity that is the sole producer of meaning is rightly rejected by poststructuralist theory, the authorial and readerly bodies Wallace's work foregrounds must be understood as lacking any firm referent in the outside world, and the resurrected author emerges as effaced yet present communicative other.

Spanning several meandering, achronologically narrated plots starring an almost unmanageably large amount of characters and filled with a highly specialized vocabulary, *IJ* is far from an easy read. As such, it resists the passive entertainment the society it describes is obsessed with. In addition, with 1079 pages, 97 of which compose an appendix of 388 small-font endnotes, about 5cm thick and at more than a kilogram, even in its pure physicality calling *IJ* unwieldy would not be an understatement.

As Vladimir Nabokov claims in his *Lectures on Literature*:

> When we read a book for the first time the very process of laboriously moving our eyes from left to right, line after line, page after page, this compli-

cated physical work upon the book, the very process of learning in terms of space and time what the book is about, this stands between us and artistic appreciation. (1980: 3)

Wallace's *IJ*, on the other hand, utilizes this "physical work upon the book" (ibid.) *for* "artistic appreciation" (ibid.), by drawing attention to the materiality of the novel and the reader's experience as an embodied subject. In particular, the novel's endnotes, a trademark of Wallace's style, involve the reader's active participation and her bodily work. As the reader is forced to continuously page back and forth between text and endnotes, the novel mimics a game of tennis. The reader's experience of materiality in the "game" of reading implies an embodied subject as "partner in the dance" (Wallace 2006: 84) on the other end of literary communication, i.e., the author. Reading, experienced as (physical and mental) work, thus forms a language game bound to arbitrary rules and conventions, such as reading from left to right, starting on the first page, and following references to endnotes from the main text into the back of the book, in which meaning is produced through the reciprocal work of coequal subjects.

When Hal Incandenza on his phone's answering machine records the response "'This is the disembodied voice of Hal Incandenza, whose body is not able...' and so on" (ibid: 845), he resembles the author's dissolution in poststructuralist theory. His message is ironically detached and transformed into text. Schtitt, on the other hand, stresses the need for "Any something. The *what*: this is more unimportant than that there is *something*" (ibid: 83, original emphasis) in tennis. Dialogic communication necessitates an 'other' as reader, a partner who cannot be assimilated to the self. Work can reveal this 'other'.

Conclusion

Even though it is not concerned with the actual Quantified Self movement, Wallace's negotiation of neoliberal conceptions of work, body, and selfhood offers an important reflection on self-quantification. As can be seen in the quantified selves of *IJ*'s laboring athletes, it is represented as a manifestation of a cultural logic of biocapitalism, postmodernism and certain ideas of poststructuralism internalized into the lived experience of an image culture. Applying a Wittgensteinian perspective, Wallace's work diagnoses US capitalism as promoting a solipsizing private language use in its equation of representation and reality, use and exchange value and, in the latest precipitate of neoliberalism, objectified body and selfhood. Biocapitalist self-quantification strips the other of its otherness and renders the self object-like. The quantified self, promising self-knowledge through the numbers it generates from the body, therefore represents a misunderstanding of the 'self' as a quantifiable object, the laboring body as private property,[6] living capital, and the neoliberal entrepreneur of the self (Foucault 2008: 226). What is called 'self-tracking' can only track the person's behavior, not the self. The quantified self project, Wallace's Wittgensteinian position would argue, constitutes a capitalist misunderstanding of the self. It misunderstands how one uses 'self' or 'I'. Self-knowledge is neither knowledge of the body nor is it a matter of self-reflexive introspection that describes an interior state in the manner of a quantifiable object only oneself has access to. Instead, self-knowledge is a product of one's relation to others. The subject, never absolute, McGinn explains, "emerges slowly as its life becomes structured through the acquisition of new and more complex language games" (1997: 52).

Nevertheless, knowledge of the body and physical work is of importance for Wallace and Wittgenstein. Self-tracking, correctly understood as body-tracking, can allow for actual self-knowledge, though not in the way of introspection. Rather tracking the body's behavior can allow oneself to treat one's self as another subject in a language game, the only place where (self-) knowledge can occur. Since it is often the case that "To attain authentic self-knowledge is typically far more difficult, not easier, than to achieve knowledge of the character, motivation, and personality of others" (Hacker 1990: 60), body tracking can allow me to enter a meaningful dialogue with myself. Therefore, while utterances such as "I love you" are, with regard to myself, expressions of my relation to you (and not so much simple descriptions of an inner state I might know or not know), others who hear me expressing my love can know that I am in love. To me, there can be no doubt, only self-deception, whether I am in love or not. Someone else may judge my behavior (of which not only my utterances but possibly my heart-rate, cheery or romantically depressed mood etc. would be useful criteria) and either know more about myself or doubt that I am in love. In the same way, body-tracking could enable me to

---

6   Marxist and Wittgensteinian notions of privacy thus converge in Wallace's analysis of neoliberal, postmodern America.

judge, and thus know, whether the other features of my behavior fits my expression or whether I am deceiving myself. The self I want to gain knowledge of here is not an object but emerges from a form of communication that needs two subjects (although in this case, both are the same person).

In *IJ*, a therapeutic recognition of the other as co-equal subject affords one's recognition of, but not reduction to, materiality. Wallace offers a solution to the danger of solipsism involved in self-quantification through the reconfiguration of the literary work as a reciprocal interaction between dialogic partners. Wallace applies the metaphor of tennis as work to the literary activity of reading and writing. As a billboard in *IJ* announces, "LIFE IS LIKE TENNIS THOSE WHO SERVE BEST USUALLY WIN" (Wallace 2006: 952). While a form of work that treats the other as an object creates a state of existential loneliness, meaningful selfhood can be found through work for and with the other. (The literary) work becomes meaningful if it is seen as a service. Rather than "body in commerce with bodies" (ibid: 160), Wallace's fiction promotes a view of human interaction as work that engages the body but does not reduce the self to object biomaterial. In Wallace's physically and mentally challenging novel, author and reader alike experience themselves as bodies put to work in order to produce a work of (moral) value.

Works Cited

Bakhtin, Mikhail (1984): *Rabelais and His World*, Bloomington: Indiana University Press.
Boswell, Marshall (2003): *Understanding David Foster Wallace*, Columbia: University of South Carolina Press.
Burn, Stephen J. (2004): "'The Machine-Language of the Muscles': Reading, Sport, and the Self in *Infinite Jest*." In: Michael Cocchiarale/Scott D. Emmert (eds.), *Upon Further Review: Sports in American Literature*, Westport, Connecticut: Praeger, pp. 41-50.
Danter, Stefan/Reichardt, Ulfried/Schober, Regina (2016): "Theorising the Quantified Self and Posthumanist Agency. Self-Knowledge and Posthumanist Agency in Contemporary US-American Literature." In: *Digital Culture & Society* 2/1, pp. 53-67.
den Dulk, Allard (2012): "Beyond Endless 'Aesthetic' Irony: A Comparison of the Irony Critique of Søren Kierkegaard and David Foster Wallace's 'Infinite Jest.'" In: *Studies in the Novel* 44/3, pp. 325-345.

___ (2015): *Existentialist Engagement in Wallace, Eggers and Foer*, New York: Bloomsbury Academic.

Foucault, Michel (2008): *The Birth of Biopolitics: Lectures at Collège de France 1978-79*, Basingstoke: Palgrave Macmillan.

Hacker, Peter Michael Stephan (1990): *Wittgenstein Meaning and Mind*, Oxford: Basil Blackwell.

Hayles, N. Katherine (1999): "The Illusion of Autonomy and the Fact of Recursivity: Virtual Ecologies, Entertainment, and *Infinite Jest*." In: *New Literary History* 30/3, pp. 675-697.

Jameson, Fredric (1991): *Postmoderrnism, or, The Cultural Logic of Late Postmodernism*, Durham, NC: Duke University Press.

Kunow, Rüdiger (2015): "Wertkörper. Zur Ökonomisierung des menschlichen Körpers im Zeichen von Globalisierung und Neoliberalismus." In: *PROKLA* 178/1, pp. 51-66.

McGinn, Marie (1997): *Wittgenstein and the Philosophical Investigations*, London: Routledge.

Nabokov, Vladimir (1980): *Lectures on Literature*, New York: Harcourt Brace Jovanovich.

Nassehi, Armin (2019): *Muster: Theorie der Digitalen Gesellschaft*, München: C.H. Beck.

Rose, Nikolas (2001): "The Politics of Life Itself." In: *Theory, Culture and Society* 18/6, pp. 1-30.

Severs, Jeffrey (2017): *David Foster Wallace's Balancing Books. Fictions of Value*, New York: Columbia University Press.

van Ewijk, Petrus (2009): "'I' and the 'Other': The Relevance of Wittgenstein, Buber and Levinas for an Understanding of AA's Recovery Program in David Foster Wallace's *Infinite Jest*." In: *English Text Construction* 2/1, pp. 132-145.

Wallace, David Foster (1997): *The Broom of the System*, London: Abacus.

___ (2006): *Infinite Jest: 10th anniv.*, New York: Back Bay Books.

___ (2012a): *The Pale King*, London: Penguin.

___ (1993): "E Unibus Pluram." In: *The Review of Contemporary Fiction* 13/2, pp. 151-194.

___ (2012b): "The Empty Plenum: David Markson's Wittgenstein's Mistress." In: *Both Flesh and Not: Essays*, pp. 73-116.

Wittgenstein, Ludwig (1986 [1953]): *Philosophical Investigations*, Oxford: Basil Blackwell.

___ (2001 [1921]): *Tractatus Logico-Philosophicus*, London and New York: Routledge.

"Quantified Self Homepage," July 9, 2019 (https://quantifiedself.com/).

Reading Chick Lit through Numbers: Postfeminist Self-Quantification in Helen Fielding's *Bridget Jones's Diary* and Karyn Bosnak's *What's Your Number?*

Regina Schober

Sunday 15 January

> 9st (excellent), alcohol units 0, cigarettes 29 (v.v. bad, esp. in 2 hours), calories 3879 (repulsive), negative thoughts 942 (approx. based on av. per minute), minutes spent counting negative thoughts 127 (approx.). (Fielding 30)

A quantified self-profile like this one typically opens the chapters in Helen Fielding's *Bridget Jones's Diary*. Often considered the prototype of 'chick lit fiction', the novel introduces many of the genre conventions that would become part of the 'chick lit formula': a female narrator who struggles to balance career and relationships as well as the temptations of consumption within a modern, urban version of the traditional courtship plot, often narrated in a confessional and self-ironic mode (Whelehan 2005; Missler 2017; Harzewski 2011; Ferris & Young 2006). Yet, *Bridget Jones* also establishes another stylistic feature, one that has only received little scholarly attention: the predominance of numerical data in the self-conceptualization of its heroine. Bridget Jones begins almost every diary entry with a list of data that pertain to her weight, the intake of drugs such as alcohol and cigarettes as well as her emotional status or, as in this example, her thought processes. If quantification has always had a particularly prominent place in autobiographical writing, it is not surprising that fictional genres that fashion themselves as 'quasi-autobiographical' also make ample use of such modes of recording the self.

Bridget Jones is a 'statistical self' par excellence. Her regular self-monitoring through the introspective mode of the confessional diary reflects the genre's investment in and negotiation of disciplinary regimes that women in particular are often submitted to: both in terms of the optimization of their bodies and of their bank accounts, as the numerous anxious comments to overspending suggest. The desire to be thin and, portrayed as a logical consequence, attractive, unites most chick lit heroines. Bodily perfection often correlates directly with economic success. The numerical charts at the beginning of *Bridget Jones's* chapters reflect the normative systems of neoliberal subject formation in which being attractive ensures a higher market value, both in a competitive job *and* marriage market. In this respect, as Stephanie Harzewski has suggested, *Bridget Jones* and other chick lit novels can be read as postfeminist retellings of the 19th century novel of manners: "With Edith Wharton and Austen as acknowledged precedents, chick lit chronicles heroines' fortunes on the marriage market and assesses contemporary courtship behavior, dress, and social motives" (4). Bridget Jones's body data is therefore part of a larger self-optimization project she has set herself at the beginning of the novel, as her New Years' resolutions list attests to: "Reduce circumference of thighs by 3 inches (i.e. $1\frac{1}{2}$ inches each), using anti-cellulite diet," followed by "Save up money in form of savings. Poss [sic] start pension-also" and, finally, "Form functional relationship with responsible adult" (3). These more or less concrete plans for a more economical, thinner, and happier new year read like a business proposal in that they contain desirable outcome and target values, each of which are continuously followed up and monitored throughout the entire novel.

However, the protagonist Bridget Jones does not simply follow the behavioral rules of a weight-obsessed, materialist society. In an ironic gesture, the data list also explicitly comments on her numbers ("excellent"/"v. v. bad" etc., 30) and, in absurd accuracy, refers to the number of minutes spent thinking "good" vs "bad" thoughts, while adding the qualifier "approx." with a pseudo-scientific formula for calculating this. Throughout the novel, it becomes clear that Bridget Jones is hyperaware of the normative definitions of what constitutes 'good' and 'bad' behavior for a modern female. Yet, her ironic comments reveal that she is both unable to reach these goals and that she does not take them as seriously as the data charts suggest.

I argue that the function of quantification of Bridget's struggle towards self-optimization is ambiguous: On the one hand she believes in the rewards of a beautiful, healthy, and productive body, using self-recording as a tool for self-discipline and -regulation. Her constant self-reflection resulting from the rationalization of eating and working habits mirrors and reinforces society's demand for the functioning (female) body. On the other hand, the ironic subtone in this list of failed achievements subverts the normative values of self-optimization. As I suggest in the following, numerical passages contribute significantly to the ambiguous politics that chick lit novels embody. As a form of narrative rupture, the data charts expose and critically subvert the logic of a rating culture, while at the same time confirming some of their underlying normative assumptions. Numbers in chick lit both discipline and liberate female characters and readers, thereby considerably informing the postfeminist agenda of these novels. In reading numerical data as key elements in chick lit's postfeminist aesthetics, I aim to shed light on the largely overlooked importance of the narrative liminality of 'data' in popular genre fiction, and more specifically in chick lit, since most of the critical discussion on quantified knowledge and data in narrative so far has focused on 'highbrow' narratives and/or genres that are typically associated with a male readership. At the same time, I seek to make productive some of the recent debates in self-tracking narratives for the field of popular women's writing, thereby raising new perspectives on the relationship between numbers, narrative, the economy, and the body. In the first part of this essay, I will refer to *Bridget Jones's Diary* in my theorization of chick lit's complicated relationship with self-quantification. Then, I will discuss another chick lit novel, one that both explicitly thematizes and implements the logic of numerical data. The protagonist in Karyn Bosnak's *What's Your Number?* (2011) deliberates on the practical value of relying on numerical knowledge in finding 'Mr. Right' after an exasperating search through her list of ex-boyfriends, all the while entrenching the view of sexuality-as-consumption, as often conveyed in postfeminist narratives.[1]

One of the few engagements with the function of quantification in chick lit fiction is Eva von Contzen's essay "Experience, Affect and Literary Lists." Von Contzen regards literary employments of lists primarily as moments of

---

1 The term 'postfeminism' comprises a plethora of different discourses and perspectives, depending primarily on the meaning of the prefix 'post', which insinuates on the one hand a rejection of feminism and on the other hand a revision of feminism under new precepts. In the context of this essay I emphasize aspects of commodification in postfeminist aesthetics, while negotiating the feminist potentials of such narratives. Therefore, I take as a vantage point Yvonne Tasker's and Diane Negra's definition of postfeminist culture as working "in part to incorporate, assume, or naturalize aspects of feminism" as well as "to commodify feminism via the figure of woman as empowered consumer" (2).

rupture: "Lists challenge our reading habits because they break open the sequential flow of the narrative. At the same time, the items that are enumerated and the list as a whole pose a challenge to the content of the narrative into which the list must be integrated" (2018: 316). These challenges, von Contzen observes, operate on the level of affective responses ("frustration, delight, interest, curiosity, and so forth" [ibid: 316]) and, more centrally, they involve a practical understanding of experientiality. Experientiality, in von Contzen's view, diverges from Monika Fludernik's conceptualization of narrative as a cognitive enactment of character's emotions and embodiment (1996: 12). Yet, von Contzen suggests, when encountering lists in narrative, the reader does not immediately perceive the protagonist's experience of lists. Rather, the experientiality of lists is enacted because the reader is fundamentally familiar with the form of the list and the practice of list-making: "Lists, then, are not only reminiscent of a real-life experience: they directly evoke a practice that mirrors an everyday, real-life experience" (2018: 318). In her discussion of what she calls the "list narrative par excellence," *Bridget Jones's Diary*, von Contzen focuses in particular on the level of reader engagement that these lists evoke. Drawing on Wolfgang Iser's reader-response theory, von Contzen argues that the many lists in this novel (including Bridget's shopping lists) contain syntactical and conceptual blanks that readers actively have to create. The ability to connect data items relies to a large extent on the reader's experience with the form of the list (ibid: 322) and on the affordances of the specific form of the list (ibid: 324).

Several implications can be drawn from von Contzen's theoretical deliberations for self-quantification in chick lit novels: Firstly, since numerical data are often presented in the non-narrative form of lists, they can equally be regarded as moments of disrupting the narrative, of evoking affective responses such as frustration, boredom, and so on. Consequently, lists can be understood as one of several devices that actively break with the normative cultural narratives of attractiveness, matrimony, and financial success which these female protagonists have internalized and which they at least partly believe to be valid. As with other disruptive devices such as irony, the insertion of non-narrative elements therefore challenges the teleology of the classic 'Cinderella plot', self-referentially drawing attention to the constructedness of both list and narrative (especially when the list is annotated with self-ironic comments).

On a formal level, lists therefore contribute to the general sense of ambiguity that chick lit novels convey. As Alison Umminger notes, chick lit certainly plays into Western beauty standards, while these narratives also "point to something greater than a narcissistic obsession with one's physique or sexual desirability; in virtually every novel, being thin has not only romantic but also financial rewards and repercussions" (2006: 240). At the same time, Umminger observes, "the women of chick lit are looking for a way out of or around the 'beauty myth', even as they unconsciously reinforce a number of its more destructive conclusions" (ibid: 241). They do so by emphasizing the importance of female labor and financial independence, by satirically exposing the destructiveness of female competitiveness and by often skeptically depicting men's potential to love or rescue females (ibid: 241). Read in this light, lists and quantification in chick lit offer moments of reflection in which the female reader can detach herself, at least momentarily, from the body cult propagated, for example, in women's magazines.

The second conclusion that can be drawn from von Contzen's model partly contradicts the first one: The accessibility of lists enables a stronger level of reader identification with the female protagonist. The imperfection of the novel's protagonist, as Suzanne Ferriss and Mallory Young note, elicits a high degree of compassion with the reader (2006: 3-4). And their heroines do so with a certain "self-deprecating humor that not only entertains but also leads readers to believe they are fallible – like them" (ibid: 4). Although lists challenge the logic of narrative and therefore function at least in part as subversive devices, their experientiality provides an entry point into the narrative, as it connects reader experience with that of the story world. Data systems such as lists or numerical charts, due to their recognizability and verisimilitude, represent modes of organization that are highly familiar to any reader and therefore render these narratives both manageable and relevant (among other features, such as colloquial language, thematization of everyday concerns, the use of multimodality etc.).

The high level of reader identification, described by Missler as "the 'that's me'-phenomenon" (2017: 10) has contributed to the enormous success of this genre. Deeply embedded in a neoliberal culture in which processes of list-making and self-quantification have become standard modes of self-observation and -optimization, readers of chick lit fiction can readily identify with the novels' protagonists. Data that relate to weight, caloric intake, and exercise, especially, are so pervasive in media discourse aimed at young women (women's magazines, makeover shows, video blogs etc.) that many readers perceive familiarity and intimacy with such discourses of project-based subjectivity.

As Rocío Montoro argues in her stylistic analysis of chick lit, the (seemingly) accessible charts remind the reader of self-help manuals or *Cosmopolitan* diet plans (2012: 24). Bridget Jones's desperate attempts to remodel herself neatly corresponds with the recommendations of self-help books. It may seem ironic that, after the second wave of feminism (1960s through 1980s), the chick lit heroine of the 1990s does not embrace the third wave of feminism (one that emphasizes intersectionality of female subjugation, for example) but rather has to rely on the authority of self-help literature. Indeed, self-help manuals' seemingly clear structure suggests a problem-solving approach to self-actualization, with a rather simple 'how to' formula of achieving bodily, relationship, and career success. However, unlike female protagonists of the 1980s, the chick lit heroine is by no means an embodiment of success. She is "neither a superwoman nor a role mode; she is in fact a rather ordinary protagonist – an Everywoman" (Missler 2017: 10). Often, she is presented (or rather, presents herself) as clumsily struggling and continuously failing (yet of course always charming and at least trying to succeed). Heike Paul suggests that chick lit explicitly parodies the predominantly male tradition of success manuals à la Benjamin Franklin or, one may add, Horatio Alger's *Ragged Dick*, since "the emphasis is always on the spectacular failure" (2007: 64). Rather than presenting a strong, powerful woman, chick lit explores the insecurities and contradicting anxieties of womanhood that result from both the 'burden' of feminism and the complexities of juggling competing female roles, such as simultaneously incorporating the desire for independence and for sustaining a meaningful relationship and/or even the desire to have a family. As Diane Negra remarks, "postfeminism often functions as a means of registering and superficially resolving the persistence of 'choice' dilemmas for American women" (2009: 2). Similarly, Imelda Whelehan notes that

> the chick lit heroine is crippled by the burden of choice – most particularly the freedom to remain single – and suffers indefinable lassitude at the prospect of career advancement. She assumes the successes of feminism without feeling the need to acknowledge the source of these freedoms; in fact, feminism lurks in the background like a guilty conscience. (2005: 176)

Read in this light, chick lit's frequent use of charts, lists, and numerical data may function as a way to both reflect and manage the fragilities of what Rosalind Gill has called the "choice biography," one of the features she assigns to the postfeminist "sensibility" (2007: 148) that can be found in many media products of the 1990s and 2000s. The contradictory nature of postfeminism, according to Gill, links a feminist desire for empowerment and individualism with a strong "emphasis upon self surveillance, monitoring and discipline" (ibid: 149). Choice, in this regard, can be both a matter of empowerment and self-determination, but, as Gill notes, postfeminism is entangled with the neoliberal narrative that success and failure can exclusively be assigned to individual responsibility, as for an "almost total evacuation of notions of politics or cultural influence... every aspect of life is refracted through the idea of personal choice and self-determination" (ibid: 153). If every decision matters in the larger project of self-optimization, choice can become overwhelming. In view of the complexities of modern womanhood, the chick lit heroine therefore often expresses a desire for structure and guidance. As Gill notes, feminist fiction of the 1980s "depict women in control of their destiny and determined to forge their own path with or without men [while] chick lit heroines appear to wish to relinquish control (ibid: 188)." The chick lit's desire for guidance makes her particularly willing to rely on seemingly objective and accessible organizational structures.

Yet, lists, diet plans, numerical data, and spreadsheets also contain a formal openness that allows for reader engagement. If "Bridget's (in)ability to navigate these controlling texts" (Smith 2008: 2), namely the many self-help manuals, magazines, and advice by others, numbers and lists can be read as a way to regain control over her life and, subsequently, provide an opportunity for readers to enter the narrative through their own engagement with these data. Playfulness, one of chick lit's central aesthetic features, can have political implications if the decidedly non-academic popularization of feminist themes allows for fresh and more inclusive perspectives (cf. Paul 2007: 61).

If, to follow von Contzen's observation that lists invite an unusual degree of reader participation, numerical data function as a counter discourse to traditional narrative as data encourages different levels of reception: Numbers are not per se meaningful but they need to be compared, calculated, put into context. In short, data need to be individually narrativized in order to become meaningful. For example, how do we know whether Bridget Jones's weight of "9 st[one]" really is "excellent" or whether this is an ironic comment? We need contextual knowledge to interpret this number, for example relational data (compared to whom?), temporal information (is this more or less than before?) as well as a general framework of reference (in what normative system are these numbers acceptable and what are the foundations of this system?).

The individual narratives that readers construct may rely just as much on their own experiences as on the invisible links between the numbers on the page. This level of reader engagement that numbers evoke reflects the participatory culture from which chick lit has emerged and in which it is embedded. As Missler has shown, chick lit fiction is surrounded by a whole array of online media like blogs, social media forums, and fan fiction platforms (2017: 49). In its participatory affordances, the ambiguous politics of chick lit is deeply entwined with their postfeminist agenda: On the one hand chick lit lends female readers agency in encouraging them to co-construct the narratives they read and, in doing so, functions as a tool of collective empowerment and identity formation. On the other hand, the willingness of a postfeminist readership to identify with a neoliberal culture for which introspection is linked to forms of consumption also shows that internalized assumptions of such a self-optimization culture are widely accepted and reproduced. Numbers may be ironically narrativized both by readers and by the narrator, and yet, they constitute a large part of these narratives and serve as generic markers to ensure recognition and stability. Although the numbers allow for reader participation and generate a sense of relatability, chick lit, to quote Lauren Berlant, remains a "commodified genre of intimacy," in which a collective female experience is produced, yet one that ultimately "sees the expression of emotional response and conceptual recalibration as achievement enough" (2008: x). Ultimately, chick lit's formulaic model of female subjectivity mirrors its own deep interlinkages with commodity culture. Not only is chick lit itself a successful commodity (to which the accessibility of numerical charts and the analogies to self-help manuals contribute), but it also frames femininity as continuously optimizing to the point of self-commodification.

The numerical conceptualization of the female protagonist is thus indicative of its rather complicated politics. As Deborah Lupton suggests, we should regard the quantified self not only as a subject who engages in self-tracking practices but also as "an ethos and apparatus of practices" (2016: 3) that, to speak with Michel Foucault, carries specific biopolitical implications. The 'good citizen' of most chick lit narratives is a female who, despite all her failings and ironic detachment, eventually finds the path to an 'acceptable' BMI, matrimony, and monetary success (usually in this order). Her journey is accompanied by more or less rigid forms of numerical self-observation and measurement, while regularly challenging the normative values of numerical systems. Numbers both disrupt *and* confirm the regulatory narratives of postfeminist womanhood and therefore serve as fascinating signifiers of chick lit's aesthetic, cultural, and political agenda.

I will now illustrate some of the complexities of chick lit's relationship with numbers in my reading of Karyn Bosnak's 2006 novel *What's Your Number?* The title alone is revealing. Female protagonist Delilah Darling, a 29-year-old project manager at a retail company in New York, worries about her 'number' in two different, yet related ways: not only is she fired from her job and is therefore under financial pressure, but also, as she openly confesses at the beginning of the novel, she is worried about her sexual 'track record'. Based on a newspaper article she has read according to which "the average person has 10.5 sexual partners in their lifetime" (3), Delilah realizes that her number is almost twice above the national average and that she needs to draw a line at no. 20 before she gets married – a number she very soon reaches, obviously to her great dismay. After a period of self-contempt, of thinking of herself as "a huge fuck-up" (ibid: 33), and of briefly considering sexual abstinence, she works out a plan:

> Tony Robbins says what separates the good from the great is the ability to take action, so that's what I'm going to do – take action! I'm going to get in a car and find these guys one-by-one. I'm going to do this and it's going to work! Celibacy is not an option, damn it – it's not! (ibid: 59)

Delilah's interior monologue oscillates between the most self-denigrating thoughts and an energetic sense of will power. The reference to bestselling life coach and author of *Unlimited Power* (1986) and *Awaken the Giant Within* (1991), Tony Robbins, underscores Delilah's newly found self-determination that enables her to embark on a major self-discovery journey. Written in diary form, the novel contains typical chick lit elements such as a courtship plot and self-ironic references to the struggles of fitting in with the image of 'perfect' womanhood. *What's Your Number?* combines the chick lit formula with the 'most American' of all genre, the road novel, and its focus on a personal quest of self-discovery – a topos that has traditionally mainly featured male protagonists (from Henry David Thoreau in *Walden* to Sal Paradise in Jack Kerouac's *On the Road*). Unsurprisingly, the novel makes ample usage of lists, references to numbers, and statistical self-observations. In fact, the novel is quite distinct in its explicit thematization of the numerical systems that structure the female protagonists' self-evaluations, anxieties, and desires. Both in its adoption and critical refusal of self-quantification, the novel therefore offers valuable insights into the forms, functions, and cultural politics of numbers in contemporary popular women's writing.

Delilah's adamant submission to her self-inflicted numerical regime evokes the Puritan rhetoric of predestination ("What if I'm supposed to marry Roger? What if last night was a sign from God ... Maybe last night was destiny" [Bosnak 2006: 38]). Her almost spiritual belief in the significance of numbers that prompts her to undergo enormous financial and logistical effort may function as a humorous device, but in its satirical manner, it also brings into sharp focus the rigid rules that women subject themselves to and that they have internalized to an extent that they no longer need an authority to explicitly remind them of these rules. Speaking with Foucault, Delilah becomes a "docile body" (1995: 135) who has adopted the disciplinary power of domination without the presence of the dominating force.

Rather ironically, the traditional sources of authority, for example parents, church etc., are much more open-minded about behavioral rules than Delilah. Early on in the novel, Delilah confesses her 'sins' to Daniel, a young Catholic priest (who, in an ironic twist, turns out to be no. 2 in her list of ex-boyfriends). Daniel's answer may come as a refreshing surprise to readers who would expect Christian morality:

> "Delilah, if you didn't have sex with Roger last night, then you wouldn't be here today confessing. Am I right?"
> "Well, yeah, probably."
> "Exactly – you weren't sorry for any of them until you slept with the last one. And the only reason you're as upset as you are about all this is because you've hit some self-imposed limit."
> "So what? I'm still sorry now. Isn't that the point?"
> "No, because if you set your limit at twenty-five, then you wouldn't be here and you wouldn't be sorry. You'd be at home, nursing your hangover, trying to forget about the gross man you woke up next to. You're not truly sorry."
> (Bosnak 2006: 46)

Rather than enforcing the disciplinary power that Delilah has subjected herself to, it is the priest, of all people, who urges Delilah to question the totalizing nature of the supposedly objective value of numbers. That he is a Catholic priest may make his sexual history with Delilah all the more ironic, yet it is exactly *not* from the position of prudery that he lectures Delilah. Intriguingly, the novel frames Delilah's problem not as stemming from an oppressive authority, at least not directly, but as emanating from her own value system. This is problematic for many reasons: First, the novel does not address Delilah's destructive self-disciplining as a form of discursive power but instead grants complete responsibility to her, suggesting that she *is* in full charge of taking action and escaping the debilitating power of normative frameworks. Second, although Daniel does not exert traditional authoritarian power, as would be associated with the Catholic Church, the Socratic dialog through which Delilah's confession takes place, still displays a hierarchical relationship between the male priest and the female penitent. More specifically, Daniel's supposition that Delilah cannot be "truly sorry" suggests that he knows more than she does, that he has already got to the root of her 'problem'. "Listen," he continues, "there's a deeper issue here that you need to explore, and until you do that, until you figure out why it is you keep going through men, I'm not going to forgive you for any of these guys" (ibid: 46).

Daniel claims that there *is* a problem to begin with. The postulation of a "deeper issue" pathologizes Delilah's sexual behavior as a form of unhealthy promiscuity. Moreover, it evokes a Protestant psychoanalytic reasoning according to which the 'cure' or the 'solution' for this alleged promiscuity is to be found by radical introspection and self-monitoring – a practice that, as Max Weber has shown, is closely linked to capitalist productivity. Through the figure of Daniel the novel thus fuses the Catholic mode of confession with a Protestant call for self-revelation, and in doing so, drastically reinscribes (patriarchal) authority into the individual practice of self-monitoring. It is noteworthy, then, that although Daniel challenges Delilah's belief in the absoluteness of her specific number system, he does *not* destabilize the underlying assumption, namely that 'too many' sexual partners are not healthy. Daniel only reluctantly contests Delilah's practice of self-quantification – only to the extent that he does not believe that numbers can adequately express the 'right' or 'wrong' limit. However, even for a rather progressive priest, he believes in the necessity of restricting the number of sexual partners.

Rather unexpectedly, then, Daniel's 'solution' for Delilah is not to pray the rosary but to make a list: "Yes, a list. Figure out why you slept with each guy on it and then analyze why things didn't work out" (Bosnak 2006: 46). The replacement of praying with list-making humorously points to the spiritual nature of what Foucault has called a Western "technology of the self," the Christian confessional mode that aims at self-knowledge as a "truth obligation" of the self (1988: 22). Paradoxically, confession does not lead to self-emancipation, as Foucault argues, but rather aims at self-renunciation and thereby reinstalls "obedience to our master in all things" (ibid: 44). Daniel's advice for Delilah to work through her list of ex-boyfriends therefore can *not* be a simple solution, as the context of Catholic confession may suggest. "Del, there's no quick-fix to make this go away," Daniel admits (Bosnak 2006: 47). Rather, in line with the Protestant tradition of deep self-investigation, Delilah's journey is expected to be a spiritual pilgrimage, thus engaging in a tradition of 19th century young women's literature such as Louisa Alcott's *Little Women* with its explicit reference to spiritual and moral pilgrimages. The list, in this context, is a crucial navigational element in this journey, both for the protagonist and the reader. As an accessible tool of guidance it helps Delilah on her pilgrimage into her own past and thereby provides an essential structuring model for the unfolding narrative.

Both Delilah and the reader literally 'work' through the list, as each chapter, another ex-boyfriend can be ticked off as a result of embarrassing, disappointing, or catastrophic reunions with the men of her past (including being caught in the act of spying, an unintended stay at a rehab clinic, and an awkward confrontation at the funeral of her gay ex-boyfriend's husband). Reading through the list becomes a form of labor, of sequential task fulfillment that reaches the point of almost algorithmic automation. The tediousness of tracking her sexual past (both for Delilah and the reader) is a performative gesture of the necessary labor of the list as a tool for self-improvement. Yet, in contrast to traditional spiritual journeys in the tradition of John Bunyan's *Pilgrim's Progress*, Bosnak continuously breaks with such conventions by humorously complicating and thereby providing comic relief as well as rearranging, modifying, and summing up the 'items' on the list. So, on the one hand, the novel fully absorbs the logic of list-making, not only by thematizing it, but also by following its sequential logic. Once Delilah sets up the list, the plot almost writes itself, since the trajectory seems to be pre-programmed: one 'item' after the other is visited, if not in chronological, but still in geographically sequential order. The list therefore epitomizes the formulaic script of chick lit, according to which the fate of the female heroine is still more or less determined by the generic conventions that require the plot to resolve in a romantic happy ending.

And yet, Delilah's list allows for a certain amount of flexibility and spontaneity, depending on newly acquired knowledge about the men's current marital status, their current location etc. The list is adaptable to the extent that if pragmatic reasons demand a change of course, modifications take place. Formally, the provisional status of the list is reflected by its frequent updates placed at chapter beginnings. For example, chapter six begins with a collage of bio summaries, a road map with an inscribed route, and an updated and manually edited list (fig. 1).

Image 1

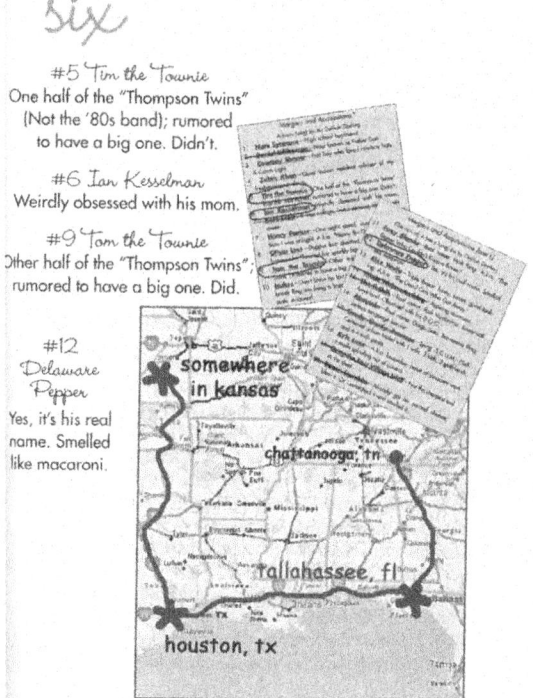

Reprinted with permission of HarperCollins

The data visualizations assorted in the chapter openings function as paratextual elements that support navigation and therefore ensure accessibility, while at the same time revealing the conditionality and contingency of such data systems. Readers encounter an updated version of the list, with slightly amended numerical order. Also, the narrative is presented as a necessary annotation to the list. Besides elaborating on and contextualizing the romantic episodes behind every number, the diary entries also explicitly refer to the specific construction of data, often inserting metacommentary on the creation of the list. Recounting the meeting with Spanish chef Abogado, for example, Delilah mentions that

> in my list of twenty, Abogado came after Rod, but almost two years after Rod. Although it was unintentional, I had a bit of a dry spell when I stopped going out every weekend. I didn't realize it at the time though. In fact, I didn't realize it until I made my list. (Bosnak 2006: 152)

For Delilah, the practice of data visualization functions as a form of self-detachment that permits her to momentarily externalize herself. Historically, as Alfred Crosby has demonstrated, the measurability and manageability of the self has resulted from the "quantitative representation of your subject that is, however simplified, even in its errors and omissions, precise...It possesses a sort of independence from you," allowing for more rigorous introspection (2013: 229). In the tradition of humanist self-observation, Delilah's lists provide access to behavioral patterns that become visible only in retrospect and in the contextual presentation of both narrative *and* numbers, rendering her self-knowledge more manageable, both to herself and to her readers.

Yet, Delilah is not the only quantified self in the novel. Her ex-boyfriends are also quantified by becoming items on her list. Self-tracking contributes to the subjectification of the female protagonist, while tracking her ex-partners objectivizes the male 'other'. Delilah more or less actively tracks herself (alcohol consumption, caloric intake, credit card debt etc.) in a process of self-optimization (all the while struggling to reject the demands of self-optimization), while the men are *being* tracked, often without their being aware of it. Yet, both forms of tracking are intricately connected. Delilah's internalized self-discipline is externalized into a form of control, as her sousveillance (in the form of tracking her own sexual history) turns into a form of surveillance of her ex-partners, especially since she collaborates with her neighbor Colin, who turns out to be a semi-professional private investigator. Both Delilah and her ex-boyfriends are commodified in the shaping of the neoliberal subject.

Yet, in the logic of the novel's autodiegetic narration, the two processes of tracking fulfill different functions. While for Delilah, self-tracking is a means of individualization, the men on her list are rather conceived of as a collective number, the sheer unmanageability of which provides one of the central challenges of the plot. On the list, men are perceived as abstract and more or less arbitrary entities more than as round characters. Supported by the internal focalization of the female protagonist, the men represent certain types that are necessarily reduced to brief profile statements ("Nate Syracus – high school boyfriend"; "Ian Kesselman – Weirdly obsessed with his mom"; "Abogado – Real name: Diego Soto. Barcelona fling"; etc.). Their status as deindividualized entities is enhanced by the fact that the first appearance of the list of men directly precedes a list entitled "Things to Do for a Road Trip," which essentially is a shopping list ("2. Buy road map for car. 3. Buy big black sunglasses, baseball hat, and binoculars for stakeouts" [ibid: 63]). The direct juxtaposition of these two lists, both framed as essential for the journey, exemplifies the commodification of male subjects. A typical feature of chick lit fiction, the commodification of mating partners has often been read in line with the genre's ambiguous postfeminism: on the one hand, it suggests sexual liberty, while on the other hand it obviously feeds into the neoliberal version of commodified sexuality. Just like the female body is rendered 'readable' and seemingly more manageable through quantification, the protagonist's dating history turns into a database that, similar to a bank statement, suggests that such data can be displayed, analyzed, and processed 'objectively' as well as managed and potentially monetized.

Simultaneously, the quantification of marriage candidates also serves to remind the protagonist of her excessive behavior and therefore functions as a means to instill normative values. The abstraction of individual experiences renders them more or less comparable in a competitive environment in which they function as markers for levels of self-perfection. Although they appear as items on the list, they are not ranked, but appear in chronological, therefore relatively arbitrary order. The non-hierarchical layout of this list makes individual men even more exchangeable, turning them into modular units that can be infinitely selected, combined, and re-assembled according to the protagonist's own taste. Adding to the commodification of men, every chapter ends with a 'balance sheet', as for example "$3,526, 37 days, 14 guys left" (ibid: 134). Delilah describes her ex-partners as resources, placed in immediate association with her financial capital and thus suggesting that finding her partner for life is a financial investment worth pursuing, since it can be profitable in the end.

Delilah's monetization of her marital quest, however, is tinged with irony. As she tells her best friend Michelle, her plan is highly strategic. Yet, Michelle reminds Delilah of the financial risk she is taking: "Del, we're not on a paid vacation. We've been laid off. You should be looking for a job, not for a ..." "A life partner," Delilah finishes Michelle's sentence, demonstrating that she *has* thought this through and that a spouse may inevitably trump such a short-term financial solution like a job (ibid: 65). The ellipsis in their conversation functions to leave room for ambiguity, as readers can decide for themselves what moral position they want to take – a strategy that reflects the structural openness of the list. Delilah reflects what Diane Negra has called a "heightened middle-class anxiety" in postfeminist depictions of female labor (2009: 91), embodying a tendency of these narratives of "moving the heroine out of a position of professional solipsism and into what they define as a more fully relational sphere" (ibid: 92). While Delilah certainly has no choice about the loss of her job, her readers do. They can decide whether they want to read Delilah's plan as a confirmation of traditional models of marriage and dependency on the male provider, as an emancipated refusal of exploitative labor, *or*, in filling in the blanks for Michelle, as a critique of economic-driven courtship, thus participating directly in their own construction of the novel's politics.

Yet, the end of the novel only seemingly resolves the ambiguity of the protagonist's relationship with quantification. Rather predictably, the road trip fails to provide a resuscitated relationship with one of Delilah's ex-partners. However, in line with the motif of the journey as a form of self-discovery, Delilah returns to her apartment in New York City to discover that Mr. Right has just been waiting for her in front of her doorstep the entire time. Preparing her readers for this romantic conclusion by admitting that what she is actually yearning for are *"real* connections" (Bosnak 2006: 225, original emphasis), as opposed to seemingly superficial/fake connections that result from her data list, the protagonist ultimately liberates herself from her self-imposed data structures and, after long deliberations, admits that she might find happiness in a relationship with no. 21. This turn is reflected on the formal level, as the book now reverts almost exclusively to the narrative mode, mostly abstaining from data charts toward the end. Colin, her neighbor who has helped her locate her ex-boyfriends, turns out to be the partner she has always been looking for. The heterosexual love plot (and, yes, again, it is the neighbor) of the chick lit is confirmed. And although *What's Your Number?*, like *Bridget Jones's Diary*, depicts the 'right' guy as more complex and less hypermasculine than all the previous, failed relationships, Colin is still a rather stereotypical character, especially with regard to his ethnicity (markers of his 'Irishness' include heavy drinking, creativity, charm, chaos etc.).

In admitting that Colin might be 'the one', Delilah realizes that numerical data regimes have obviously failed her. Yet, just when she begins to accept the deviation from her self-imposed numerical framework, the narrative restores normative order. In the epilogue, a final twist ultimately reinstates the logic of quantification. Delilah receives a phone call from one of her (alleged) sexual partners, Jim Nukerson, who informs her that they have never had sex. Looking at Colin, she realizes that her world, after all, is in order: "I snuggle into him, my #20... not that it matters anymore" (351). Again, she qualifies her statement, leaving it open to readers whether they want to 'buy' in to the alleged security of a numerical system or whether they want to read it as an ironic comment of a female character who has matured enough to dismiss this belief system as an unhealthy delusion.

The function of (self-)quantification in chick lit novels, as the analyses of *Bridget Jones's Diary* and *What's Your Number?* have suggested, depends to a large extent on reader participation. The confessional and often self-ironic tone of self-tracking in chick lit oscillates between reproducing and playfully questioning the neoliberal approach to the (female) body as a project which can be managed like a bank account and which requires self-responsible adjustment. Yet, not least because of the seamless integration of diary like passages like these, chick lit novels largely operate within and affirm such discourses of the quantified self as a commodified self, reinforcing the intrinsic value of self-optimization and financial as well as matrimonial success. It therefore remains for the reader to be determined how they will read the numbers and what narrative they will opt for in the ambiguous spaces between data and fiction.

Works Cited

Berlant, Lauren (2008): *The Female Complaint: The Unfinished Business of Sentimentality in American Culture*, Durham, NC: Duke UP.
Bosnak, Karyn (2006): *What's Your Number?* (previously titled *20 Times a Lady*), New York: Harper Collins.
Crosby, Alfred (2013): *The Measure of Reality: Quantification and Western Society 1250-1600*. Cambridge UP.
Ferriss, Suzanne/Young, Mallory (eds.) (2006): *Chick Lit: The New Woman's Fiction*, London, New York: Routledge.
Fielding, Helen (1996): *Bridget Jones's Diary*, London: Picador.
Fludernik, Monika (1996): *Towards a 'Natural' Narratology*, London: Routledge.
Foucault, Michel (1990): *The History of Sexuality. Vol. 1: An Introduction*, 1976, Robert Hurley (transl.), New York: Vintage Books.
___ (1988): "Technologies of the Self." In: Luther H. Martin/Huck Gutman/Patrick H. Hutton (eds.), *Technologies of the Self. A Seminar with Michel Foucault*, London: Tavistock Publications, pp. 16-49.

___ (1995 [1977]): *Discipline and Punish: The Birth of the Prison*, Trans. Alan Sheridan, New York: Vintage Books.

Gill, Rosalind (2007): "Postfeminist Media Culture: Elements of a Sensibility." In: *European Journal of Cultural Studies* 10/2, pp. 147-166.

Harzewski, Stephanie (2011): *Chick Lit and Postfeminism*, Charlottesville: University of Virginia Press.

Lupton, Deborah (2016): *The Quantified Self: A Sociology of Self-Tracking*, Cambridge: Polity.

Missler, Heike (2017): *The Cultural Politics of Chick Lit: Popular Fiction, Postfeminism and Representation*, London, New York: Routledge.

Montoro, Rocío (2012): *Chick Lit: The @stylistics of Cappuccino Fiction*, London: Continuum.

Negra, Diane (2009): *What a Girl Wants? Fantasizing the Reclamation of Self in Postfeminism*, London, New York: Routledge.

Paul, Heike (2007): "Feminist Chicks?: Chick Lit Als (Post)Feministische Populärliteratur." In: Heike Paul/Alexandra Ganser (eds.), *Screening Gender: Geschlechterszenarien in der gegenwärtigen US-Amerikanischen Populärkultur*, Münster: LIT, 59-74.

Smith, Caroline J. (2008): *Cosmopolitan Culture and Consumerism in Chick Lit*, London, New York: Routledge.

Tasker, Yvonne/Negra, Diane (eds.) (2007): *Interrogating Postfeminism: Gender and the Politics of Popular Culture*, Durham, NC: Duke University Press.

Umminger, Alison (2006): "Supersizing Bridget Jones: What's Really Eating the Women in Chick Lit." In: Suzanne Ferriss/Mallory Young (eds.), *Chick Lit: The New Woman's Fiction*, London, New York: Routledge, pp. 239-252.

von Contzen, Eva (2018): "Experience, Affect and Literary Lists." In: *Partial Answers* 16/2, pp. 315–27.

Whelehan, Imelda (2005): *The Feminist Bestseller: From Sex and the Single Girl to Sex and the City*, Houndmills, New York: Palgrave Macmillan.

"I Track my Cycle Religiously": Representations of Fertility Tracking and Childlessness in Contemporary Graphic Memoirs

Dorothee Marx

In recent years we have developed manifold ways of quantifying our lives, often with the help of smart devices. We use apps on our phones, watches or activity trackers like FitBit to count our steps, measure our calorie intake, track our weight or our workouts. The basis of our apparent need to self-track seems to be a wish for "self-control and improvement" (En/Pöll 2016: 45) and "self-optimisation" (ibid: 47) that leads to "the kind of self-knowledge that will create a fitter, happier, more productive person" (Crawford et al. 2015: 480). Other than tracking calorie intake or weight, or, in the era of smart devices, steps or heartrate, the female body offers further potential for quantification in terms of the menstrual cycle and fertility. While women have of course 'logged' their cycles long before the advent of smart phones (Ajana 2017: 3; Lupton 2015: 445), app creators have realized the market value of digitalizing the pen-and-paper cycle calendar and numerous apps and new smart devices for menstrual and fertility tracking have become available of late. They promise the user the advantage of a "more exact, detailed, and scientific approach that is able to produce data on a range of bodily functions that, when aggregated can provide greater accuracy than more traditional forms of self-tracking" (Lupton 2015: 445).

This article analyzes the assumptions and expectations about female fertility that become manifest in such fertility tracking apps and connects them to two contemporary graphic memoirs about infertility. I begin my analysis by examining three popular period/fertility tracking apps, namely *Clue*, *Glow*, and *Kindara*, and the way these apps are marketed and presented with the following questions in mind: What implications do these apps create for women, especially for women who are trying to conceive? On which assumptions about the able-bodied, cis-gender female body are these apps based? Can contemporary discourses about motherhood and fertility be inferred from these apps? I argue that the self-disciplining inherent in fertility tracking practices mirrors the surveillance of pregnant women that Molly Wiant Cummins illustrates in her article (2014), which shows how (self-)surveillance begins even prior to conception. In a second step, I connect the presentation of these apps and the image of in/fertility they create to the depiction of fertility tracking and childlessness in two contemporary graphic memoirs, namely *Good Eggs* (2010) by Phoebe Potts and *Broken Eggs* (2014), a webcomic by Emily Steinberg. Through this comparison, I examine in how far cultural representations of the female body, in this case in graphic narratives, are related to current practices of self-quantification and the image of the docile body that these practices create.

'Normalcy' and Responsibility in Self-Tracking

Before coming to the analysis of the apps and the two memoirs, I will briefly consider the historical origins of self-quantifying practices and their connection to concepts of 'normalcy'. Self-quantification is done primarily through numbers, as Gary Wolf made clear when he declared the official slogan of the Quantified Self-project to be "self-knowledge through numbers"' (Crawford et al. 2015: 490). Boka En and Mercedes Pöll (2016) describe self-quantification as the "scientisation of the self with the help of digital devices in self-tracking, based on valuing measures that provide reliable means of attaining self-control – like the supposed neutrality and credibility of numbers" (44). However, to be able to use numbers to quantify the body, one needs a baseline, that is, a 'normal', against which to measure and compare one's own numbers. The concept of normalcy developed in the 19th century (cf. Davis 1995) and many of the implications of contemporary self-tracking can be traced back to the origins of this concept. For example, Kate Crawford, Jessa Lingel, and Tero Karppi illustrate in their 2015 article how the development of the weight scale at the end of the 19th century, together with an "industry standard" table of weight and height became a "powerful dual technology for defining normalcy" (2015: 483). Marketing for the weight scale, initially aimed towards male customers, shifted towards women in the 1920s with the development of the domestic weight scale "where value and self-worth [could] be attached to the number of pounds weighed" (ibid). Before the 1920s, women had not been encouraged to diet (ibid), thus, this change in marketing reflects a shift in the public image of the female body that was reinforced by advertisements that showed women "in lingerie [...] posing provocatively on the scale" (ibid). This early history already illustrates how self-tracking, even through non-digital devices, is connected to "controlling" and "normalizing" bodies (ibid: 484) and showcases the powerful emotional impact self-tracking can have.

The concept of norm or average, which also lies behind the success of the weight scale, is connected to the rise of statistics in the 19th century (Davis 1995: 25f). In his seminal study of the construction of normalcy and disability, Lennard Davis, referring back to the appearance of terms like 'norm' and 'normality' in the English language and the establishment of statistics as a discipline, dates the "coming into consciousness of 'the norm' over the period 1840-1860" (1995: 24). Showing the connection between the quantification of the body and the commercialization of the collected data, Davis points out that many of the leading members of the first British statistical societies which formed in the 1830s and 40s were closely connected to industries or industrialists themselves (ibid). This indicates that the collection of numbers (read: data) was from the beginning connected to economic endeavors.

L'homme moyen, the average man of the Belgian statistician Adolphe Quetelet, consisted of a combination of the morally and physically average man (ibid: 26), which demonstrates the significant moral component that played into the construction of normalcy – a link which clearly resurfaces in contemporary self-quantification practices. Simultaneously, Quetelet's construct helped support the rising middle class:

> In formulating the idea of *l'homme moyen*, Quetelet is also providing a justification for *les classes moyens*. With bourgeois hegemony comes scientific justification for moderation and middle-class ideology. The average man, the body of the man in the middle, becomes the exemplar of the middle way of life. (Davis 1995: 24f)

Thereby, the norm or average becomes a desirable ideal (ibid: 27). Thus, "norming" the population becomes an enticing goal as well, so it should come as no surprise that most of the British industrialists in the statistical societies that Davis mentions also were eugenicists (ibid: 30), who conceived "of the body as perfectible but only when subject to the necessary control of the eugenicists" (ibid: 32).

As becomes evident, statistics and the quantification of the human body are from their beginnings linked to population control, (self-)improvement, and ideas of becoming a better member of the human race, or, in Foucauldian terms, a better biocitizen. Self-quantifiers turn their bodies into docile bodies, bodies "that may be subjected, used, transformed and improved" (Foucault 1995 [1975]: 136). While subscribing to bodily standards, for example of health, beauty or fitness (En/Pöll 2016: 40), users are attracted by a "promise of agency through mediated self-knowledge, within rhetorics of normative control and becoming one's best self" (Crawford et al. 2015: 494).

Deborah Lupton emphasizes how biopolitics and social sanctions for 'good' and 'bad' health behavior play into contemporary practices of self-quantification, underlining the

> emphasis on self-responsibility and self-management on which self-tracking rationales and devices tend to rely, the biopedagocial function of self-tracking (teaching people about how to be both healthy and productive biocitizens) and the reproduction of social norms and moral meanings concerning health states and embodiment (good health can be achieved through self-tracking, while illness can be avoided or better managed). (Lupton 2017: 3)

Lupton's analysis shows that self-tracking practices are embedded in a complex web of social processes. People who self-track to gain control over their bodies and seemingly gain an identity as free agents are in fact subjecting themselves to a highly moralized, normative behavior that is deeply interlaced with neoliberal concepts of citizenship. Btihaj Ajana argues along a similar line when she claims that

> practices of the Quantified Self can thus be seen as an instantiation of a 'biopolitics of the self' in which the body is made amenable to management techniques according to a set of agreed upon [...] norms. [...] In internalizing such norms, the self-quantifier ends up conforming to a pre-given standard of health and fitness and being normalized and (self)assessed according to an idealized numeric identity. (2017: 6)

This conformity has taken on a growing significance in recent decades. Responsibility for one's own health has become a central feat of neoliberal societies, as Rose Galvin lays out in her 2002 article, showing how the idea that "health and illness are matters of personal responsibility" has morphed into "a culture of victim blaming" (108), in which health and fitness are presented as "a matter of individual choice" (ibid: 109). Those who fail to comply with these demands, for example by having a non-conforming, 'fat' body, are blamed for not exercising and not eating 'healthy' and are shamed publicly or on social media. People who become ill are often blamed for their illness and are accused of having brought it on themselves, through said lack of compliance or risky health behavior (ibid: 115; 119-21), such as drinking, smoking or consuming 'junk food'.

Especially chronic illness is "defined as an instance of personal moral failure" (ibid: 119). This, in turn, makes it reasonable to cut welfare programs for people with chronic illnesses or disabilities, because those who have become ill are to blame for their illness and thus need to be disciplined into seeking work and acting "responsibly" (ibid: 126-27). As Galvin writes: "The healthy person is, in effect, symbolic of the ideal neoliberal citizen, autonomous, active, and responsible and the person who deviates from this ideal state is, at best, lacking in value and, at worst, morally culpable" (2002: 117).

Cultural Implications of Motherhood and In/fertility

Amanda J. Grigg and Anna Kirkland emphasize that within the growing promotion of health responsibility, women are positioned as "model health citizens" who adopt practices of "self-monitoring, anxiety, obedience and moralism," while men often oppose or disregard these prescriptions (2016: 332-33). Women, Grigg and Kirkland write, "are awash in exhortations about health and many of them come from women, focus on women, and address women as mothers and responsible caretakers" (ibid: 340). Nevertheless, women continue to experience discrimination in health care settings. Studies have shown that "women are less likely than men to receive more advanced diagnostic and therapeutic interventions" (Hamberg 2008: 237) and, when comparing treatment for a number of conditions, women are treated less invasively than men who show the same severity of symptoms (ibid: 238). As the groundbreaking 2001 study "The Girl who cried Pain: A Bias Against Women in the Treatment of Pain" by Diane E. Hoffmann and Anita J. Tarzian illustrates, women's pain is often managed less efficiently than the pain of men. Thus, generally speaking, women often receive less than optimal healthcare treatment. Part of this discrimination is linked to the fact that for the longest time, medical studies were performed predominantly with young white male test subjects with the results being generalized for entire populations (ibid).

Especially women of color, women with disabilities, and/or trans women are at risk for delayed or withheld treatment: For example, African-American and Native American women are up to three times more likely to die of pregnancy-related causes than white women (Petersen et al. 2019), a problem that is mirrored by the disparate access to fertility treatments or birth control:

> Like any other instantiation of power, the regulation of reproduction and the surveillance of pregnant bodies are not distributed equally. The history of reproductive rights in the United States and its territories, for example, is rife with examples in which calls for the individual right to birth control have been transformed into racist practices and eugenic policies of population control. (Johnson 2018: 3)

Often, women's treatment focuses on the preservation of their fertility over their quality of life, as, for example, Abby Norman describes at length in *Ask Me About My Uterus. A Quest to Make Doctors Believe in Women's Pain* (2018). This persistent centrality of reproductive capacity for the construction of contemporary female identity is epitomized by the importance motherhood takes in American culture. Sara Ahmed identifies motherhood as one of the central feats of the "gendered [...] 'happiness scripts'" that "provid[e] a set of instructions for what women and men must do in order to be happy, whereby happiness is what follows being natural or good" (2010: 59). Motherhood, in short, continues to be intertwined not only with ideas of womanhood but also with ideas of happiness and morality. As Cecil Helman writes: "In the USA, as elsewhere, the ability to nurture others, and thus to be fertile, is the very basis of womanhood" (2007: 176).

These cultural scripts have clear repercussions for women experiencing infertility: "Given the continued emphasis on biological motherhood in United States culture, it is not surprising that many studies indicate women feel marginalized and viewed as deviant or abnormal when they cannot or do not become pregnant and give birth to children" (Sternke/Abrahamson 2015: 6). Predictably, "the social stigma of childlessness persist at the same time as technological advances in treatment are being made," despite the fact that more couples experience fertility issues (ibid). Even though men also experience infertility, the stigma continues to be placed on women:

> Though the feminist movement and health activism have made substantial headway, it is women who are disproportionately burdened by infertility, making this uniquely a 'women's problem'. Put differently, beyond a biological impediment, infertility has become a cause for psychological and social oppression constituting a cultural drama of sorts. (Venkatesan/ Murali 2018: 610)

Research has shown the "emotional rollercoaster" (Watkins/Baldo 2004: 394) that infertility and its treatment can cause for couples (and singles), who may experience "guilt, shame, inadequacy, stigmatization, anxiety, stress, fear of spousal rejection, devastation, rage, anger, isolation, helplessness, powerlessness, loss of control, doom, despair, mourning, depression, frustration, feeling cheated, fatigue, moodiness, tenseness, disappointment, and loneliness" (ibid: 397).

With its historically grown implications of control and success, self-quantification in the form of fertility tracking appears as a countermeasure to the immense psychological impact of infertility, countering the feeling of helplessness and loss of control. The following section therefore turns to a number of fertility apps and analyzes which implications this contemporary form of (self)control over the female body creates.

There's an App for That: Fertility Tracking

As pointed out in the introduction of this paper, the female body lends itself to a specific kind of quantification, namely the tracking of the menstrual cycle and fertility. App creators have responded to this potential and Android and iPhone offer a variety of apps to track menstruation and fertility. However, these apps go beyond the mere charting of *when* menstruation occurs and usually include the possibility to log the severity of bleeding and additional symptoms such as cramps, nausea or mood swings, as well as sexual activity. Many of these apps enable the user to track basal body temperature, monitor birth control (with a pill reminder), and predict the user's ovulation window. Therefore, these apps can be and are used to prevent pregnancy or to help with conception. Other apps are even more directly marketed to help with conception, with some offering the ability to connect to other smart devices, such as the Apple watch (*Clue*) or the basal thermometer *Wink* by *Kindara* (available for $129).

These apps are marketed and reviewed with an emphasis on control, self-knowledge (that leads to self-control), and the early recognition of possible health problems through regular tracking of the period. Leanka Sayer, author of the web article "5 Reasons Tracking your Menstrual Cycle will change your life" that promotes the app *Clue*, writes: "You're in control of your body, your schedule, your well-being, and you avoid period surprises" (2016). Ignoring her period was "pretty harmful in terms of body acceptance" and she felt "that

[she] was in control of [her] menstrual cycle for the first time" (ibid). A review of "The 10 best period tracking apps" on *Medical News Today* further underlines this. *Clue* is presented there as follows: "Your health and menstrual cycle will no longer be a mystery [...]. The app's unique algorithm learns from the data that you add, which means that the more you use Clue, the smarter it will become" (Nichols/Collier 2018). Thus, the more users track, the more 'successful', i.e. in control of their body, they are likely to be.

It appears that even though these apps seem to depart from a presentation of menstruation as a "hygienic problem in need of solutions that promote secrecy" (Stubbs 2008: 60), they perpetuate deep-seated negative attitudes towards menstruation and construct the female body as 'mysterious' and in need of control. Online resources show how these apps follow the neoliberal ideals of health self-management and risk minimization through control (cf. Galvin 2002). An online article about *Clue*, "The Clue app saved my life," underlines how *Clue* can help to detect diseases early through constant self-monitoring and period tracking (Avey 2017). It describes how the app helped a woman recognize that the irregularity of her cycle had a dangerous dimension and how she used the app's data to convince her doctor to order more tests that revealed a tumor. Incidentally, the article also illustrates how the neutral, scientific numbers of self-quantification are promoted and valued over women's instinctive perception of their bodies (cf. Lupton 2015: 446-447). Apparently, women need the help of digitalized, neutral data to convince medical professionals that something is 'really' wrong with them.

Clue is presented as "a global movement to revolutionize female health, powered by data" (Tin 2015). On their website, the company's CEO, Ida Tin, writes:

> We work closely with respected universities and scientists to improve female health and to find insights that benefit our users. The more reproductive health data scientific researchers have access to, the better they will be able to conduct targeted research that might someday lead to significant improvements in female health. [...] When tracking your cycle, you're not only helping yourself, you're also helping other people and scientific research. (ibid)

This corresponds to what Ajana has identified as "data philanthropism": "Individuals who are willing to share their self-tracking data for research believe that their data will contribute to advancing knowledge in fields relating to healthcare" (2017: 9). Not only do the apps in question collect highly sensitive data, but the app creators use this fact to market their apps, causing women to perceive their data tracking efforts as contributions to improvements in female health care.

The focus on control illustrated with regard to *Clue* also becomes visible in the marketing of the other two apps, *Glow* and *Kindara*, that are more specifically marketed to couples who are trying to conceive. Regarding *Glow*, the authors of "The 10 best period tracking apps" write that "Glow's data-driven menstrual and ovulation calculator helps women to take control of their reproductive health" (Nichols/Collier 2018). According to a *YouTube*-demo video, *Glow* comes with a male and a female version that makes sure the male partner is up to date about the woman's fertile window and will also send the partner a reminder for that (TechCrunch 2013). The CEO, Michael Huang, who presents the app in the video reports that *Glow* has a calendar so that couples can schedule sex (e.g. if partners are away for business) (ibid). Both partners can log a huge variety of symptoms, among them sexual activity (checking boxes for: had sex, no sex, multiple sessions) and the position of the female partner during ejaculation (on bottom, on top, in front, other) and whether or not there was a female orgasm, or generally any physical or emotional discomfort (ibid). With regard to female orgasm and sexual position, Huang explains that they added in these points to gather the user data to be able to answer the question whether or not female orgasm and position during ejaculation influence the success of conception, because there had been a lack of studies regarding this in the past (ibid). Like the creators of *Clue*, the *Glow* creators openly admit that they are mining their user data to optimize the app and to "help the users better conceive" (ibid). Making one's highly sensitive data available is sold to the users as a way of improving their chances of conception (since they will profit from an optimized app), framing the sharing their user data as a small price to pay.

The last app I want to briefly present here is *Kindara*, which is promoted together with the wireless oral thermometer *Wink* that is used to track women's basal body temperature. The wireless thermometer transfers the temperature directly to the app that uses it to chart ovulation. The description in the app store reads: "Better data means you can take better ownership of your reproductive health and achieve your fertility goal with more ease." The *YouTube*-advertisement promises: "Kindara puts women in the driver's seat of their bodies," the "freedom to make choices" and "a sense of power and ownership of their body" (Kindara Fertility 2014). *Kindara* assures users that they will "take [their] fertility in [their] hands" and "get pregnant faster or avoid pregnancy naturally without side effects or better understand [their] body" (ibid). The video shows several women waking up in the morning and reaching for the thermometer on their nightstands, as well as a health care practitioner who is discussing the temperature curve on a tablet with one of the women (ibid). Control of the medicalized body is achieved through regular use of the thermometer. These presentations and the use of words such as "ownership" or "fertility goals" show how the app is linked to current neoliberal discourses of health that stress the individual's responsibility (En/Pöll 2016: 41). Users do not only purportedly achieve more control over their bodies, they also conform to the expectations of the medical profession to participate actively in keeping healthy and documenting their fertility.

When looking at examples of how apps like *Kindara*, *Clue*, and *Glow* are presented to the users, it becomes clear how the developers subscribe to a "desire for control" that Ajana locates "at the heart of the Quantified Self-movement" (2017: 6) and that Lupton frames as "people's response to the problem of dealing with the uncertainties and openness of choice in late modernity" (2016: 76). With regard to the tracking of the female body, Lupton points out that "many of these self-tracking apps seek to impose order on otherwise disorderly or chaotic female bodies, using data to do so" (2015: 447). Rachel Sanders is even more critical of the controlling potential of these practices when she writes that "As digital-era technologies of gender that facilitate increasingly rigorous and intricate body projects, digital self-tracking devices are instrumental to contemporary patriarchy" (2017: 48). She argues that these devices help sustain so-called "body projects" aimed at the attainment of the "medical and aesthetic imperative" of the "thin female body" and that they help "re-stabilize status-quo gender arrangements" (ibid: 39).

The controlling potential of these tracking practices becomes especially apparent with regard to women who are pregnant or trying to conceive. Cummins, in her analysis of the surveillance of pregnant women, highlights the ways in which women's bodies are disciplined to ensure successful reproduction:

> [...] women's bodies are continually seen as lacking, as needing work, and as requiring external help. In the case of pregnant bodies, panoptic discipline is a literal reproduction, both as a disciplining of the pregnant body, as well as through the "production" of a child. [...] This policing is present in moments such as making choices that benefit the fetus only or following Western medical advice over other types of advice [...]. (2014: 36)

As pointed out in the introduction, I argue that the surveillance of pregnant women is mirrored in the (self-)disciplining of women who are trying to conceive, so that (self-)surveillance begins even prior to conception. The data collection of fertility tracking apps assists in this disciplining. Lupton describes the docile body that these apps create as follows:

> [...] when the focus is on women's bodies there is more emphasis on medicalization and risk. The ovulation and fertility apps and devices represent a female body that is amenable to intense data collection and self-surveillance in the interests of providing better knowledge about the reproductive cycles and ovulation symptoms of the user. [...] Women who are attempting to conceive are positioned as ideally taking responsibility to achieve an ideal, timely pregnancy by avoiding risks (such as stress or not sleeping enough).
> (2015: 447)

Accordingly, women who fail to conceive are often perceived as not taking enough responsibility for their reproductive health and failing to control their unruly bodies. This further underlines the body normativity of the apps and shows that they are clearly designed to add to the productivity of the good female biocitizen: the apps produce self-knowledge that leads to the users' self-control. The ideal user will buy the premium features, produce useful data by logging meticulously, and will be rewarded for their data by being able to produce a baby. This shows the connection between consumption and productivity that Alvin Toffler has named "prosumption" (1980) that is inherent in these apps.

A 2016 evaluation of the available menstrual tracking apps of the free apps from the iTunes store in *Obstetrics & Gynecology* confirms that many of the apps are highly problematic:

> Most available menstrual cycle tracking apps are inaccurate, contain misleading health information, or do not function. We found only 20 free, English-language apps that allowed for accurate menstrual cycle tracking based on cycle length averages. Few apps cited literature used or were developed or recommended by reproductive health experts. [...] Nineteen percent of apps evaluated for accuracy contained erroneous medical information.
> (Moglia et al. 2016: 1157)

Contrary to advertisements and popular perception, researchers caution that "Paper calendars may remain the best option for some patients until data use is more transparent" and point out that "Information contained in menstrual cycle tracking apps should not take the place of medical advice" and that they do not "advocate use of these menstrual cycle tracking apps as a primary tool to *prevent or achieve* pregnancy (ibid: 1159; my emphasis).

Additionally, researchers have pointed out that these apps are normative, and I would like to add, ableist, with regard to their presupposition of a regular, 28-day-cycle (cf. Lupton 2003: 153) and because they entail the assumption of a clear binary gender identity that conforms to a homogeneous body type that erases people outside of the normative male-female gender binary and the general heterogeneity of different bodies (En/Pöll 2016: 47). These apps also reinforce the ableist belief that all young (i.e. fertile) female bodies are healthy and function 'normally'.

Having illustrated the implications of control, discipline, self-improvement and economic entanglement that the apps entail, I will now turn to the representation of childlessness and infertility in the graphic memoirs *Good Eggs* by Phoebe Potts (2010) and *Broken Eggs* by Emily Steinberg (2014). Both works depict the emotional strain of infertility and childlessness and engage with the pressure that the self-quantification of the female body and the 'doability' of fertility tracking and treatments create.

Good Eggs and *Broken Eggs*: Two Representations of Fertility Tracking and Childlessness

For some years now, the emerging field of graphic medicine has brought more scholarly attention to comics that narrate stories of illness or disability, so-called pathographies, both in the healthcare professions and in academia (Williams 2015: 133). As the recent publication of *Graphic Reproduction. A Comics Anthology* (Johnson 2018) highlights, comics' power to "[challenge] the dominant methods of scholarship in healthcare, [to offer] a more inclusive perspective of medicine" (Czerwiec et al. 2015: 2) can also be made fruitful to interrogate discourses surrounding (women's) reproductive health. As Ian Williams suggests, authors of pathographies "might be subtly altering the discourse of health and the social mediation of illness outside the clinic" (2015: 118). Among the many contemporary publications in graphic medicine are also numerous graphic narratives by women (and some men) who describe experiences of infertility, pregnancy, miscarriage, abortion, childbirth, and motherhood. For example, Teresa Wong writes about her experience of postpartum depression in *Dear Scarlet: The Story of my Postpartum Depression* (2019) and Lucy Knisley relates the complications caused by her overlooked preeclampsia in *Kid Gloves: Nine Months of Careful Chaos* (2019). Among the many publications dealing with infertility are Sheila Alexander's *I(v)f. A Memoir of Infertility* (2019) and Paula Knight's *The Facts of Life* (2017). These topics have also been explored online; most recently Sarah Glidden published a webcomic about her infertility experience (and subsequent motherhood) titled "Barren: How an expensive path to fertility highlights the price of pregnancy" (2019), which also discusses the financial aspects of the treatment, illustrating how "human reproduction is a place where the boundaries between biological, social, technological and political life collapse" (Johnson 2018: 3).

Good Eggs and *Broken Eggs* are both graphic memoirs in which a successful, white middleclass woman describes her experiences with infertility and chronicles her attempts to become pregnant and carry to term. Both Potts and Steinberg are diagnosed with "unspecified infertility," which means no medical explanation for their infertility can be found. This diagnosis undermines their belief in the omniscience of science and also means that, since no obvious obstacle can be found, the women are left to exhaust all possible options to achieve pregnancy.

Steinberg's webcomic *Broken Eggs: A Visual Narrative* (2014) consists of a set of 67 images that are "designed as an egg" and accompanied by text that "condemns the glorification of motherhood and the commercialization of infertility care" (Venkatesan/Murali 2018: 610; 612). In a style reminiscent of "underground women artists," Steinberg uses "colors, varied fonts, font sizes handwriting, and other strategies to convey her biological horror and emotional turmoil" (ibid: 612). Potts's *Good Eggs: A Memoir* (2010) is a book-length graphic novel that also chronicles Potts's youth, her relationship with her Jewish faith and her search for her identity as an artist. While Potts employs "conventional panels with a discriminate use of splash pages" (ibid: 613), the handwritten style and rich metaphorical black and white drawings powerfully convey the pain and pressure of infertility. As Sathyaraj Venkatesan and Chinmay Murali write, "Dark lines, uneven grids, handwriting and various affordances of the medium used in these narratives convey the subjective experiences of infertile women in raw honesty" (ibid: 620). In terms of their depiction of the artists' experiences with infertility both comics reproduce many of the features of the fertility tracking discourse that I have highlighted so far. While Steinberg, in contrast to Potts, does not depict herself tracking actively, her memoir, like Potts's, illustrates the pain of unwanted childlessness and the pressures that medicine and society put on women who are trying to conceive.

Image 1 Emily Steinberg (2014): Broken Eggs #8.

Reprinted with permission from Cleaver Magazine

At the beginning of their respective narratives, both Steinberg and Potts describe how their inability to get pregnant comes as a surprise to them, and both artists illustrate their belief that their childlessness can be solved through science and money. In her first image, Steinberg portrays her narrator figure sitting down with her arms hugging her knees, next to a large caption that reads: "I'm part of that generation of women who were raised to believe unfalteringly in the exalted truth of science" (2014: #1). In another image she draws herself next to a baby and two representations of the Virgin Mary, accompanied by the captions: "I mean, come on, we're surrounded by mommy images from the day we are born. We're saturated with paintings of the mother and child in art history. It was a no-brainer. Of course I'd get pregnant. But nothing happened" (#8; Image 1). So Steinberg turns to a fertility clinic and, drawing herself cradling a huge egg, she writes that "I will be the one to beat the odds" (#16). She will become pregnant through "the miracle o'science" (#12), adhering to the taxing regime of fertility treatments. She pictures becoming pregnant as yet another business project that the successful middleclass woman will complete: "Schedule mein Baby. Have my people talk to your people" (#2). She writes: "It all seemed eminently doable" (#2; Image 3).

Potts has been raised on a similar note of seeing motherhood as something that should be easy to achieve. She writes: "My attitude isn't so weird when you consider that I've been steeped in the 2 Great American myths: You can do it. Cash is king. Combine the two and you get this easy-to-remember mantra: You can buy it!" She continues in the caption of the next panel: "With that logic instilled in me, I've got a classic case of middle-class entitlement. I should be able to pick up a few toddlers at IKEA" (2010: xvi-xvii). Like shopping at IKEA, having a baby would illustrate Potts's status as a successful, middle class woman. Babies, that is, become a "middle- class accessory" (xvi).

Potts's and Steinberg's assertion of the "doability" of becoming pregnant corresponds to Lupton's assessment: "In the culture of individualism and achievement which obtains among many members of the middle class in particular, not being able to have a child at the right time, as planned, is difficult to accept and seems 'unfair'" (2003: 171). The failure to become pregnant and have biological children thus corresponds to a failure to perform the function of a 'normal' middle class woman.

Images 2 and 3 Steinberg (2014): Broken Eggs #46 and #2.

Reprinted with permission from Cleaver Magazine

Both Potts and Steinberg also add a moral component to their story early on, describing how they felt that they "deserved to get pregnant" because of their former achievements, lifestyle and because of their past and future 'goodness'. Steinberg pictures herself kneeling on the ground, with a halo around her head, and her left hand raised in the air, swearing an oath: "How can this be? I swear I'm a good person. I swear I would be a good mother. I promise I won't be one of those horrible women who scream at their kids in grocery stores" (2014: #46; Image 2).

On a splash page, Potts draws herself as a kind of shiva-character, sitting in a yoga-pose on a fitness ball, with her many hands pointing to her achievements: "I worked for the poor! I married a nice (partially) Jewish boy! I recycle! I vote! I eat my greens! I go to yoga! I went to Smith! I untangled my issues in therapy!" (xviii). On the next page, Potts pictures herself standing on a small earth, screaming: "So...Where's my baby?" at the universe (Image 4). Potts controls her psyche through therapy and her body through exercise and healthy nutrition but has to realize she still cannot bend her biological function to her will (cf. Benedicks 2012). Of course, as I have shown, fertil-

Representations of Fertility Tracking and Childlessness in Contemporary Graphic Memoirs   157

ity tracking apps suggest exactly that. After all, they promise women to give them full control over their body to achieve their fertility goals.

Image 4 Potts (2010): Good Eggs, xviii-xix

xviii   xix

Used by permission of HarperCollins Publishers

Not surprisingly, both women perceive a deep loss of control over their bodies (cf. Lupton 2003: 171), which Potts tries to counteract through measures of self-tracking. Potts, in contrast to Steinberg, pictures herself tracking, thermometer in mouth, in front of a calendar: "We have to maximize our chances of getting pregnant. To find my most fertile time of month, I track my cycle religiously and take my temperature with a basal thermometer every morning" (2010: xii; Image 5). Here, Potts's narrative figure is shown with a thought bubble that reads: "So much for romance." The next panel caption reads: "… and I pee of hundreds of dollars' worth of sticks waiting for little blue lines to appear on them to know when would be the optimal time to sleep with Jeff" (xii). In the image, the stick reads: "Try again later." The two panels already indicate that fertility tracking requires a high amount of discipline from women, is financially straining, and that it might put pressure on the couple and take away "romance" from sexuality. On the next page, Potts draws herself and her husband in bed over several days, with visibly sinking enthusiasm. In the panel captioned "Day 10" Jeff is pictured saying: "I think I'd rather be just friends for a while," which shows that Potts's partner suffers as well (xiii).

Image 5 Potts (2010): Good Eggs, xii

Used by permission of HarperCollins Publishers

Potts continues to illustrate the effect that the fertility treatments have on both her and her husband throughout the narrative. Towards the end of the story, she draws the couple having a fight about the constant pressure of trying to achieve pregnancy. While Jeff argues: "It's not relaxing to think I always have to do it," Potts's angry character who "wanted a break [...] from everything! The drugs, the charting, the hormones, the blood tests, the sonograms, the... SCRUTINY ..." yells at Jeff that "It's not relaxing to CHART!!" (229). On the following page, Jeff expresses his anger and frustration over a coworker who brought his baby to work. He, like Phoebe, cannot understand why the couple cannot conceive, despite "doing everything right" (230), which illustrates the moral component of "deserving" a child Potts expressed earlier.

When they do not become pregnant, with their beliefs in the 'doability' of achieving pregnancy and their trust in science and money, both Potts and Steinberg turn to the medical-industrial complex and the professionals take over to 'solve' their fertility problem. The industrial aspect of the medical infertility treatment is illustrated in *Good Eggs* when Potts draws herself opening the door to the clinic labeled "New England Fertility Factory" (91).

After a conversation with a fertility specialist who tells Potts to "test the system" and come back in six months, she still seems to believe that even stricter tracking and more self-control will lead to pregnancy: "I will chart my ovulation to the nano-second! We'll try harder" (94). When "trying harder" does not work out, Potts and her husband undergo various procedures, from hormone treatments to artificial insemination, to IVF (In-Vitro Fertilization). The certainty of tracking clashes with the repeated uncertainty of the success of the procedures and the repeated failures which are met with attempts at even more meticulous self-quantification. Potts illustrates her repeated attempts to become pregnant and her disappointment in two ways. She repeatedly draws a panel of herself sitting on toilet, reaching for a tampon behind her and cursing "Rats" (xiv, 137). Later, when phone calls from the fertility clinic confirm that she is not pregnant (a situation she also draws several times) the panels of the phone call are followed with up to four completely blackened panels, illustrating her hopelessness and frustration (139, 140).

Especially Steinberg illustrates how the numbers and statistics that the "white coats" present her with keep her hopeful enough to continue try new treatments after one has failed. She is left devastated when the attempt to implant a fertilized donor egg fails. Believing in science, Steinberg had thought that the procedure sounded "doable" (2014: #54). She draws herself cowering on the ground, surrounded by the caption: "But what about the 70% success rate? We didn't even achieve a fertilized egg, let alone a viable pregnancy. It was a total dud" (#61). Potts also illustrates her belief in statistics when she draws her husband asking her doctor: "What's your success rate?" (37). The apparent reliability of numbers that lies at the heart of self-quantification practices is exposed as a treacherous claim of putative safety that women who are trying to conceive can ultimately not depend on. Lupton comments that

> the concept of 'odds', or statistical chances, was a constantly used rhetorical strategy in conversations about IVF, used to organize and condense various statements about the individual chances of becoming pregnant, [...] and the probability attached to technological intervention. The health professionals involved tended to use a statistical meaning of odds, even comparing the procedure to a gamble equivalent to a roulette wheel stake. (2003: 171)

Both Steinberg and Potts take up the gambling rhetoric; for example, Steinberg writes that she "felt like an addict or a compulsive gambler, aching for one more spin of the roulette wheel" (2014: #26). She illustrates the dehumanizing effects of the treatment when she draws herself as a lab rat walking out of the fertility clinic cage (cf. Venkatesan & Murali 2018: 616), surrounded by the large words: "And then I became ... a Fertility Guinea Pig" (#17), showing the depersonalization the medicalization of her body causes; something that both women experience.

Image 6 Potts (2010): Good Eggs, 143

Used by permission of HarperCollins Publishers

Potts, like Steinberg, chronicles the medicalization of her body and the uncomfortable procedures that she undergoes in detail. For example, during the first embryo transfer after IVF, she draws the nurse who has brought in a "straightener" for Potts's tipped uterus as a torturer, speaking with a German accent, wearing an executioner's mask and carrying a hugely drawn instrument. The insertion of the instrument is illustrated with the sound effect "THUPK" and Potts's head seems to jump out, her eyes and mouth open with wordless pain, while a speech bubble next to the doctor reads: "That's better" (2010: 149; Image 6).

Potts, listing the numericals of the last cycle her insurance company will pay, also uses the gambling rhetoric when she writes that she and her husband cast their "last lot with biotech baby engineering": "And I laid 20 eggs! Of which 18 became embryos! After the genetic testing, 10 came back from the lab normal! A grand total of 4 were transferred to my long-suffering uterus. Resulting in... Zero. Zip. Zilch. Nada. Nothing. None. Nil. Not" (ibid: 233-34). The repetition illustrates Potts's frustration and the finality of the last unsuccessful cycle. Even the most sophisticated science has not worked for Potts and her husband, despite Potts's adherence to science and self-discipline.

Ultimately, both women experience their inability to get pregnant as a personal failure. Potts writes: "I can't fulfill the most basic of biological functions" (152), which presents a deep challenge to her identity as a woman (cf. Benedicks 2012). When the final procedure has failed, Steinberg draws herself upside down, tears falling from her eyes, surrounded by the words of the doctors who proclaim her "damaged goods" (2014: #63). Steinberg also decides to discontinue the treatment: "But then I said: No more! I was done," disentangling herself from the fertility gamble (#65). The active decision to discontinue fertility treatments is the way in which both women can take back control, not of their fertility, but of their bodies and their identities as women. Potts expresses her relief over the end of the treatments: "This process has been like structured insanity. I think I'm relieved it's over – I would never have had the resolve to end it myself" (2010: 235). Drawing on the biblical narrative of the journey to the Promised Land, Potts ultimately frames her narrative as a growth experience with religious resonances and ends on a note of hope and acceptance.

Conclusion

As I have illustrated, the autographic representations of childlessness in the comics by Potts and Steinberg correspond to the implications of the fertility tracking apps marketed to women who are trying to conceive. The apps promise women "success" (in the sense of conception) through self-control and the objectivity and the scientific "truth" of numbers. The apps help commodify conception, creating the belief echoed by Potts's credo: "You can buy it." Becoming pregnant becomes just another project that a successful middle class woman will complete, with the help of science, money and self-discipline. However, to become pregnant, both artists have to submit their bodies to the medical regimes of infertility treatment, turning their unruly bodies that do not conform to the expectations of regular womanhood into docile bodies that can be improved – and made fertile – through science. When Potts and Steinberg repeatedly fail to become pregnant (or, in the case of Potts, suffer several miscarriages) they have to redefine their identity as women; an identity that is based on "a script that turns out to be predicated on a 'normative' female body defined by reproductive ability" as Crystal Benedicks writes (2012: n. pag.). Through the narratives in question, both artists expose the emotional hardship of unwanted childlessness and the struggles of infertility treatments and "deconstruct the myth of motherhood and destigmatize infertility" (Venkatesan/Murali 2018: 620).

The medium of comics seems particularly suited for the women artists to regain part of their agency that they lose in the fertility treatment process. When drawing, the women are able to turn the tables on the medical professionals that measure and examine their bodies and expect the women to participate in this process of quantification and qualification. The writing of autobiographical narrative and the documenting of life experiences also constitute different kinds of self-assessment, forms of artistic introspection that differ from the numerical, rational self-quantification processes of fertility tracking.

The artists can represent their own bodies, their emotions and thoughts in the process and show the financial strain as well as the physical discomfort and alienation of their bodies during the medical treatment. As Jenell Johnson, another comic artist writes about drawing her own infertility memoir:

> To put it bluntly, I never felt more like a body than I did while undergoing fertility treatment. Constantly monitoring and dutifully reporting my bodily processes [...] getting injected, swabbed, poked, prodded, and measured both quantitatively ("this follicle is 3.5") and qualitatively ("your lining is beautiful"); undergoing invasive procedures [...]: when trying to conceive, I was a (female) body first, and most important, I was a body that didn't work the way I "should." [...] there was something thrilling about taking the instru-

ments of representation into my own hands. In the pluripotent space of the comic panel, I had the power to represent not only my body and my experiences, but also my doctors, nurses, friends, and husband. Confronted daily by a pronatalist world that reminded me how abnormal I was [...] my pencils, pens, paints, and paper offered a quiet place to work out what was happening to me with some measure of critical distance. (2018: 2)

Williams has also suggested that the creative process of drawing a comic may be well suited for some artists to work through grief and that "some artists find some therapeutic effect" (2011: 365). Other than the therapeutic effect, the production of the comic might also be read as linked to the wish of the women to refute their stigma as unproductive citizens. Benedicks, in her review of Potts's graphic novel, underlines that the creative process of producing a work of art also corresponds to a "fertile activity": "Above all, [the artists] give the slip to the insidious notion that to be labeled 'infertile' or 'barren' or 'sterile' is, literally, to be unproductive. Writing a book is a productive, creative, deeply 'fertile' enterprise – indeed, one that many authors have metaphorically likened to giving birth" (2012: n. pag.). Potts echoes this sentiment, when she says in an interview that her 6-word-memoir would be: "Tried for baby, had book instead" (Lehmann-Haupt 2010: n. pag.).

Works Cited

Ahmed, Sara (2010): *The Promise of Happiness*, Durham and London: Duke University Press.
Ajana, Btihaj (2017): "Digital Health and the Biopolitics of the Quantified Self." In: *Digital Health* 3, pp. 1-18.
Alexander, Sheila (2019): *If. A Memoir of Infertility*, New York: Archway Publishing.
Avey, Erica (2017): "'The Clue App Saved My Life': Early Detection through Cycle Tracking." In: *Clue* September 25, (https://helloclue.com/articles/cycle-a-z/clue-app-saved-my-life-early-detection-through-cycle-tracking).
Benedicks, Crystal (2012): "Review of Potts, Good Eggs: a Memoir & Tsigdinos, Silent Sorority: A (Barren) Woman Gets Busy, Angry, Lost and Found." In: *Disability Studies Quarterly* 32/3.
BioWink GmbH (2019): Clue (Version 5.12.) Mobile application software. Retrieved from http://itunes.apple.com.

Crawford, Kate/Lingel, Jessa/Karppi, Tero (2015): "Our Metrics, Ourselves: A Hundred Years of Self-Tracking from the Weight Scale to the Wrist Wearable Device." In: *European Journal of Cultural Studies* 18/4-5, pp. 479-496.

Cummins, Molly Wiant (2014): "Reproductive Surveillance: The Making of Pregnant Docile Bodies." In: *Kaleidoscope: A Graduate Journal of Qualitative Communication Research* 13/4, pp. 33-51.

Czerwiec, MK/Williams, Ian/Squier, Susan Merrill/Green, Michael J./Meyers, Kimberly R./Smith, Scott T. (eds.) (2015): "Introduction." In: *Graphic Medicine Manifesto*, University Park, PA: The Pennsylvania State University Press.

Davis, Lennard (1995): *Enforcing Normalcy. Disability, Deafness, and the Body*, London and New York: Verso.

En, Boka/Pöll, Mercedes (2016): "Are You Self-tracking? Risks, Norms and Optimization in Self-Quantifying Practices." In: *Graduate Journal of Social Science* 12/2, pp. 37-57.

Foucault, Michel (1995 [1975]): *Discipline and Punish. The Birth of the Prison*, translated by Alan Sheridan (1977), New York: Random House.

Galvin, Rose (2002): "Disturbing Notions of Chronic Illness and Individual Responsibility: Towards a Genealogy of Morals." In: *Health: An Interdisciplinary Journal for the Social Study of Health*, Illness and Medicine 6/2, 107-137.

Glidden, Sarah (2019): "Barren: How an Expensive Path to Fertility Highlights the Price of Pregnancy." In: *The Nib* April 10.

Glow (2019): Glow Cycle & Fertility Tracker (Version 7.7.4). Mobile application software. Retrieved from http://itunes.apple.com.

Grigg Amanda J./Kirkland, Anna (2016): "Health." In: Lisa Disch//Mary Hawkesworth (eds.), *The Oxford Handbook of Feminist Theory*, Oxford: Oxford University Press, pp. 326-345.

Hamberg, Katarina (2008): "Gender Bias in Medicine." In: *Women's Health* 4/3, pp. 237-243.

Helman, Cecil G. (2007): *Culture, Health and Illness*, London: Hodder Arnold.

Hoffmann, Diane E./Tarzian, Anita J. (2001): "The Girl Who Cried Pain: A Bias Against Women in the Treatment of Pain." In: *Journal of Law, Medicine and Ethics* 29, pp. 13-27.

Johnson, Jenell (2018): "Introduction." In: Jenell Johnson (ed.), *Graphic Reproduction: A Comics Anthology*, University Park, PA: The Pennsylvania State University Press, pp. 1-16.

Kindara Fertility (2014): "Wink by Kindara." YouTube October 7 (https://www.youtube.com/ watch?v=47mvygsKo_Q).

Kindara, Inc. (2019): Kindara: Fertility Tracker (Version 6.5.2) Mobile application software. Retrieved from http://itunes.apple.com.

Knight, Paula (2017): *The Facts of Life*, University Park, PA: The Pennsylvania State University Press.

Knisley, Lucy (2019): *Kid Gloves: Nine Months of Careful Chaos*, New York: First Second.

Lehmann-Haupt, Rachel (2010): "Interview: Phoebe Potts, Author of Good Eggs." In: *Smith Mag* September 28 (http://www.smithmag.net/memoirville/2010/09/28/interview-phoebe-potts-author-of-good-eggs/).

Lupton, Deborah (2003): *Medicine as Culture: Illness, Disease and the Body in Western Societies*, London, Thousand Oaks, and New Delhi: Sage.

___ (2015): "Quantified Sex – a Critical Analysis of Sexual and Reproductive Self-Tracking Using Apps." In: *Culture, Health & Sexuality* 17/4, pp. 440-453.

___ (2016): *The Quantified Self*, Cambridge: Polity.

___ (2017): "Self-tracking, Health and Medicine." In: *Health Sociology Review* 26/1, pp. 1-5.

Moglia, Michelle L./Nguyen, Henry V./Chyjek, Kathy/Chen, Katherine T./Castaño, Paula M. (2016): "Evaluation of Smartphone Menstrual Cycle Tracking Applications Using an Adapted APPLICATIONS Scoring System." In: *Obstetrics & Gynecology* 127/6, pp. 1153-1160.

Nichols, Hannah/Collier, Jasmin (2018): "The 10 Best Period Tracking Apps." In: *Medical News Today* January 19 (https://www.medicalnewstoday.com/articles/320758.php).

Norman, Abby (2018): *Ask Me About My Uterus: A Quest to Make Doctors Believe Women's Pain*, New York: Nation Books.

Petersen, Emily E./Davis, Nicole L./Goodman, David/Cox, Shanna/Mayes, Nikki/Jonston, Emily/Syverson, Carla/Seed, Kristi/Shapiro-Mendoza, Carrie K./Callaghan, William M./Barfield, Wanda (2019): "Vital Signs: Pregnancy-Related Deaths, United States, 2011–2015, and Strategies for Prevention, 13 States, 2013–2017." In: *CDC Morbidity and Mortality Weekly Report* 68, pp. 423-429.

Potts, Phoebe (2010): *Good Eggs: A Memoir*, New York: Harper Collins.

Sanders, Rachel (2017): "Self-tracking in the Digital Era: Biopower, Patriarchy, and the New Biometric Body Projects." In: *Body & Society* 23/1, pp. 36-63.

Sayer, Leanka (2016): "Five Reasons Tracking Your Menstrual Cycle Will Change Your Life." In: Rubycup July 19 (http://rubycup.com/blog/5-reasons-tracking-menstrual-cycle-will-change-life/).

Steinberg, Emily (2014): "Broken Eggs. A Visual Narrative." In: *Cleaver Magazine* September, with an introduction by Tahneer Oksman (http://www.cleavermagazine.com/broken-eggs-by-emily-steinberg/).

Sternke, Elizabeth A./Abrahamson, Kathleen (2015): "Perceptions of Women with Infertility on Stigma and Disability." In: *Sexuality & Disability* 33/1, pp. 3-17.

Stubbs, Margaret L. (2008): "Cultural Perceptions and Practices around Menarche and Adolescent Menstruation in the United States." In: *Annals of the New York Academy of Sciences* 1135, pp. 58-66.

TechCrunch (2013): "Glow Fertility App Demo" YouTube August 8 (https://www.youtube.com/watch?reload=9&v=DLbEun8uBZ8).

Tin, Ida (2015): "About Clue. Why Clue will revolutionize global female health." Helloclue.com December 22 (https://helloclue.com/articles/about-clue/why-data-will-revolutionize-global-female-health).

Toffler, Alvin (1980): *The Third Wave: The Classic Study of Tomorrow*, New York: Bantham.

Venkatesan, Sathyaraj/Murali, Chinmay (2018): "Infertility Comics and Graphic Medicine." In: *Perspectives in Biology and Medicine* 61/4, pp. 609-621.

Watkins, Kathryn J./Baldo, Tracy D. (2004): "The Infertility Experience: Biopsychosocial Effects and Suggestions for Counselors." In: *Journal of Counseling & Development* 82, pp. 394-402.

Williams, Ian (2011): "Autography as Auto-therapy: Psychic Pain and the Graphic Memoir." In: *Journal of Medical Humanities* 32, pp. 353-366.

___ (2015): "Comics and the Iconography of Illness." In: MK Czerwiec/Ian Williams/Susan Merrill Squier/Michael J. Green/Kimberly R. Meyers/Scott T. Smith (eds.), *Graphic Medicine Manifesto*, University Park, PA: The Pennsylvania State University Press, pp.115-142.

Wong, Teresa (2019): *Dear Scarlet: The Story of my Postpartum Depression*, Vancouver: Arsenal Pulp Press.

Compulsive Self-Tracking: When Quantifying the Body Becomes an Addiction

Katharina Motyl

There can be no doubt that biometric self-tracking has helped numerous groups improve their health: diabetics, recovering drug addicts, individuals suffering from hypertension, to name but a few. However, in the realm of non-medical self-monitoring, for some, striving for self-optimization and better health qua self-tracking has, in fact, resulted in 'self-disimprovement', that is, in deteriorated (mental) health and a diminished quality of life. I refer to those whose practices of self-tracking are no longer a matter of volition, but of compulsion: quantifying their bodies has become an addiction. Consider the experience of Jeff Foss, a self-described "Strava addict (Foss 2014), who recounts that he realized his use of the fitness-tracking app had become compulsive when he felt the urge to track his physical activity whilst out on a rescue mission to find a friend who had gone missing on a hike. As he relates in an article published in *Wired* titled "The Tale of a Fitness-Tracking Addict's Struggles With Strava,"

> This summer, two episodes brought my excessive tracking habit into sharp focus. The first was on a family hike in Rocky Mountain National Park. I was carrying my 14-month-old son on my back, and I suddenly caught myself (...) pausing and un-pausing the app every time we stopped to inspect a wildflower or wave at a marmot. For this I was duly scolded by my wife, and I began to think more critically about my relationship with tracking. The more I attempted to track every minute, it seemed, the less engaged I became from the moment. A few weeks later I hit rock bottom. I was on a mountain bike trip in Southern Colorado with friends, and one of the guys decided to climb Mt. Harvard (...) [and] got lost. The next morning, as we geared up for an emergency ascent with the local search and rescue team, I had to resist the urge to use Strava. On a rescue mission! (Foss 2014)

Or take the grave case of William Flint, who died racing down a descent on his bicycle in the Berkeley Hills in 2010, having propelled himself to reckless speed while seeking to reclaim Strava's 'King of the Mountain' award for the fastest time on a particular route; Flint had been notified on the morning of his death that another user had broken his record.

As these examples illustrate, for some users, self-tracking is no longer a matter of volition: much of their day revolves around self-tracking, they perceive the tracking device's malfunctioning or running out of battery as catastrophic, and they would feel tremendous anxiety and discomfort if they were somehow prevented from monitoring their bodies through wearable devices and apps. In other words, for these users, quantifying their bodies has become an addiction. In the following article, which situates itself in the field of Critical Digital Studies, I will first discuss the dimensions that make the practice of self-tracking potentially addictive, and highlight the convergence effects between self-tracking and users' immersion in social media environments that fuel lifelogging's addictive potential. I will then theorize compulsive self-trackers as neoliberal capitalism's perfect subjects: whereas all self-trackers can be read as seeking to discipline their bodies in accordance with the neoliberal norm of productivity, compulsive self-trackers have additionally subjected their quest to become better neoliberal subjects to the repetitive and constant rhythm of the capitalist mode of production. Last, I will turn to a creative-aesthetic negotiation of self-tracking's addictive allure; in her autobiographical poem "Why I Stopped Tracking," Alexandra Carmichael, one of the pioneers of the Quantified Self movement, illuminates the self-alienation and diminished quality of life she faced while self-tracking compulsively.

I would like to preface my analysis by some remarks on my use of the term 'addiction': The semantic field of 'addiction' is prominently mobilized for figures of speech in cultural discourses of the 21st century – for instance, when someone exclaims "These Cookies Are So Addictive!," to highlight that the baked goods in question are hard to resist, or a user confesses "I'm Addicted to Game of Thrones!," on a fan site to compliment the TV series' compelling storytelling.[1] In this essay, however, I am *not* interested in addiction

---

1   The scenarios I conjure up here imply that neither of the two imagined speakers is pathologically dependent on sugar or watching TV. However, it is common knowledge that the food industry produces foods high in sugar content to increase demand for its products, while the makers of serial TV mobilize strategies such as cliffhangers to amplify consumers' desire to 'binge-watch' their products. The prevalence with which individuals today reference *addiction* to characterize a need or an activity on which they

as a metaphor used to characterize self-tracking and other aspects of digital technology, but in instances of *actual* addiction to digital self-monitoring, which significantly impacts affected individuals' well-being (I cited some symptoms above, e.g. experiencing intense anxiety when prevented from self-tracking). While the hegemonic narrative in the (US-American) medical and life sciences community today frames addiction as a brain disease (cf. Leshner 1997), the competing theory of addiction as a learned behavior also enjoys considerable support, particularly in the discipline of psychology (cf. Heyman 2009). For the purpose of my discussion, the question whether addiction is a neurological disorder or a learned behavior, is negligible. To illustrate, what centrally interests me is that a fitness-tracking app's reward system may encourage a user's compulsive return to said app; whether the app 'achieves' this by rewiring the user's brain or by conditioning the user's behavior, is not of concern to my analysis. The perspective I bring to bear on addiction in the following analysis, then, is best approximated by the processual approach outlined by literary critic Susan Zieger: addiction can be defined as the compulsion and need to engage in an activity as a result of having engaged in it in the past (Zieger 2008: 3).

Self-Tracking's Addictive Potential

What constitutes self-tracking's addictive potential? First, self-tracking technologies feature built-in reward systems (positive reinforcement), as well as admonitions when targets haven't been met (negative reinforcement). The fitness-tracking device FitBit, for instance, vibrates to let a user know they have reached their daily health goal; calorie-tracking apps will display a congratulatory message at the end of a day when a user has managed to stay below their calorie target. In the blog entry "Why I Broke Up With My FitBit" on her blog "hello spoonful," self-described nutritionist and health coach Elizabeth

---

are not actually dependent, is perhaps best understood as a consequence of advertising strategies. The advertisement industry has interpellated consumers as lacking something that could be fixed by purchasing a particular good. Addiction is likewise rooted in the need for 'a fix,' that is, in the desire to escape circumstances perceived as deficient or painful. When individuals characterize a thing or an activity as addictive, they seek to express how small their power to resist it is. They have thus internalized as self-image the ad industry's interpellation of consumers as deficient.

recalls the effects the fitness-tracking device's negative-reinforcement feature had on her:

> Fitbit also has a feature where it vibrates on your wrist when you haven't gotten your 250 steps for the hour. It will buzz and then say something goofy like "It's step o' clock!" (...) I'd be completely immersed in a task, making huge strides on a project and then BOOM — It's step o' clock! I'd freak out and have to get my 250 steps fast before the hour was up. My focus would disappear and my mind would get stuck on how many steps I *hadn't* taken that day. (Elizabeth 2017; original emphasis)

Elizabeth's account of FitBit's negative-reinforcement component, first, highlights that the app inserts itself in a disruptive manner into users' daily lives; whereas someone following a non-digitally supported fitness regimen might allocate an hour after work to exercise on three days a week, FitBit and other fitness-tracking technologies interrupt users' work routine, time with family, etc. to remind them to be more active. It is easy to see that by fragmenting users' daily lives, such apps and devices heighten users' reliance on them, furthering their immersion in an algorithmically mediated form of self-perception and simultaneous alienation from immediate lived experience. Second, the quote illustrates that although Elizabeth made "huge strides on a project," a sense of achievement in the 'real world' was drowned out by the digital reminder of her failure to meet a certain (arbitrary) target. The fact that while she practiced self-tracking, Elizabeth's sense of self-worth was influenced much more by numbers displayed on a digital device than by her own awareness of her achievement, is certainly remarkable.

This tension throws into sharp relief the Quantified Self movement's slogan "Self Knowledge through Numbers."[2] According to the movement's logic, only that knowledge about oneself counts which is both quantifiable and indexical of the body, whereas qualitative knowledge (about one's deeds, one's personality, etc.) appears as negligible. The self that is contoured in this technology-derived, data-based, and supposedly objective self-knowledge, is thus effectively reduced to the body. Deborah Lupton observes that while "[t]echno-utopian discourses" in the early days of the internet

> were particularly evident in discussions of the freedoms and liberation from the confines of the body offered by writers on cyberspace and the posthu-

---

2   Cf. https://quantifiedself.com/

man body [...] the kind of techno-utopian discourses evident in discussions of biometric self-tracking [...] privilege an intense focus on and highly detailed knowledge of the body, in which it is suggested that possession of this knowledge of one's body offers a means by which illness and disease may be prevented. (Lupton 2013: 396)

I would go a step further than Lupton and argue that striving for better health qua self-monitoring is not only an end in itself, but also represents a means to approximate the neoliberal norm of productivity. Second, the logic on which the slogan "Self Knowledge through Numbers" is built, de-individualizes persons, since it disregards what makes each individual unique in favor of a (quantified) perspective that allows for comparing persons with one another at a glance (or perhaps 'at a click' is the better metaphor in this context). The quantified self, that is, a person both reduced to their somatic dimension and rendered comparable with the aid of technology and data, epitomizes what Gilles Deleuze (fore-)saw happening to the individual in neoliberal, technology-driven "societies of control" (Deleuze 1992): "the corporation," which Deleuze identifies as determining the governing logic in control societies, "constantly presents the brashest rivalry as a healthy form of emulation, an excellent motivational force that opposes individuals against one another and runs through each, dividing each within. [...] Individuals have become '*dividuals*'" (Deleuze 1992: 5, original emphasis). Perhaps it is unsurprising that in thoroughly neoliberalized societies, which place the highest premium on productivity as well as performance, and assess a person's work by 'objectifiable' data such as number of customers or length of publication list, some people think it opportune to base their self-image on quantified data rather than on their qualitative knowledge about themselves.

Why did I characterize the health targets that fitness-tracking apps deploy as *arbitrary* before? The conventional wisdom that 10,000 steps a day 'keep the doctor away,' which FitBit adopted as default health-target setting, is not, in fact, based on science, but an arbitrary result of a marketing campaign. According to I-Min Lee, a professor of epidemiology at Harvard University, "It turns out the original basis for this 10,000-step guideline was really a marketing strategy [...] In 1965, a Japanese company was selling pedometers, and they gave it a name that, in Japanese, means 'the 10,000-step meter'" (qtd. in Mull 2019; cf. Lee, Shiroma and Kamada 2019). Apparently, the Japanese character for '10,000' visually resembles a man walking (cf. Mull 2019). Not only has the 10,000-step norm never been validated by medical research (cf.

Lee qtd. in Mull 2019); there are concerns in the medical community that the guideline might actually discourage those not exercising at all from engaging in physical activity, and even have adverse consequences for the elderly and those who are chronically ill or have type 2 diabetes (Cox 2018). Catrine Tudor-Locke, a professor of public health at the University of Massachusetts, Amherst, advocates reframing Western societies' dominant approach to encouraging fitness:

> We know that sedentary lifestyles are bad, and if you're taking fewer than 5,000 steps a day on average this can lead to weight gain, increase your risk of bone loss, muscle atrophy, becoming diabetic [...] But, at the same time, there seems to be an obsession about 10,000 and how many steps are enough, *yet it's more important, from a public health point of view, to get people off their couches. The question we should really be asking is: how many steps are too few?* (qtd. in Cox 2018; my emphasis)[3]

In addition to featuring the reward and admonition mechanisms outlined above, self-tracking devices may also compel individuals to rely on them obsessively by encouraging competitiveness, thus offering users the opportunity to 'win' or to 'beat' their own record/the performance of others. Crucially, self-tracking apps not only store a user's own past data so that fitness self-trackers, for instance, can compete against their own high score; they also allow users to share their data so that someone tracking their calorie intake can see how little others managed to eat that day. In the context of calorie-tracking apps, physician Debbie Mueller maintains that connecting with other users has little to do with mutual support of the self-help variety, but is driven by competitiveness (qtd. in Newman 2015) – and competitiveness without moderation can easily turn into a health risk. Blogger Elizabeth reflects on the emergence of her obsession with FitBit:

> Everything was normal at first. I'd feel accomplished when I felt my wrist vibrate letting me know I hit my goal of 10000 steps for the day, but then I read somewhere how 10000 steps really wasn't THAT great of a number so I'd adjust my goal to 15000 steps a day. Suddenly 15000 wasn't enough either because you could add your 'friends' on the Fitbit app and I'd see people averaging 18000, 20000 and even 30000+ steps a day. (...) The competitive side

---

3   Moreover, the question remains whether fitness-tracking is sustainable. For instance, a study conducted by Jordan Etkin has shown that fitness-tracking takes the fun out of exercising and may thus lead to a less active lifestyle in the long run (Etkin 2017).

of me started coming out and I wanted to be up there, too. If 'Sally' and 'Tom' could average 25000 steps per day then darn it so could I! (Elizabeth 2017)

This quotation discloses the arbitrary origin of Elizabeth's temporary need to walk 25,000 steps per day (the approximate equivalent of 9.5 miles or 15 kilometers): the urge to outdo others. Even if Elizabeth's walking had been motivated by wishing to attain a certain health outcome, say, to maintain a certain weight, the question remains whether a cardio workout combined with weight lifting three times a week might not have achieved the same health result, at a fraction of the time she spent walking per week and at far less disruption to her daily life. Some self-tracking technologies even feature reward systems that are predicated on users' sharing data, thus encouraging competitiveness among users to the extreme; Strava's 'King of the Mountain' award, which William Flint strove to reclaim on his fatal descent down the Berkeley Hills, is one such example.

The compulsion to digitally monitor one's body also seems to be rooted in a cultural anxiety that is widely observable in the age of mobile digital devices: digitally documenting life is more important than experiencing life 'in the flesh'. Jeff Foss – the self-described Strava addict – reflects on what caused his fixation on the fitness-tracking technology: "for me, an active but undistinguished runner and cyclist with no KOM [King of the Mountain] ambitions, the compulsion seems to lie *in the tracking itself*—the physical act of starting and stopping the clock. If Strava wasn't active and my numbers were slipping away unrecorded, *some small part of the activity felt wasted*" (Foss 2014; my emphasis). Elizabeth, too, recounts that during her fitness-tracking obsession, she considered as meaningful merely those of her activities that were validated in the realm of technologically mediated 'reality': "I refused to take my Fitbit off. Heaven forbid when the light would flash 'battery low' and my charger wasn't around!? *It was as if the steps I took that day didn't count unless they were logged properly by this tracker*" (Elizabeth 2017, my emphasis).

The anxiety that becomes apparent in these two accounts of compulsive self-tracking – an experience is not considered actual unless it is digitally recorded – seems to be a variation on the 'recording frenzy' so easily observed in the era of smartphones with high-resolution cameras: rather than study da Vinci's "Mona Lisa" at the Louvre with their own eyes, for instance, many museum visitors will take a selfie in front of the painting, indexing that in the digital era, *recording* an event is more important than *experiencing* the event. Just like a tourist might post a selfie with the "Mona Lisa" to her

Instragram account to prove to herself and others the veracity of her experience, a fitness self-tracker needs to see their step count climb on a device while walking – with the added twist that the fitness tracker's experience is not only recorded, but also quantified. That is, whereas smartphone cameras record an experience in a medium that resembles reality (photography),[4] self-tracking technologies translate an experience into a numerical sign system. Both practices can be read as cultural responses to the logic of neoliberalism in that they represent a turn away from intuitive self-knowledge and experience-based identity towards a self-concept anchored in visual evidence (selfie) or data evidence (quantified self): in light of the neoliberal belief in data as a basis for comparability and competition as well as the neoliberal obsession with performance assessment, these practices disclose a self-concept that only validates the measurable, comparable, and recorded. There is a considerable degree of convergence between these two modes of neoliberal self-fashioning: many fitness self-trackers will post their day's exercise tally to their social media accounts at the end of a day, for instance.[5]

Indeed, self-tracking's addictive potential appears to be intensified by the fact that users of specific lifelogging technologies tend to immerse themselves in social media environments dedicated to related content; for instance, fitness self-trackers will often follow 'fitspiration' feeds on pinterest and those using apps such as 'Clean Eating Meal Plan' will participate in #cleaneating threads on Instragram and twitter (cf. Simpson and Mazzeo 2017b). As Pixie Turner and Carmen Lefevre have shown, the higher users' immersion in #cleaneating feeds on Instragram is, the higher is their risk for *orthorexia*

---

4   In her seminal study *On Photography*, Sontag argues that the seductive character of the photograph is located in its carrying a trace of reality (Sontag 2019: 165). This is not to deny the staged and curated character of selfies, most of which are subjected to digital editing before being posted on social media; rather, selfies' deceptive power is grounded in their photographic mediality, appearing to represent the real.

5   In the instant that they are being posted online, the selfie and the tracking score become forms of self-commodification, since in the Web 2.0 subbranch of digital capitalism – the 'like economy' – data posted online spells symbolic capital for users and some, e.g. influencers, additionally accrue economic capital (cf. Bourdieu 1984). It feels almost superfluous to point out that tech giants such as Facebook generate vast surplus by users' sharing personal data online. One could make the case that (non-medical) fitness tracking, calorie tracking, etc. already amounts to self-commodification since practitioners can be read as seeking to turn themselves into more beautiful commodities for visual consumption.

nervosa, an obsession with healthy eating.[6] The prevalence of *orthorexia nervosa* among those following #cleaneating accounts on Instragram is 49 per cent, which is significantly higher than among the general population, for which it is smaller than 1 per cent (Turner and Lefevre 2017: 277). Moreover, as a study by Courtney Simpson and Suzanne Mazzeo underscores, the use of fitness-tracking technologies is a predictor for 'exercise addiction' (the medical term is 'exercising for appearance') and eating disorders (2017a: 91).[7] However, the authors stress that fitness-tracking devices do not 'give you' these mental health disorders, but pose a considerable risk to those already vulnerable to 'exercise addiction' and eating disorders (Simpson and Mazzeo 2017a: 91). In conclusion, not only is compulsive self-tracking – as addictive behavior – injurious to mental health *per se*; the compulsive drive to ride faster, consume fewer calories, or eat healthier than one's past self/other users may also entail mental and physical comorbidities, such as eating disorders, or even result in death, as in William Flint's case.

Remarkably, tech companies seem to purposefully design their products in a fashion that encourages compulsive use, if Anna Wiener's account of her work experience at a digital start-up she provides in her memoir *Uncanny Valley* is remotely representative of Silicon Valley at large. The start-up had developed a feature that would allow app-developing companies to ascertain how frequently an app was used – its name: Addiction. Wiener writes: "Addiction graphs displayed the frequency with which individual users engaged, visualized on an hourly basis – like a retention report on steroids. [...] Every company wanted to build an app that users were looking at multiple times a day" (Wiener 2020: 140-141). Although Wiener, "to promote Addiction, [...] ghostwrote an opinion piece for the CEO that described, dryly, the desirability of having people constantly returning to the same apps, multiple times

---

6   *Orthorexia nervosa* (ON) is defined as "an unhealthy obsession with eating healthy food" (Turner and Lefevre 2017: 278). Although it does not yet appear in the Diagnostic and Statistical Manual of Mental Disorders (DSM), the condition has been well-researched. The proposed diagnostic criteria for ON include "obsessive focus on healthy eating, food anxiety, and dietary restrictions, with these behaviours causing clinical impairments" (Turner and Lefevre 2017: 278). While *anorexia nervosa* entails preoccupation with the *quantity* of food, ON entails preoccupation with the *quality* of food (Turner and Lefevre 2017: 278-279; cf. also Klotter, Depa, and Humme 2015).
7   Interestingly, calorie tracking was not found to be a predictor for eating disorders: "fitness tracking, but not calorie tracking, emerged as a unique indicator of ED [eating disorder] symptomatology" (Simpson and Mazzeo 2017a: 91).

an hour" (141), she had qualms. The app's "premise made me uneasy," Wiener recalls (141). "I already tied myself in dopamine knots all too often: I would email myself a link or note, feel a jolt of excitement at the subsequent notification, then remember I had just triggered it. *App addiction* wasn't something I wanted to encourage" (141; my emphasis). Here, Wiener's objection to Addiction seems grounded in a perception that the feature fuels *actual* addiction to digital technology. However, in the passage that directly follows, Wiener seems to change course, now taking issue with the feature's *name*, which she frames as *figuratively* referencing addiction, and thus perceives as trivializing experiences of *actual* addiction:

> The branding also vexed me. I knew multiple people who had decamped for pastoral settings to kick dependencies on heroin, cocaine, painkillers, alcohol – and they were the lucky ones. Addiction was a generational epidemic; it was devastating. The Tenderloin was five blocks away from our office. There had to be higher aspirations. *At the very least, there were other words in the English language.* (141; my emphasis)

It's hard to argue against the assessment that heroin addiction diminishes someone's quality of life more drastically than app addiction, and I have no intention of doing so; yet dismissing the notion that addiction to digital technology exists, belittles what those whose technology use is out of their control are going through and, not least, absolves tech companies of accountability towards these very users: the demand that companies take responsibility for designing technology in a fashion that encourages compulsive use, which potentially has legal ramifications, is thus downgraded to a rebuff for being insensitive towards drug addicts, which remains solely in the realm of morality.

Tellingly, when Wiener brought up the issue with the head of her unit, going with the 'inappropriate name'-angle ("It wasn't just insensitive, but sheltered, embarrassing, offensive," 142), his answer is revealing: "Kyle listened patiently while I ranted. [...] 'I hear you,' he said. 'The question of addiction is a big thing in gaming. It's nothing new. But I don't see any incentive for it to change. [...] We already call our customers "users"'" (142). Highlighting the polysemous character of the term 'user,' which both denotes those engaging with digital technology and those consuming drugs, the head of the unit in blasé fashion discloses that tech companies welcome the slippery slope between metaphorical references to addiction to advertise their products and their products' fueling actual technology addiction. This reaction casts online-gaming addicts, compulsive self-trackers, and other technology addicts as collateral damage of Silicon Valley's success: according to the logic underlying this mindset, if tech companies are to operate in economically viable fashion (and continue to develop technology that drives civilization forward, as believers in techno-salvation would have it), they need to develop 'sticky' products, and it is to be expected that this 'stickiness' will compel some individuals to engage in addictive use.

Compulsive Self-Trackers as Neoliberal Capitalism's Perfect Subjects

While some may consider compulsive self-tracking an excessive aberration from an otherwise beneficial practice, I contend that compulsive self-tracking takes the rationale underlying the practice of self-tracking in neoliberal societies to its logical conclusion. Self-tracking represents a "technology of the self" (Foucault 1988), whereby users mobilize quantifying their bodily activities to discipline their bodies in accordance with the ideological regimes of productivity and beauty concomitant to the neoliberal economic order. By seeking to increase their bodies' productivity and to transform their bodies into more beautiful commodities for visual consumption, of course, (non-medical) self-trackers turn themselves into "docile bodies" (Foucault 1995: 135), who discipline themselves according to the norms stipulated by the dominating entity, which they have internalized. This holds for all non-medical self-trackers. In the following, I want to suggest a way to theorize the specificity of the self-disciplining regime involved in *compulsive* self-tracking.

My argument operates on two presuppositions. First, capitalism necessitates the continuous production of goods through repetitive steps. Second, as mentioned before, addiction can be defined as the compulsion and need to engage in an activity as a result of having engaged in it in the past. In light of these tenets, compulsive self-trackers appear as neoliberal capitalism's 'perfect subjects': whereas all non-medical self-trackers discipline their bodies in accordance with the cultural norms of productivity and physical attractiveness concomitant to the neoliberal economic order – as probably most of us socialized in neoliberal societies discipline our bodies in some fashion, even if we don't self-track – compulsive self-trackers have additionally subjected their striving to become better neoliberal subjects to the repetitive and constant rhythm of the capitalist mode of production.

Some may object that the emergence of wearable technologies in the age of the Internet of Things has precisely intersected with a neoliberal, post-Fordist economic order. In other words, isn't speaking of the repetitive and constant rhythm of the capitalist mode of production *so* 1970s, *so* pre-Reaganite? I would counter this by arguing that in the neoliberal age, the body itself has become the object of production, with labor and body entering into a new relation. In this context, Rüdiger Kunow has maintained:

> In light of the neoliberal polemic against the welfare state, securing the living of the individual diverges from the relations of production outlined in classical political economy: the means of life are no longer being secured primarily through labor *of* the body, but increasingly through labor *on* the body, through constant monitoring of its vital functions, through self-imposed fitness regimes, but also increasingly through the use of biotechnological 'enhancement procedures,' which increase the body's capacity for productivity beyond what it is normally capable of. (Kunow 2015: 54, original emphasis; my translation)

Kaushik Sunder Rajan and others have theorized the centrality of the body to the neoliberal economic order and the dominant position biotechnology assumes in contemporary neoliberal markets, as "biocapitalism" (Rajan 2006: 184). In this inflection of neoliberal capitalism, human bodies have been transformed into "lively capital" (Rajan 2012: 1).

Under the Fordist paradigm, workers, who ideally possessed strong bodies so as to achieve maximum production output, as a collective made up of shifts physically labored without cease and by going through repetitive motions to produce goods. In neoliberalism, the body is no longer primarily the means of labor, but has been turned into an object of labor, as Kunow so astutely points out. Self-tracking constitutes a form of labor on the body that serves to render it more productive and a more beautiful commodity for visual consumption. Attaining a more productive body in neoliberalism is only partly motivated by the desire to increase the body's performance capacity – after all, self-tracking is mostly practiced by the middle and upper classes, the vast majority of whom don't have occupations involving physical labor; rather, attaining a more productive body has become an end in itself in "the age of fitness" (Martschukat 2019), which, according to Jürgen Martschukat, commenced in the 1970s and thus, "not at all coincidentally" emerged alongside the age of neoliberalism (Martschukat 2019: 10, my translation). Those seeking to attain a fit body have turned themselves into docile bodies by internalizing the neoliberal ideology that "the individual has to work on themselves, be in control of their life, keep fit, be responsible for their own performance capacity and literally embody the latter" (Martschukat 2019: 10, my translation). Laboring on one's body to increase its fitness is also a highly conspicuous practice: a fit body can be regarded as "symbolic capital" (cf. Bourdieu 1984), that is, as one of the most prized status symbols in neoliberal societies. Compulsive self-trackers unwittingly embody (and thus make visible) the groundedness of neoliberal ideologies in the base, as Marx would have it, of the capitalist economic order, as they have subjected their laboring to attain fitter and more beautiful bodies to the constant and repetitive rhythm of the capitalism mode of production.

A Negotiation of Compulsive Self-Tracking in Expressive Culture

The poem "Why I Stopped Tracking" by Alexandra Carmichael, an associate of the Quantified Self movement since its infancy,[8] was published on the QS website in 2010 (Carmichael 2010). Best conceptualized as an autobiographical poem in the vein of confessional poetry, its speaker, a recovering compulsive self-tracker, seeks to come to terms with having developed a sense of self entirely dependent on the data generated through digitally monitoring her body's labors. While the poem's aesthetic merit is admittedly limited, it nonetheless affords an insightful glimpse into the consciousness of an individual whose practice of self-tracking had become pathological and hence, psychologically damaging. Carmichael powerfully draws attention to the ways in which a practice aimed at self-optimization can lead to a diminished quality of life, a life devoid of spontaneity and immersion in the world of lived experience (as opposed to technologically mediated 'reality'), a life in which trust in one's intuition has become replaced by self-loathing over failing to meet norms:

> Yes, I did it.
> On a crisp Tuesday morning
> After 40 measurements a day for 1.5 years
> I. Stopped. Tracking.

---

8   Further information on Alexandra Carmichael's role in the QS movement can be found here: https://quantifiedself.com/blog/alexandra-carmichael/.

Why?
When I first wrote about my tracking
People thought I was narcissistic
What they didn't see
Was
The self-punishment
The fear
The hatred behind the tracking
I had stopped trusting myself
Letting the numbers drown out
My intuition
My instincts
I was afraid
Of not being in control
Of becoming obese like my genetic predecessors
I was addicted
To my iPhone apps
To getting the right numbers
To beating myself up
Each day
My self-worth was tied to the data
One pound heavier this morning?
You're fat.
2 g too much fat ingested?
You're out of control.
Skipped a day of running?
You're lazy.
Didn't help 10 people today?
You're selfish.
I'm starting to realize
That I need to
Trust
Listen
Accept myself
That I'm more than the numbers
That I'm beautiful, strong, and super smart
I don't need data to tell me that
And I don't need to punish myself anymore

> Will I ever track again?
> Yes, probably
> For a specific goal or experiment
> Or to observe a pattern
> I'll try to keep an objective, non-judging eye
> But then I'll stop
> When I've seen what I needed to see
> And learned what I wanted to learn
> Like any tool
> Self-tracking can be used for benefit or harm
> I won't let it
> Be an instrument of self-torture
> Any. More. (Carmichael 2010)

Significantly, the speaker, who managed to stop self-tracking upon realizing that taking "40 measurements a day" was effectively a form of "self-punishment" and thus, injurious to her mental health, identifies her former condition as an addiction "To getting the right numbers" *as well as* "To beating myself up."[9] The speaker thus maintains that she self-tracked obsessively because it allowed her to prove to herself that she was "in control," that is, she was able to meet the norms that (supposedly) spell success in a neoliberal society, *but also* because it allowed her to engage in self-loathing. Significantly, while substance addiction often originates in the desire to numb emotional pain (and later might become the attempt to stave off the physical pain of withdrawal), the speaker portrays the self-inflicted emotional pain that lifelogging affords when one has failed to adjust one's behavior to a norm, as fueling self-tracking's addictive potential. The two impetuses the speaker identifies at the heart of her former compulsive self-monitoring – meeting norms to prove that one is in control, and the opportunity to engage in self-flagellation – seem contradictory at first glance, as they involve diametrically opposed emotional states: when someone meets their daily fitness goal, satisfaction ensues, whereas failing to do so will result in self-loathing. However, upon closer consideration, both impetuses can be traced to a weak sense of self and a conception of oneself as deficient.

---

9   I will comment on Carmichael's use of the past tense when referring to her experience as a compulsive self-tracker ("I was addicted") in due time.

An insecure sense of self appears to have been involved in the speaker's development into a compulsive self-tracker: "Each day / My self-worth was tied to the data." The self-worth, and possibly even the identity, of users who self-track compulsively, it appears then, is entirely wedded to the quantification of their bodily activities. This is underscored when the speaker asserts that upon quitting self-tracking, she had to learn "That I'm more than the numbers." Unsurprisingly, then, the poem portrays compulsive self-tracking as a condition in which trust in one's intuition is entirely replaced by 'faith in numbers': "I had stopped trusting myself / Letting the numbers drown out / My intuition / My instincts." Obsessive self-trackers, the speaker maintains, purposefully disregard qualitative self-knowledge in favor of what the data gleaned from monitoring their bodies 'knows' about them, and their encounter with the world is mediated by digital technology to an extraordinary degree. Moreover, the speaker discloses that while she was self-tracking compulsively, any minute behavioral deviation from the norm was magnified into a severe personality shortcoming ("2 g too much fat ingested? / You're out of control"). This indexes that compulsive self-trackers take the ideology of perfectionism demanded by neoliberalism to the extreme, which backs up my claim that compulsive self-trackers can be read as neoliberal capitalism's perfect subjects.

In light of compulsive self-trackers' difficulty to immerse themselves in their sensual and intuitive experiences, it is significant that the speaker maintains she decided to stop self-tracking "On a crisp Tuesday morning." Her decision, we can infer, was made in a moment of sensual experience, when she either visually beheld the weather outside her window or haptically sensed the cool temperature while outside. In other words, a bodily, non-technologically mediated encounter with nature is what triggered the speaker's resolve to quit digitally monitoring her bodily activities and the regime of self-punishment it engendered for her.

Ending the poem with a dialectical assessment of the practice of self-tracking per se ("Like any tool / Self-tracking can be used for benefit or harm"), the speaker's optimistic outlook that she will probably self-track again in the future "For a specific goal or experiment" while keeping "an objective, non-judging eye," and "stop / When I've seen what I needed to see," warrants some skepticism. To elaborate, Carmichael's use of the past tense when referring to her experience as a compulsive self-tracker early in the poem ("I was addicted") already notably diverges from the perspective embraced by most addiction-recovery programs that a person remains an addict for life even after discontinuing the compulsive behavior in question. For instance, a person who has managed to stay off heroin for ten years will still introduce themselves as "My name is x and I'm an addict" at Narcotics Anonymous meetings. Accordingly, most addiction recovery programs recommend abstinence from the substance / compulsive behavior in question if freedom from addiction is to be achieved in the long run. By contrast, Carmichael seems to believe that her addiction to self-tracking became a thing of the past when she stopped digitally monitoring herself. However, if we take compulsive self-tracking seriously as an addiction disorder and are mindful of Carmichael's self-described personality disposition, it seems doubtful that as a personality with rigid, perfectionist, and competitive tendencies, she will be able to track a parameter without developing the urge to perfect the behavior in question, thus paving the way for a relapse into self-tracking obsessively.[10]

An App to Optimize Self-Optimization Gone Awry?

From self-punishment over failing to meet norms to self-alienation due to an inability to trust one's intuition, Carmichael's poem highlights the psychological toll many aspects of compulsive self-tracking I have discussed in this article, take on individuals. I have endeavored to show that lifelogging devices compel users to return to them frequently, potentially giving rise to compulsive self-tracking, because these devices feature reward and admonition systems, the latter of which are particularly disruptive to users' daily lives. These technologies also encourage compulsive use in that they give individuals the opportunity to 'beat' their former selves/others, thus affording the illusion of success, this key value of neoliberal societies. Further, self-monitoring devices allow users to record their lives in the algorithmically mediated realm, thus giving in to the cultural anxiety of the Internet of Things-era that life does not count unless digitally documented. Self-tracking's addictive potential, I have demonstrated, is further fueled by users' simultaneous immersion

---

10   Granted, the analogy between technology addiction and substance dependence does not hold all the way; while a recovering heroin addict has millions of other individuals as role models who go through their days without consuming heroin, Western societies are technology-saturated to such an extent that recovering tech addicts will face tremendous difficulty cutting digital technology out of their lives entirely. Self-tracking does not, however, qualify as one of the digital practices without which life in the twenty-first century is practically impossible.

in thematically related content on social media, as in the case of fitness self-trackers who follow #fitspiration threads on Instragram.

In light of Silicon Valley's techno-optimism, it is perhaps unsurprising that a tech company should have developed an app that promises to deliver individuals from excessive use of digital technology: users who self-identify as addicted to digital technology and others who would like to curb their time online now have the app Flipd at their disposal. "Flipd nudges you to spend less time on your phone — helping you to be present, productive, and happy. Enjoy life offline with Flipd," reads the company's ad for its app.[11] Although it is quite remarkable that a tech company should semantically equate the use of digital technology with unhappiness, this move is necessary for the company to land their product's sales pitch: our tech product is vital in order for you to navigate life in times of overabundant digital services and technologies. The narrative underlying this sales strategy, however, rings familiar: Users are promised that the app will help them lead happier and, crucially, more productive lives. In other words, the app allows individuals, who are presupposed to be deficient, to self-optimize into better neoliberal subjects; the app thus shares the same premise as fitness-tracking devices and calorie-tracking apps. The only – and highly ironic – difference is that while those tracking their fitness or calorie intake (for non-medical reasons) mobilize digital technology to fashion themselves into healthier, more productive neoliberal subjects and more attractive commodities for visual consumption, users of Flipd rely on digital technology to become more productive neoliberal subjects in an age of tech overload.

In contrast to compulsive self-tracking, the obsessive use of Flipd might actually increase users' quality of life and lead to their heightened immersion in intuitive and sensual experience. In principle, the compulsive use of Flipd thus represents a subversive cultural technique (but only as far as users' relationships to themselves are concerned, since the ultimate goal of Flipd use, as already mentioned, is to increase users' productivity). And yet, it is doubtful that compulsive Flipd use exists empirically, rather than as a mere theoretical possibility. While Flipd inserts itself into users' daily lives via push notifications ("This is your reminder to unplug for 30 minutes today") and allows users to track their time spent away from their smartphone, thus enabling them to compete against their own record of time spent in digital detox, it is highly

---

11 www.flipdapp.com

unlikely that users become addicted to Flipd because the app, per unique selling proposition, can precisely not display the same degree of 'stickiness' that drives some users to engage compulsively with self-tracking apps, social media platforms, etc. Those in need of digital proof that their lives are happening are probably not easily 'cured' by using Flipd, but rather quite likely to add ever more apps to Flipd's exceptions list in order not to miss out on 'life'. The truly subversive practice would be to put one's phone on 'mute', place it on the shelf, and read Henry David Thoreau's *Walden* for a while – I am, of course, suggesting this approach after checking my work e-mail inbox at least five times over the last two hours while writing this piece.

Works Cited

Bourdieu, Pierre (1984): *Distinction: A Social Critique of the Judgement of Taste*, Trans. Richard Nice, Cambridge, MA: Harvard University Press.

Carmichael, Alexandra (2010): "Why I Stopped Tracking", April 10 (https://quantifiedself.com/blog/why-i-stopped-tracking/). Access January 27, 2020.

Cox, David (2018): "Watch Your Step: Why the 10,000 Daily Goal is Built on Bad Science." In: *Guardian* September 3 (https://www.theguardian.com/lifeandstyle/2018/sep/03/watch-your-step-why-the-10000-daily-goal-is-built-on-bad-science). Access February 23, 2020.

Deleuze, Gilles (1992): "Postscript on the Societies of Control." In: *October* 59, pp. 3-7.

Elizabeth (2017). "Why I Broke Up With My FitBit." In: Blog "Hello Spoonful" December 22 (https://www.hellospoonful.com/blog/2017/12/22/10000-steps-fitbit-obessed/). Access February 23, 2020.

Etkin, Jordan (2016): "The Hidden Cost of Personal Quantification." In: *Journal of Consumer Research* 42/6, pp. 967–984.

Foss, Jeff (2014): "The Tale of a Fitness-Tracking Addict's Struggle with Strava. In *Wired* March 10 (https://www.wired.com/2014/10/my-strava-problem/). Access May 18, 2018.

Foucault, Michel (1995 [1977]): *Discipline and Punish: The Birth of the Prison*, Trans. Alan Sheridan, New York: Vintage Books.

___ (1988): "Technologies of the Self." In: Luther H. Martin/Huck Gutman/Patrick H. Hutton (eds.), *Technologies of the Self. A Seminar with Michel Foucault*, London: Tavistock Publications, pp. 16-49.

Heyman, Gene M. (2009): *Addiction: a Disorder of Choice*, Cambridge, MA: Harvard University Press.

Holcombe, Brian (2013): "Strava Wins Dismissal of Civil Suit over Berkeley Death. In: *Velonews* June 4 (http://www.velonews.com/2013/06/news/strava-wins-dismissal-of-civil-suit-over-berkeley-death_289714#VQZiBSQdhcU19YoD.99). Access May 20, 2018.

Klotter, Christoph, Julia Depa, and Svenja Humme (2015): *Gesund, gesünder, Orthorexia nervosa: Modekrankheit oder Störungsbild? Eine wissenschaftliche Diskussion*, Wiesbaden: Springer.

Kunow, Rüdiger (2015): "Wertkörper. Zur Ökonomisierung des menschlichen Körpers im Zeichen von Globalisierung und Neoliberalismus." In: *Prokla: Zeitschrift für kritische Sozialwissenschaft* 45/1, pp. 51-66.

Lee, I-Min, Eric J. Shiroma, and Masamitsu Kamada (2019): "Association of Step Volume and Intensity With All-Cause Mortality in Older Women." In: *JAMA Internal Medicine* 179/8, pp. 1105-1112.

Leshner, Alan I. (1997): "Addiction Is a Brain Disease, and It Matters." In: *Science* 278/5335, pp. 45-47.

Lupton, Deborah (2013): "Quantifying the Body: Monitoring and Measuring Health in the Age of MHealth Technologies." In: *Critical Public Health* 23/4, pp. 393-403.

Martschukat, Jürgen (2019): *Das Zeitalter der Fitness*, Frankfurt am Main: S. Fischer.

Mull, Amanda (2019): "What 10,000 Steps Will Really Get You." In: *Atlantic* May 31 (https://www.theatlantic.com/health/archive/2019/05/10000-steps-rule/590785/). Access February 23, 2020.

Newman, Judith (2015): "Why We're Addicted to Health-Tracking Apps." In: *Allure* January 4 (https://www.allure.com/story/tracking-fitness-progress). Access May 18, 2018.

Rajan, Kaushik Sunder (2012): "Introduction: The Capitalization of Life and the Liveliness of Capital." In: Kaushik Sunder Rajan (ed.), *Lively Capital: Biotechnologies, Ethics, and Governance in Global Markets*, Durham, NC: Duke University Press, pp. 1-41.

___ (2006): *Biocapital: The Constitution of Postgenomic Life*, Durham, NC: Duke University Press.

Simpson, Courtney C., and Suzanne E. Mazzeo (2017a): "Calorie Counting and Fitness Tracking Technology: Associations with Eating Disorder Symptomatology." In: *Eating Behaviors* 26, pp. 89-92.

___ (2017b): "Skinny Is Not Enough: A Content Analysis of Fitspiration on Pinterest." In: *Health Communication* 32/5, pp. 560-567.

Sontag, Susan (2019 [1977]): *On Photography*, London: Penguin Books.

Turner, Pixie G., and Carmen E. Lefevre (2017): "Instragram Use Is Linked to Increased Symptoms of Orthorexia Nervosa." In: *Eating and Weight Disorders* 22, pp. 277–284.

Wiener, Anna (2020): *Uncanny Valley: a Memoir*, London: 4th Estate.

Zieger, Susan (2008): *Inventing the Addict: Drugs, Race, and Sexuality in Nineteenth-Century British and American Literature*, Amherst: University of Massachusetts Press.

The Portable Peoplemeter Initiative: Wearable Sensor Technologies and Embodied Labor

Jennifer Hessler

Contemporary wearable gadgets that monitor our biometrics, map our movements, track our exposure, or remind us about the tasks we need to complete have become part of our everyday outfitting. While these wearable devices enhance the efficiency with which we accomplish our goals and even empower us with deeper, datafied insights about ourselves, they also further implicate us as laborers, extending the hours that we are 'on' at work, and entrench us within corporate consumer data regimes. These 'sensing technologies' that we wear, which detect and store information about our bodies or environments, reconfigure our experience of embodiment, labor, and space. In fact, these devices are so pervasive that scholars like Mark Andrejevic and Mark Burdon (2015) have argued that contemporary society, especially in regard to surveillance culture, is best characterized as a "sensor society."

While the ubiquity of wearable sensor-technologies seems like a contemporary phenomenon, the first consumer-purchasable sensor microelectronics were available in the late-1970s, including digital watches that could tell you the temperature or turn your household lights on/off; pagers that could let you know if your car has been broken into; and 'jogging computers' that could emit a beep tone in accord with your pre-entered pace and distance goals for you to run in-rhythm to (*Chicago Tribune* 1978; "Display Ad 23" 1975: 4). These precursory technologies had numerous functional issues; they were overall difficult for consumers to integrate into their daily activities, and thus many of them failed to achieve market success. Nonetheless, following a wide scale turn toward biometrics in the consumer information industries in the 1980s, data collection companies and audience measurement firms spent the latter part of the 20th-century experimenting with how to put wearable sensors to use as data trackers.

In this essay, I use media archeology and posthumanist frameworks to analyze the design and implementation of one of the most prominent wearable trackers used by the consumer research/audience measurement industry: the portable people meter (PPM), which Arbitron field-tested throughout the 1990s and brought to market in 2003. The PPM is a fruitful case study in the history of wearable tracking technologies because of its well-documented design challenges and innovations, which have spanned across three decades. To work sufficiently as an audience measurement device, the PPM had to be able to detect media engagement (while, theoretically, in motion), it had to work well with the technologies and audience assessment practices already being used by broadcasters, and it had to be user-centric and engaging enough that participants would want to wear it consistently. Thus, the long and politically fraught endeavor of engineering and implementing the PPM offers valuable insights into the complex negotiations of user embodiment, spatiality, and corporate practicality that go into engineering wearable tracking technologies. In relation to other contemporary wearable gadgets like smart watches, glasses/ headsets, and biomedical clip-ons, the PPM is different in that it doesn't offer any functional benefits to users; PPM wearers don't even have access to the data they produce. Yet, the device is contingent on users' willingness to wear the device every day (which, as I discuss, is procured through a variety of technological and rhetorical strategies). As a surveillance mechanism then, the PPM is not a self-tracker nor is it 'imposed' panoptically (users agree to be audience ratings panelists). The PPM is also different from other mobile gadgets because its data collection mechanisms are not hidden; in fact, wearing the device comes with an awareness that one is an active participant in the system of broadcast audience measurement. These unique elements are perhaps what makes the PPM particularly valuable for conceptualizing the 'politics of design' that go into wearable trackers.

In the first part of this essay, I track the broadcast audience measurement industry's turn toward biometrics and body/tech throughout the 1980s, which combined with other industrial factors, such as the fragmentation of audiences and proliferation of media in public places, led to the creation of the PPM. I then use industry archival documents and technology patents to detail the process of designing and implementing the PPM. Arbitron managed two central design elements – body attachment and exposure-based tracking – by working to create an "interfaceless interface" (Bolter/Grusin 1999: 23), field-testing form factors, and engineering sensor-based audio and movement trackers. The engineering challenges that Arbitron faced in creating the

PPM are emblematic of the fragile negotiations of body/tech interfacing that mobile data tracking requires.

In the second part of this essay, I analyze the unique modes of surveillance and forms of embodied labor that the PPM relied on. The PPM ultimately entrenched users within a trans-spatial surveillance enclosure, implicating even activities that are unrelated to television viewing or consumption under corporate surveillance, thereby turning the body itself into a round-the-clock technology of commodification.[1] The work that the PPM's design features and Arbitron's promotional rhetoric had to do to procure its participants' complicit labor is perhaps best seen in the numerous patented, sensor-based 'compliance incentives', ranging from motion trackers to gamification mechanisms such as giving users points, that Arbitron incorporated into the device to help motivate panelists' cooperation. Indeed, beyond tracking participants, the PPM relied on the labor of participants' bodies to extend the capabilities of the machine, even policing them as 'employees' by tracking the time they put in and offering them incentives to work harder. While the employment of sensor mechanisms to extend the spatiality and temporality of surveillance and gamification features to procure users' loyalty are often taken as unique features of the contemporary self-tracking movement, here I demonstrate that corporate consumer tracking firms like Arbitron spent the latter part of the 20th-century testing the utility of these features for mitigating the limits of body/tech interfacing and labor in ways that were both prescient of and influential to contemporary practices of mobile tracking.

Broadcast Audience Measurement and the Turn to Body/Tech

Audience ratings are the foundation of the United States' commercial broadcast industries; they operate as a supposed third-party entity and establish the currency with which commercial spots (which fund radio and television programs) are sold to advertisers. Since the early-1950s, the broadcast audience ratings market in the US has been dominated by two major firms:

---

1   Michel Foucault argues that the body serves as "instrument or intermediary" of capitalist production that "becomes a useful source only if it is both a productive body and a subjected body" (Foucault 1995, 11, 26). Foucault's description of the body as a "political technology" informs my conceptualization of the body's role – more specifically in the context of data economies – as a "technology of commodification."

Nielsen and the American Research Bureau (which changed its name to Arbitron in 1973). The ratings firms used similar methods of collecting listening/viewing data from relatively small but 'statistically representative' panels of households, congregating the data into program ratings, and selling them to clients. Within a couple of decades, each ratings firm had established its relative niche. Nielsen used mechanical meters to measure television audiences in its national panel and viewer diaries to measure television audiences in local markets. Arbitron, on the other hand, focused its efforts on local television markets and radio, using viewer diaries in both cases.

Throughout the late-1970s and 1980s significant changes within the television industry brought this relative stability in the ratings market to an end. Between 1975 and 1985, the number of cable subscribers in the US increased from 9.2 million to 54.9 million, and cable penetration increased from 13 percent to 46 percent. Whereas in 1980, most cable systems were 12-channel, by 1985 more than half offered more than 20 channels. With this additional competition, the network share decreased from 90 percent in 1975 to 73 percent in 1985 (Poltrack 1986; Mullen 2003: 128-137). The increasingly fragmented television market created demand for more specific viewer demographics. Additionally, the proliferation of remote controls (in 1983 1/3 of new color television sets came equipped with a wireless remote control) created industry concern over viewers' ability to 'zap' past commercials (cf. J. Walter Thompson USA 1987).

The widespread agreement among network executives and advertisers was that established audience measurement systems were not equipped to keep up with these changes. In 1985 Audits of Great Britain (AGB), a British audience measurement firm, introduced their peoplemeter to the US market, and Nielsen followed, introducing its own peoplemeter device in 1986. Peoplemeter systems marked a turn toward measuring individuals (whereas the previous household meters merely recorded what the television set was tuned to); they were also active, requiring each viewer to push a remote-control button every fifteen minutes to confirm their viewing. While peoplemeters were better suited for the new multi-channel, fragmented audience experience, they begot new challenges. In particular, the decrease in ratings resulting from the introduction of peoplemeters motivated criticism about whether viewers could reliably push the buttons.

In response to the widespread critiques of the peoplemeter, the decade between 1985 and 1995 marked a period of competition in the ratings industry, which the press referred to as the "peoplemeter wars" (Broadcasting 1988:

62; Buzzard 2002). During this time, audience measurement companies like Nielsen and Arbitron, but also newcomers Smart and Percy Co., raced to develop a viable passive peoplemeter device, a system that could still measure audience viewing on an individual level, but without relying on their active participation. Elsewhere, I refer to this period as a "biometric turn" in audience measurement (Hessler 2019). Drawing inspiration from the increasing popularity of biometrics in the healthcare and banking industries, ratings firms experimented with things like body heat sensors, motion detectors, and facial recognition technologies to surveil television viewing and collect audience demographic information (Gates 2011; Hessler 2019). In general, during this period, the audience measurement industry responded to the proliferating array of television choices and new forms of viewer agency by using biometric surveillance technologies to re-discipline consumers. As the task of datafying viewing practices became increasingly difficult, the body itself became a technology or tool; through it, audience measurement firms could reembody the disarray of viewing information and bind it to specific individuals.

The task then, for ratings firms, became how to engineer a common body/machine language – how to create a technology that could work seamlessly enough with the body to create usable data. Especially given the relatively primitive technological state and expensive cost of biometric technologies at the time, this task proved difficult. Journalists covered these increasingly invasive experiments with both criticism and sarcasm. In 1992, Elizabeth Jensen wrote, "The TV Industry has been on a quest for years for a so-called passive system that would require little or no effort on the part of the person whose viewing habits are being measured. The goal is so elusive that TV executives occasionally joke about wishing they could implant computer chips under viewers' skin to ensure an absolutely accurate and complete measurement of who watches what and when" (Jensen 1992: B8). Ultimately, none of the aforementioned biometric body heat sensing, motion detecting, or facial recognition ratings systems actually made it to market. But this period of experimentation taught ratings firms and their engineers a lot about the opportunities and limits of biometrics, and they remained devoted to the potential of body-tech for audience surveillance.

While the efforts to create a viable biometric passive meter were mostly focused toward capitalizing on the body to measure television viewing within the living room space, throughout the 1980s television viewing was becoming increasingly public, with a proliferation of TV screens in airports and bars and portable television sets at 10 percent penetration by the end of the decade.[2] Moreover, portable television viewers consisted of some of the most 'valuable' audiences for advertisers: usually younger, more tech-savvy, and having higher income. While the "peoplemeter wars" had centered on the efforts to create a new measurement system for television, the industry was equally dissatisfied with Arbitron's continued use of viewer diaries to measure radio listening. In the past, radio's more stringent financial constraints (radio brings in much less advertising money than television) meant that Arbitron did not have the financial backing to experiment with technologies beyond the viewer diary. But by the late-80s, glimpses of the digital transition were already in sight. The industry was increasingly aware of the impending proliferation of media options, which would beget increasingly fragmented and intractable audiences. Nielsen and Arbitron were under pressure to engineer a measurement technology that could not only address the current limitations of audience measurement (such as the inability to capture media consumption outside the home) but also offer forward thinking solutions for the digital age. Both ratings firms envisioned a portable meter to be the solution, and their design efforts focused on two elements connected to portability: first, the meter's epistemological and physical attachment to 'the person/the body', and second, its turn to exposure-based measurement.

Manufacturing an "Interfaceless Interface": Designing the Portable Peoplemeter

In accord with the aforementioned prophetic invocations of body attachment, throughout the late-1980s and 1990s, both Nielsen and Arbitron worked to develop a peoplemeter that could attach to the body. In addition to the challenge of designing a body-attachable device that was durable enough to work with the body's movement, perhaps a greater challenge would be creating one that users would cooperate with – one that users would not find burdensome to wear. Any viable body-attachable meter would have to work like a prosthetic; it would have to be almost invisible, seemingly operating as one with the body. In this way, portable meters relied on a third design element that is central

---

2   Between the mid-1980s and mid-1990s, portable television sets such as the Sony Walkman, which were the size of a walkie-talkie and designed for users could carry with them outside the home, were gaining popularity in the United States (Roberts 1986).

to digital tracking: creating what Jay David Bolter and Richard Grusin call the "interfaceless interface" (1999:23), where users are meant to be practically unaware of the gadgetry as they engage with it, interacting with gadgets as seamlessly as they do with the physical world. Indeed, in the contemporary digital age, ubiquity and inconspicuousness go in hand. As Jason Farman explains, "Ubiquitous or pervasive computing often seeks to create an environment in which the technologies remain invisible. Instead of being conscious of our interactions with the interfaces, we simply act intuitively with our environment and it responds accordingly" (Farman 2012: 7). But this trend is owed to more than mere practicality. This evolution toward miniaturization and ubiquity enables surveillance to weave through our lives unnoticed; the more technology feels like a normal part of 'the self', the less it's recognized as a corporate onlooker. Through miniaturization and ubiquity this stealthy gadgetry goes unnoticed in its role as 'employer', but nonetheless it procures participants' labor through a combination of incognizance and distraction.

Throughout the late-1980s, Nielsen experimented with a range of possible 'form factors' for a wearable device, fashioning devices in the functional form and style of familiar accessories. Gina Neff and Dawn Nafus describe form factors as "the material envelopes for the technology inside." They write, "Technological innovations make smaller devices conceivable, but it is the social and material envelopes for them that help us imagine wearing them on our bodies" (Neff/Nafus 2016: 110). Accordingly, Nielsen experimented with giving a panel of viewers rings to wear, which picked up frequencies from the TV set. However, Jensen mentions that the participation rate was low: "half the participants lost them." Nielsen tried watches as well, fashioning the gadgets to a test-panel of users in London, but panelists frequently neglected to wear them (Jensen 1992). In 1987, writing about the abundance of "outside the box" experimentation with portable meter technologies, *Variety* teased, "Word has spread that the next wave of [experiments] will be to generously give a semi-precious birthstone ring or bracelet to members of measured families with the proviso they wear it all day" (Variety 1987: 72).

On the matter of the second design goal – the move to measure 'exposure' – the ratings industry possessed a patent trail of technologies going back to the mid-1950s that utilized audio detection (Evans 1960).[3] And throughout

---

3   In 1956 Nielsen filed a patent for a device that emitted an audio pulse in the voice coils of the speakers in panelists' radios or televisions in accord with whichever channel the set was tuned to. The resulting audio pulse could not be heard by listeners/viewers,

the late-1980s, Nielsen and another competitor, Pretesting Company, which was working to bring an audience measurement system called Whispercode to market, both experimented with using audio detection in portable meters with middling success (Pretesting Co. v. Arbitron Co. 1996; Stamler 2000).[4] Audio detection was promising because it could be used with both radio and television, in a cross-platform environment; it enabled mobility since it didn't require a meter to be tethered to a physical media source; and it had body/tech design elements. However, the task of creating a code that was durable enough and could be detected unabridged in a variety of acoustic settings proved to be an engineering feat.

While Nielsen wasn't able to design a viable portable meter, Arbitron was more successful. In 1992, Arbitron partnered with Martin Marietta Corporate – a contracting company that designed the audio transmission technologies that the US military used to communicate with submarines during the Cold War – to create a unique identifying code for radio and television broadcasters to embed in the soundtracks of their programs (R&R 2000a: 114). Lockheed Martin of Martin Marietta conducted proof-of concept testing for two different systems before settling on a design that uses psychoacoustic masking, which takes advantage of the human ear's inability to discern a slightly weaker frequency that is immediately adjacent to a strong frequency. As indicated in Arbitron's patent, "The coded message [would] either have a very low frequency (e.g. 40 Hz) or be at an audible frequency, but at a very low level (the sound signal from -50 to -60 d B)" (The Arbitron Company 1995: 1). This type of acoustic masking is also the core technical basis for AAC, mp3, and a host of other data-rate reduction schemes. The code that Arbitron and Lockheed Martin engineered would eventually become known within the industry as a Universal Program Code, and often referred to simply as an audio "watermark."

Engineering the audio code required a fragile manipulation of the body/technology interface. The code had to be completely inaudible to the human ear in all listening and viewing environments and had to be capable of being integrated into a soundtrack without degrading the sound quality of the program. It also had to be able to survive in any techno-acoustic environment, including format conversions and compression; conform to all

---

but would be transmitted via a phone line to Nielsen, where it would be matched to its corresponding broadcast station.

4   Whispercode would later lose a patent infringement case against Arbitron in 1996.

current (and possible future) industry standards; and be capable of encoding monophonic, stereophonic, and multichannel signals. Finally, the design had to be impervious to any attempts to tamper with or corrupt the embedded signal (R&R 2000b: 114).

Despite their promising developments with the PPM, Arbitron was struggling financially. The company had suffered from the failure of another system they had tried to bring to market during the "peoplemeter wars," a device called ScanAmerica, which attempted to integrate television viewership data with information about panelists' grocery purchases. Moreover, due to the increased expenses expected with the rumored implementation of peoplemeters in local markets, many local stations ceased subscribing to two networks, and Arbitron's subscriber base fell drastically between 1985 and 1992. In 1993 Arbitron announced that it would cease measuring local television ratings and focus exclusively on radio ratings, freeing Arbitron up to invest more money in the PPM (Jensen 1993, B2).

In late-1993, Arbitron contracted with engineering firm Intellisys Automation to create the first hardware prototypes for the device which consisted of three pieces: the PPM, which participants would carry with them or wear on their person, a base station for each PPM, and a household hub. Whenever panelists were within audio range of a radio or television program, the PPM would detect the inaudible high frequency code, time-stamp, and store it. At the end of the day, participants would return the PPM to its docking station, which was connected via wire to the household hub. The household hub then uploads the information to Arbitron's central facility via a dial-up line running through public telephone infrastructure. In original prototypes, the PPM itself was about the size of a small brick – useful for laboratory testing, but not suitable for body-attachment. From there, early hardware design efforts focused on miniaturizing the device, and experimenting with field tests to figure out the best shape, size, and form function for it. By the fourth generation of the prototype, the device was the size of a pager, three cubic inches and $2 \frac{1}{2}$ ounces (The Arbitron Company 1996; Moss 2002: 16-17).

Ensuring that station chief engineers encoded their programs properly and that all audio configuration could be detected by the PPM with equal efficiency was another ongoing challenge; it required collaboration among a variety of station personnel and compatibility across multiple technological assemblages. As Arbitron found out during their very first panel test-run with the PPM in Manchester, England, a single encoding error could fail the whole system. Arbitron Vice President Bob Michael's explains that during the Manchester test-run, "An isolated problem with a single recording on the BBC Classical Network caused the five BBC networks to turn off their encoders about a week into the test" (R&R 2000b: 112). Ultimately, it was found that a manufacturing defect was at fault. Since the BBC accounted for 55 percent of the radio market, the error made the data from the test-run unusable. In fact, encoding/decoding issues were common throughout the PPM's test-runs, and they remain common today. Michael LeClair wrote in *Radio World*, "Some radio engineers joke that if a PPM encoder were to break, they might as well turn the transmitter off; advertisers will never know if anyone is listening anyway. Radio stations invest in backup encoders and even specialized monitors to ensure their encoding is always working, and their engineers jump to repair it when something goes wrong" (LeClair 2015: 32). In 2009, former MIT Professor and Director of Engineering at 25-Seven Systems, Inc., Barry Blesser, published a white paper titled "Technical Properties of Arbitron's PPM System," offering an analysis of the PPM's technical functions. In the report, Blesser concluded that while the PPM is overall reliable, certain sound properties could affect proper detection of Arbitron's watermark. He writes:

> Because fricative phonemes (such as /s/, /z/, /th/, and /f/) contain a broadband hissing component that is like white noise, they can encode large amounts of data. But some announcers may have weak or rapid articulation of such fricatives. Consonants, although short in duration, are good for PPM; pregnant pauses and halting delivery are not. Speaking style matters. While the typical radio program may produce perfect watermarking performance, and while the average reliability over the universe might be 99 per cent, there are likely to be some announcer voices, vocal articulation styles, and specific genres of music that belong to the 1 per cent failure cases. (Blesser 2009: 4)

Blesser concludes that elements that are due to chance, like a presenter's voice qualities or rhythms of articulation, could affect code detection and thus lower a station's or program's ratings. In addition to program content, Blesser concluded that the environment in which an audience member listens to radio may affect the ability of their PPM to properly capture and decode Arbitron's watermark. He explains that since the usable signal-to-noise ratio between 1.0 and 3.0 kHz varies dramatically depending on the environment, programs that are encoded within a wider range of the available spectral channels have a higher chance of being detected and decoded in hostile sound environments (Blesser 2009: 4-5).

In 2015, 25-Seven Systems, Inc. presented a product called Voltair at the National Association of Broadcasters. Voltair helps stations ensure that their encoded watermark is transferred as clearly and efficiently as possible (LeClair 2015: 33). The Voltaire website describes the system's functions as follows:

a) Monitors and analyzes the robustness of watermark encoding across all program content.
b) Offers visibility into how listening environments may influence watermark decoding, using models of acoustic spaces where listeners are wearing or carrying their devices.
c) Includes advanced audio signal processing to enhance the detectability of the watermark codes within the context of your programming objectives.
d) Empowers programmers to make informed decisions to address potential weaknesses in either encoding or decoding. ("Voltair-In Dept" 2019)

Blesser's white paper and Voltair's PPM audio code detection troubleshooting system shed light on the intra-industry cooperation and constant technological troubleshooting that characterize the PPM system. These continued issues also exemplify the challenge of designing body tech – in this case, the audio code's necessary inaudibility makes it vulnerable to a number of (often unnoticed) transferal issues – and also of engineering an exposure-based tracking system.

The PPM's reliance on the mobile body to capture exposure wrought additional design challenges for Arbitron. First, since each family member over the age of six was assigned their own PPM, it was possible that family members could accidentally swap meters. Regarding this challenge, Michaels explains, "If someone in the household switches the meter, we would notice that by an abrupt change in the stations the person listened to and other indications. People can write their name on it or do whatever they need to do to make sure it's theirs" (*R&R* 2000b: 133).[5] Second, since the PPM picks up all audio exposure (even when it is docked), Arbitron had to build mechanisms into the PPM

---

5   The deleterious effect of meter swapping amongst family on the reliability of PPM data foreboded similar issues that streaming services like Netflix face regarding the detrimental effects of profile-sharing on data collection and the function of algorithmic recommendations. Notably, Bob Michaels's dubious defense of the PPM system—that oversight will catch any data irregularities – is also mirrored by Ted Sarandos's regarding Netflix. (Lawler 2013)

system to distinguish the parameters of what constitutes 'listening'. To avoid counting ambient sound that the wearer is exposed to while strolling through the mall or pulling up alongside another vehicle at a stop light, Arbitron only includes 'listening' of a minimum duration of 5 minutes in its metrics. On the other hand, the PPM is limited in that it cannot measure multiple sound sources at once. If, for example, a participant is both watching television and listening to the radio, the PPM will record only the louder audio signal (Bray 2009: B.5.). In addition to this wide array of technological obstacles, Arbitron had to overcome users' social and behavioral disinclinations to cooperate with the PPM. To accomplish this, Arbitron tapped into strategies that have become fundamental to contemporary digital tracking such as offering users tangible incentives and employing gamification elements to disguise panelists' labor as participatory diversion rather than surveilled work.

Incentivizing Compliance: Embodied Audience Labor Under PPM Surveillance

Regardless of the amount of effort and testing that went into creating a viable PPM device, its functionality was still contingent on panelists consistently carrying the device around. In other words, the second half of the PPM system was the labor of the user's body. The PPM is a unique case study because it neither offers users tangible benefits like many contemporary self-tracking gadgets nor is it panoptically imposed, since users agree to be ratings panelists. I contend, however, that the rhetoric that ratings firms use to convince panelists to sign on is similar to that used by peddlers of contemporary self-tracking gadgets. Ratings panelists are sold on the promise of self-elevation – by having their listening/viewing tracked, panelists are made to believe that they are no longer anonymous, passive consumers of the media they love, but rather are transformed into important agents who help influence media. They are also sold on the promise of community – by participating as ratings panelists they are members of a very exclusive club, and further, their data contributes to a larger compilation that is meant to signify overall audience taste. However, while these might be adequate psychological incentives for participants to sign on with Arbitron, the lack of material incentives for (and the fatigue of) consistent participation means that the ratings industry is perpetually dealing with a crisis of cooperation. Thus, it is necessary for ratings firms to not only make the labor of participating as seamless as possible (through technological design) but also to manufacture continued psychological incentives.

As the PPM was a novice technology, the onus was on Arbitron to demonstrate that panelists would indeed cooperate with the system. Journalist Roberta McConochie wrote, "One of the obvious, critical keys to Arbitron's new pocket people meter program is respondent cooperation. Some in the industry have speculated that wearing a pocket meter could be easier than filling out a diary. Others have asked, 'Will survey participants accept the high-tech method? Will they keep the meter with them all the time?'" (McConochie 1993: 26). To answer these questions, between 1992 and 1995 Arbitron's methods researchers conducted 25 different field tests during which they provided participants with portable devices that emulated the size and shape of the PPM and asked them to wear the device for time periods ranging from one week to two months. The simulated PPM devices contained small motion detectors and clocks so that Arbitron representatives could determine how long they were carried.

Following these tests, Intellisys and Arbitron incorporated a number of patented features into the PPM to help motivate and ensure participant compliance. The first was (similar to what was used during the trial) a motion detector, which could reportedly detect movement as small as breathing, and a clock that generated a time stamped record of panelists' movement. In their patent, Arbitron referred to this movement policing mechanism as a "compliance incentive." The patent describes it as follows:

> A sense signal is provided indicating whether the device is being carried with the person of the audience member, and a time signal corresponding with the sense signal is also provided. An indication to the audience member of whether the audience member's usage of the device has been in accordance with the predetermined usage criterion is provided based on the sense signal and the corresponding time signal. (The Arbitron Company 1996: 1)

Essentially, whenever a meter is removed from the docking station a green light turns on. If an undocked meter goes more than three minutes without being moved the green light starts blinking to alert the user, and after a few more minutes of immobility the green light shuts off. During this time the meter still picks up audio signals, but the record shows Arbitron that the meter was dormant, and the data is discarded. This allows Arbitron to track whether participants were complying with carrying the device around. A PPM has to register as being in motion at least eight hours a day for its results to be considered valid, or 'in-tab', for that day (R&R 2000a: 114).

Another way to characterize the exposure-based mode of tracking that the PPM relies on is as a turn toward sensor-based surveillance. Andrejevic and Burdon argue that the interactive and participatory modes of surveillance that predominated throughout the late-20th century have been somewhat supplanted by a sensor-society, consisting of networked, interactive devices that sense and relay data about how the device itself is used, about the user, or about the user's environment. Sensor devices, they argue, can obtain vastly larger quantities of (meta-) data. They write, "These days, we *generate* more than we participate – and even our participation generates further and increasingly comprehensive 'meta'-data about itself'" (Andrejevic/Burdon 2015: 20). While the examples of sensor devices that Andrejevic and Burdon give are quite contemporary – "car seats with heart-rate monitors, desks with thermal sensors, phones with air quality monitors, [and] tablets that track our moods" (Andrejevic/Burdon 2015: 22) – the PPM, and even Nielsen's body heat sensing and facial recognition systems that pre-dated it, are exemplary of the ratings industry's turn to sensor-based systems. The PPM, in particular, with its reliance on sensing audio codes to measure media consumption and its time-stamped sensing motion detector, is emblematic of a sensor-based data tracker in both function and effect. Andrejevic and Burdon argue that the goal of sensor-directed surveillance is to capture a "comprehensive portrait" (2015: 23) of a particular ecosystem or population. Indeed the dual-functioning sensing mechanisms of the PPM tracks the entire ecosystem of media exposure that a user might encounter and also comprehensively manages the user him/herself: recording when the user is carrying the device, whether they are dormant or mobile, on a minute by minute basis – even using its sensor to elicit immediate compliance from the user. Thus, just as Andrejevic and Burdon say that "sensor-derived surveillance can be untargeted, non-systematic, and often opportunistic" (2015: 23), the PPM's sensors enable its surveillance mechanisms to discreetly seep into almost every facet of a user's daily existence.

The PPM's exposure-based tracking system altered dynamics of audience labor and its implication in surveillance. By carrying the PPM measurement device around on their person, Arbitron panelists implicated their entire daily activities within a regime of audience surveillance even when they were not acting as television viewers. Through their technological prosthetic, panelists enact an identity of permanent audiencehood. Scholars have argued that the proliferation of mobile electronic devices like pagers, cellphones, and smart watches enable workplace tasks to creep into our familial life and demand our attention at all hours, keeping us tethered to labor even in our leisure (cf. Turkle 2008). In a similar vein, with the PPM, users move through life always marked and measured as 'consumer' or 'audience', implicated as a neverending data node in the commercial (media) economy. Andrejevic uses the term "digital enclosure" to describe "a process whereby activities and transactions formerly carried out beyond the monitoring capacity of the Internet are enfolded into its virtual space" (2004: 35). I argue that a similar occurrence of surveillance enclosure is evident there, one that participants enter when they agree to become an Arbitron family. Part of an 'exposure-based' media audience measurement system entails implicating and enclosing even activities that are unrelated to television viewing or consumption under corporate surveillance. In its early years, the ratings industry and the press often referred to the PPM interchangeably as both the "portable people meter" and the "personal people meter"; this slippery semantics gestures to the conjointness of audience measurement's reliance on an exposure-based mobile omnipresence with manufactured intimacy and trespass of the personal.

In accord with these manufactured intimacies, the PPM display directly addressed its user, with notes like "Hello Maddy" and "Congratulations Maddy, you have completed your upload." Natasha Dow Schüll argues that tracking technologies often function as tools for "relationship management," where corporations strategically employ the intimate details they collect about users in an affective manner in effort to procure their loyalty (2012: 152). By using direct address, Arbitron also leans into the promise to transform users from anonymous consumers to sanctioned agents.

Arbitron also utilized gamification strategies, turning PPM use into play, to motivate panelists' consistent use of the device and loyalty to the process.[6] For example, the compliance incentive patent also included mechanisms for giving users positive feedback in the form of points earned for carrying the

---

6 In her study of gambling machines, Natasha Dow Schüll uses the concept of gamification to explain the contemporary trend in technological design toward incorporating affective and reward-based mechanisms meant to psychologically motivate (often subliminally) users to spend ever-more time using the machines. And others, like Jennifer Whitson have identified gamification as a primary strategy of digital self-tracking tracking apps.

device for the duration of the day. Arbitron Vice President Bob Michaels explains,

> On the docking stations is an LED readout that congratulates them and shows them the number of points they earned that day [...] The point system is not based on how much [they] listen to the radio or watch television, but rather on keeping the green light lit on the meter, and the way they do that is to carry it with them wherever they go when they are awake. (R&R 2000a: 114)

The compliance incentive patent describes this as a pre-stored message that reads: "Because you have correctly used your 'meter' for (X) consecutive days, you have won a prize. Please call [...]" (The Arbitron Company 1996: 6). There is an inherent affective dimension to these feedback mechanisms, as Jennifer Whitson illustrates:

> The lovely sound of simulated coins clinking, or bars levelling-up, or an encouraging simulated voice, provides the feedback and support I crave, bringing me into this relation with myself and the machine, and persuading me to stay. These sounds, colours, badges, etc. let me know that the system is listening to me, that it is reading me, that its sensors are working. This feedback feels *good*. (2013: 171)

With the PPM, positive affiliation with the device and good affect is cultivated with bright green lights associated with progress and congratulatory phrasing associated with accomplishment.

Importantly, like employees, PPM users were rewarded for "time on task." Further, Michaels' clarification that "the point system is not based on how much [they] listen to the radio or watch television, but rather on keeping the green light lit" coincides with Schüll's description of reward systems for gamblers being based not on the amount they wage, but on the time they spend playing (2012: 144). In both cases, the rewarded behavior is consistency; like conventional capitalist labor, being a good employee means supplanting leisure time with labor time. Whitson points out that virtual rewards and reputation scores have the benefit of not costing the corporation anything (2013: 168); however, at times PPM users were also rewarded monetarily. By accumulating points, PPM panelists could win rewards of $12 to $17 a month and become eligible for monthly sweepstakes. Michaels continues, "Think back to when you first started traveling and earning frequent-flyer points. Every time you flew somewhere, rented a car or stayed at a hotel, you were probably thinking about how many points you were earning. It's the same with the PPM" (R&R 2000a: 114). Whitson argues that gamification is reliant on quantifying users' activities which in turn "enables cycles of feedback and behavior modification that are propagated as play" (2013: 167). Ultimately, the PPM system uses gamification mechanisms to generate behavior modification, provoking users to carry the PPM on their person more consistently and remember to plug the PPM into the docking station at night so that their data can be downloaded.

Later, after the PPM's wide scale implementation, panelists were given access to a members' only site called "meandmymeter.com" where they could see up-to-the-minute graphs detailing how many points they have accumulated. In addition to rewarding panelists for good behavior over time, the incentive strategy incorporated randomized bonus awards or money "given to a randomly selected audience member who was either carrying the device with her or his person at a particular time or whose monitoring device was re-charging after being carried" (The Arbitron Company 1996: 6). By offering a member's only community (that also contains a larger quantity of feedback than the device itself can display) and randomizing prizes, Arbitron cultivates panelists' awareness that they are part of an exclusive community and that their data is part of a greater whole, further eliciting their loyal participation. This too is a common strategy of gamification. Whitson writes that "Games create a shared social space... One becomes immersed, engrossed in the game and the social interactions that the game system's rules and goals evoke" (2013: 165). Through the incentive of community, Arbitron strategically employs two psychological motivations – duty and competitiveness – to motivate panelists' cooperation in the task.

The patent's description of this array of mechanisms designed to ensure cooperation as 'compliance incentives' itself encapsulates the ambiguous forms of labor the PPM entailed. On the one hand, the term 'compliance' denotes an expectation of obedience to a contract, a dynamic that the patent further emphasizes when it describes the green sensor light as indicating "whether the audience member's usage of the device has been in accordance with the predetermined usage criterion" (The Arbitron Company 1996: 1). But on the other hand, the 'incentives' – denoting the array of positive messages, bonuses, and prizes – work to disguise both the participant labor and surveillance mechanisms and even to recast them as leisure. Moreover, while the accumulation of points and surprise bonuses reward participants for being 'good employees', they also enhance the surveillance enclosure properties of the system, ensuring that participants are always on and active. In actuality, the PPM facilitates a dialectic between manufactured incognizance, where the device is meant to integrate with participants' bodies seamlessly enough that they forget it is there, and attentive labor, where the system's constant compliance alerts and point notifications constantly remind users that they are under task.

The ambiguous forms of labor that the PPM relied on resulted in disagreements in the industry about whether the device was a passive or active peoplemeter. Arbitron originally marketed the PPM as a passive peoplemeter: Vice President Michaels explained,

> The Portable People Meter is as close to passive audience measurement as we can get. Consumers don't have to press buttons every time they start or stop watching TV. Nor do consumers have to write an entry in a paper diary every time they watch TV or listen to radio. (R&R 2000b: 116)

The press followed this characterization, emphasizing the PPM's ability to eliminate "the risk that a lazy viewer would slack off and ignore punching in" (Jensen 1992: B8). On the other hand, Nicholas Schiavone, vice president of media and marketing for NBC, stated, "The fact that one has to wear the new Arbitron meter makes it a highly active device, not a passive one" (1992). Schiavone had a point, since even the PPM's time stamping function could not ensure compliance. For example, one former Arbitron family admitted to frequently circumventing the time stamp monitor by attaching the device to their dog's collar (Hessler 2016).

Donna Haraway lists "active/passive" as one of the dualisms that facilitate domination in Western traditions. She says, "high-tech culture challenges these dualisms in intriguing ways. It is not clear who makes and who is made in the relation between human and machine" (Haraway 1991: 177). Is it the PPM machine doing the labor of measuring the body's exposure, or is it the body doing the labor for the machine? This dialectic is the operating logic of mobile tracking, where the two often conflate in perpetual conflict. Through its integration into these "interfaceless interfaces" that we interact with seamlessly, surveillance normalizes its place within our everyday movements and tasks. Yet the actuality of embodied experience is that interfacing with technology is rarely seamless; thus, in the moments when the barriers between our 'selves' and our wearable prosthetics become apparent, mobile tracking becomes laborious and must be mitigated with a host of design assemblages and manufactured incentives.

Implementing the PPM: The Cultural Politics of Audience Surveillance

Arbitron conducted their first test-runs with the PPM in Manchester, England in 1999. While the system experienced the aforementioned technology issues with watermark codes, the test-run demonstrated a high participant cooperation rate – the percent of survey respondents who carried or wore the PPM at least eight hours a day averaged around 86 percent to 89 percent, which is similar to other established audience measurement practices (Moss 2002: 17; Billboard 1999: 59). According to Arbitron, in debriefing interviews, "Ninety-nine percent of participants agreed that participating in the ratings panel was a positive experience, and over 80 percent said that they could easily have participated for as long as six months" (R&R 2000b: 116).

In 2000, Arbitron started their first PPM test run in America, fastening approximately 300 panelists in Philadelphia with peoplemeters for periods of time ranging from one to three months. Around 38 radio stations watermarked their programs in order to participate in the trial (Geist 2000: 4; Young 2001: C.2.). By January 2001, Arbitron had increased the pool of panelists in Philadelphia to 1,500, and after a short break to work out technological quirks, in 2004 Arbitron started trial runs in Houston. By the end of 2007, Arbitron had completed transitioning their radio ratings panels from diaries to PPMs in both the Philadelphia and Houston markets, with plans to implement the device wide scale (Goldsmith 2004: 6; Billboard 2008: 10).

The ratings data derived with PPMs diverged in significant ways from that collected from viewer diaries. The PPM found that "overall listening time" was similar to that reported by the diary, but the number of "listening episodes" (unique tune-ins) increased by 135 percent. Further, the number of channels listened to was greater, while the duration of each listening episode decreased by 57 percent (Billboard 2008: 10). Essentially, PPM data indicated that audiences listened to more channels, but for a shorter duration of time than previously thought. Some programming formats and genres also saw significant changes in their ratings. In many markets, Rock and Top 40 stations performed better in PPM data than they typically did with diaries, while Hispanic and urban stations saw significant drops in their ratings (Lewis 2008: E.1.).

In addition to the predictable pushback from stations that saw their audience share fall, cultural critics and diversity advocates campaigned against Arbitron's continued roll-out, warning that the decrease in ratings for minority-oriented stations could further diminish the already limited ad revenue these stations were bringing in. In response to the criticism, Arbitron increased the number of Black and Hispanic households in its PPM panels, but nonetheless, the pattern persisted with the PPM roll-out in New York. After the New York ratings were released, the *New York Times* reported: "WPAT 93.1, a Spanish-language adult contemporary station, was ranked No. 7 in Arbitron's summer ratings but fell to No. 19 in October's personal people meter test among 25- to 54-year-olds. Sister station WSKQ 97.9 dropped from No. 4 to No. 7" (Stelter, 2007: C11.). A similar drop occurred with urban adult contemporary stations, with WBLS 107.5 dropping from its number 1 rank to number 12 and WRKS 98.7 falling from number 3 to number 9 (Stelter, 2007: C11.).

In *Sounds of Belonging*, Delores Innes Casillas offers a more complete analysis of these criticisms and of Arbitron's longer history of undercounting Hispanic audiences. Casillas argues that Arbitron's proposed solutions to the racial discrepancies in audience data – more follow-up with Black and Hispanic panelists, for example – rhetorically positioned the problem as a "perceived disorganization, idleness, and irresponsibility" of nonwhite listeners rather than an issue with Arbitron's method or the PPM device (2014: 138). Casillas's argument highlights the fact that while Arbitron has always promoted the PPM as a 'passive' device that mitigates audience noncooperation or fatigue, this rhetoric carries additional racial underpinnings. For people of color, part of the hidden embodied labor of being a PPM panelist means that even with a so-called 'passive' device, one is always actively performing race – fair cultural representation under neo-liberal datafication regimes requires minority panelists to not only be ultra-cooperative under consumer surveillance, but also to consume the cultural products that are meant to be representative for their identity group (i.e. represent Black, Hispanic, etc. tastes) lest they go further undervalued in the market.

On October 10, 2008, both the New York State Attorney General Andrew Cuomo and the New Jersey Attorney General Anne Milgram filed two separate suits against Arbitron for its undercounting of minority viewers. In the suit, Milgram described the PPM as a "new, unaccredited system for measuring listenership [that] harms minority consumers and violates New Jersey's consumer fraud, advertising and anti-discrimination laws" (Billboard 2008: 10). Ultimately Arbitron settled, agreeing to pay $260,000 to resolve the suit and $100,000 to trade groups associated with minority radio stations. Arbitron also agreed to pay for an advertising campaign supporting minority radio. As part of the settlement, Arbitron also committed to paying for a study overseen by Attorney General Cuomo to "determine and cure" any measurable bias against racial minorities that could result from PPM implementation (Stelter 2009: Stelter 2007: C.11.).

Despite the controversy, throughout 2006 and 2007, both CBS Radio and Clear Channel signed multi-year contracts; collectively these two conglomerates account for over 50 of the US's largest radio markets, ensuring a wide adoption the PPM system (Ovide 2007: A.8.; Lewis 2008: E.1.). By the end of 2008, Arbitron replaced the diary system with the PPM in eight new markets: New York; Los Angeles; Chicago; San Francisco; Nassau-Suffolk, New York; Middlesex-Somerset-Union, New Jersey; Riverside-San Bernardino, California; and San Jose, California (Billboard 2008: 10). Despite its shortcomings, industry professionals lauded the PPM's forward-thinking, digital-apt design. For example, even Nielsen spokesman Jack Loftus commended the device for being "designed to meet the challenges of digital and satellite distributed content, as well as the convergence of media and the Internet" (Gentile 2002: F.10.). Since 2010, the PPM operates in 48 of the largest radio markets (which comprise ~90 percent of the listening public), and it is the main mechanism for collecting radio ratings.

Conclusion: The Future of the PPM

In 2013 Nielsen bought Arbitron, in hopes of utilizing Arbitron's expertise in mobile tracking methods to enhance their own cross-platform measurement capabilities. The PPM panel, and radio ratings in general, now operate under a new arm of Nielsen called Nielsen Audio. Nielsen is currently working on a revamp of the PPM, called the "next-generation PPM," which they hope will become the main mechanism for measuring both radio and television audiences across a variety of platforms. In 2017 Nielsen demoed the next-gen PPM at industry trade events, and physical models of the device were passed around for the first time at the National Association of Broadcasters show in April 2019. The wearable watch-like device was developed in partnership with various smart watch companies. However, during testing Nielsen found that, while a watch seems to be the most functional form for the device, some panelists were strongly averse to wearing stuff on their wrists or didn't want to replace their own smart watches. Thus, Nielsen also plans to make the PPM available in the form of a pendant or a clothing clip for panelists who request it ("Nielsen Exhibit" 2018; Inside Radio 2019b). The PPM watch contains Bluetooth, enabling it to connect to panelists' set top meters, allowing Nielsen to congregate the data and ascertain a single metric for in home and out of home television viewing. Moreover, the Bluetooth connection removes the need for a push button registry because it enables Nielsen to automatically know which individuals are in the room with the television (Inside Radio 2017).

The next-gen PPM will also have a companion mobile app that panelists will download onto their smartphones. When panelists attach their next-gen PPM to their phone via a charger, the app will upload the media consumption data to Nielsen. In an interview with Inside Radio, Nielsen senior VP of Local Product Leadership Bill Rose explains that the smart phone app also enables two-way communication between Nielsen and panelists: "It allows us to have messaging and go back and forth with them in ways that you don't have with today's device" (Inside Radio 2019a). Moreover, the PPM smartphone app measures content watched on the smartphone itself. Nielsen is currently running the device through field tests in America, Australia, and parts of Europe to work out kinks with the device's battery life, waterproof function-ability, and microphone capabilities.

In addition to detecting audio watermarked codes to measure all radio and television consumption, some planned prototypes of the next-gen PPM would also have the device double as an activity tracker. Thus, under the neoliberal, techno-utopian guise of multi-functionality, Nielsen would hypothetically have access to panelists' health data, such as their heart rate, fitness level, and certain illnesses or disabilities that they may have. This would be in addition to information about panelists' spatial movements and geographical location, the latter of which Nielsen would get through the app, by tapping into panelists' phone GPSs ("Nielsen Exhibit" 2017; Inside Radio 2017).

Since Arbitron's process of designing the PPM has spanned three-decades, the PPM offers an ideal case study for how the technology, embodied labor, and culture of mobile tracking have evolved across the millennium into the contemporary data-driven digital landscape. The design experiments that firms like Arbitron were conducting throughout the late 20th-century – drawing from and building on a history of technology patents, experimenting with form factors, and improving sensor trackers – inform the mechanisms of today's many mobile-tracking gadgets. Moreover, in addition to establishing the precursory technology, consumer-tracking firms like Arbitron also tested the limits of participant cooperation with wearable devices, experimenting with ways to mitigate the labor and manufacture incentives to keep participants willing to be tracked. Many of the incentives that drive the contemporary popularity of self-tracking technologies, including the desire for some sort of self-elevation and the appeal of being part of a data collective community, were the same incentives that motivated participants to sign on as PPM panelists. Yet, Arbitron quickly found that these original motivations would not sustain PPM panelists' cooperation; thus, the firm was on the forefront of experimenting with digital-age tools like sensor-based feedback mechanisms and manufactured psychological incentives (like building gamification elements into the design of the PPM).

While 20th-century consumer tracking devices like the PPM were precursory in many ways to contemporary wearable gadgets, the ratings industry's investment in the next-gen PPM is ultimately due to the wide scale cultural normalization and proliferation of wearable tech. The self-tracking industry's and Quantified-Self movement's success at validating tracking as a tool of self-improvement and community building, popularizing consumers' outfitting in wearable gadgets, in turn has influenced even legacy consumer surveillance firms to venture further into wearable sensor-based tech. Ultimately, Nielsen endeavors to convert their entire national television ratings panel away from television/computer installed meters to wearable, sensor-based next-gen PPM trackers. With this evolution, broadcast audience measurement is becoming almost indistinguishable, as a part of our mobile sensor society, among the plethora of other forms of data tracking and mobile surveillance that the public participates in on a daily basis.

Works Cited

Andrejevic, Mark (2004): *Reality TV: The Work of Being Watched*, Lanham, Maryland: Rowman and Littlefield.
Andrejevic, Mark/Burdon, Mark (2015): "Defining the Sensor Society." In: *Television & New Media* 16/1, pp. 19-36.
Billboard (1999): "Device May Replace Diaries." In: *Billboard* 111/44 October 30, p. 59.
___ (2008): "Tuning Out the Static." In: *Billboard* 120/43 October 25, p. 10.
Blesser, Barry (2009): "Technical Properties of Arbitron's PPM System." 25-Seven Systems, Inc. August 18, pp. 4 (www.telosalliance.com/images/25-Seven/Voltair/25-Seven_Tech_Paper_Arbitron_PPM.pdf).
Bolter, Jay David/Grusin, Richard (1999): *Remediation*, Cambridge, MA: MIT Press.

Bray, Chad (2009): "Arbitron Settles Ratings Suit." In: *Wall Street Journal* January 8, p. B.5.

Broadcasting (1988): "Arbitron to Go with Peoplemeter." In: *Broadcasting* June 27.

Buzzard, Karen (2002): "The Peoplemeter Wars: A Case Study of Technological Innovation and Diffusion in the Ratings Industry." In: *Journal of Media Economics* 15/4, pp. 273-91.

Casillas, Delores Innes (2014): *Sounds of Belonging: U.S. Spanish-Language Radio and Public Advocacy*, New York, NY: New York University Press.

Chicago Tribune (1978): "Brains in Boxes" (1978): In: *Chicago Tribune* June 18.

"Display Ad 23: Digital Watch Breakthrough!" (1975): In: *Wall Street Journal* June 3, p. 4.

Evans, Chauncey Richard, assignor to A.C. Nielsen Company (1960): "Automated Audience Rating System." U.S. Patent 2,958,766, filed November 26, 1956, and issued November 1, 1960.

Farman, Jason (2012): *Mobile Interface Theory: Embodied Space and Locative Media*, New York: Routledge.

Foucault, Michel (1995): *Discipline & Punish*, Alan Sheridan (trans.). 2nd edition, New York: Vintage Books.

Gates, Kelly (2011): *Our Biometric Future: Facial Recognition Technology and the Culture of Surveillance*, New York, NY: New York University Press.

Gentile, Gary (2002): "Audience Tracking Becomes High-Tech." In: *Los Angeles Times* May 6, p. F.10.

Geist, Laura Clark (2000): "Who Watches What?" In: *Automative News*, August 21, p. 4.

Goldsmith, Jill (2004): "Radio Bix Picking Up Static on Rating Gauge." In: *Variety* 395/7 June 28 – July, p. 6.

Haraway, Donna J. (1991): *Simian, Cyborgs, and Women: The Reinvention of Nature*, New York: Routledge.

Hessler, Jennifer (2016): Personal Interview Conducted with "Michael," former "Arbitron PPM" panelist, March 30.

___ (2019): "Peoplemeters and the Biometric Turn in Audience Measurement." In: *Television and New Media* October 21.

Inside Radio (2017): "Nielsen Looks to Change Game with Next-Gen PPM." In: *Inside Radio* May 22.

___ (2019a): "Testing, Testing: Nielsen Puts Wearable PPM Devices Through Their Paces." In: *Inside Radio* January 7.

___ (2019b): "The Big Reveal: Nielsen Demos New Wearables PPMs at NAB Show." In: *Inside Radio* April 9.
Jensen, Elizabeth (1992a): "Arbitron TV Ratings Service to End, Leaving Rival Nielsen as Sole Provider." In: *Wall Street Journal* October 19, p. B2.
___ (1992b): "Nielsen Rival to Unveil New 'Peoplemeter'." In: *Wall Street Journal* December 4, p. B8.
J. Walter Thompson (1987): "Flippers: Changes in the Way Americans Watch TV." A Study by J. Walter Thompson
Lawler, Ryan (2013): "Netflix Makes Recommendations More Personalized By Adding Individual User Profiles." In: *Tech Crunch* August 1.
LeClair, Michael (2014): "So How's Your PPM?" In: *Radio World* 39/8 March 25, p. 32.
Lewis, Randy (2008): "Fresh Data Changes Radio's Numbers Game; Programmers Act on Arbitron's Portable People Meter Results." In: *Los Angeles Times* December 15, p. E.1.
McConochie, Roberta M. (1993): "Arbitron's Pocket Peoplemeter: The Question of Cooperation." In: *Radio & Records* July 16, p. 26.
Moss, Linda (2002): "Does Arbitron Have a Better Mousetrap?" In: *Broadcasting & Cable* February 11, pp. 16-17.
Mullen, Megan (2003): *The Rise of Cable Programming in the Unites States: Revolution or Evolution?*, Austin, TX: University of Texas Press.
Neff, Gina/Nafus, Dawn (2016): *Self-Tracking*, Cambridge, MA: MIT Press.
"Nielsen Exhibit" (2017): All Access Worldwide Radio Summit (Burbank, California) April 20.
___ (2018): All Access Worldwide Radio Summit (Burbank, California) April 23.
Ovide, Shira (2008): "Arbitron Scores a Hit as Clear Channel Picks Radio-Ratings System." In: *Wall Street Journal* June 23, p A.8.
Polrack, David (1986): "The US – The Impact of Cable and More Stations." In: *Television Today* January 3.
Pretesting Co. v. Arbitron Co. (1996): U.S. Dist. LEXIS 12329, 1996 WL 480899 (United States District Court for the Southern District of New York. August 23, 1996. filed).
Roberts, Johnnie L. (1986): "As Pocket TVs Catch On, Owners Adopt Some Unconventional Viewing Habits." In: *Wall Street Journal* March 5.
R&R (2000a): "The Development Of The Arbitron People Meter." In: *R&R* September 15, p. 114.
___ (2000b): "The Revolution of the Personal People Meter." In: *R&R* September 15, pp. 112, 114, 116, 133.

Schiavone, Nicholas (1992): Speech Delivered at the Television Bureau of Advertising Convention. October 4.

Schüll, Natasha Dow (2012): *Addiction by Design: Machine Gambling in Las Vegas*, Princeton, New Jersey: Princeton University Press.

Stamler, Bernard (2000): "Who Pays Attention to Television and Radio Commercials? Whispercode is Watching." In: *New York Times* August 16.

Stelter, Brian (2007): "New Way of Counting Radio Listeners May Cut Ad Income." In: *New York Times* 12 November 12, p. C11.

___ (2009): "Arbitron Settles Suit Over Ratings." In: *New York Times* January 7.

The Arbitron Company (1995): "Apparatus and Methods for Including Codes in Audio Signals and Decoding." United States Patent number: 5,450,490, filed March 31, 1994, and issued September 12, 1995.

___ (1996): "Compliance Incentives for Audience Monitoring/Recording Devices." United States Patent number 5,483,276, filed August 2, 1993, and issued January 9, 1996.

Turkle, Sherry (2008): "Always-on/Always-on-you: The Tethered Self" In: Katz, James (ed.), *Handbook of Mobile Communications and Social Change*, Cambridge, MA: MIT Press.

Variety (1987): "Microchip Off The Ol' Peoplemeter." In: *Variety* May 27.

"Voltair-In Dept" (accessed July 2019): The Telos Alliance (www.telosalliance.com/25-Seven/Voltair).

Whitson, Jennifer R. (2013): "Gaming the Quantified Self." In: *Surveillance & Society* 11/1, pp. 163-176.

Young, Doug (2001): "New Audience Measurement Device Tested." In: *Los Angeles Times* December 26, p. C.2.

Instant Nerve-Ana: Biofeedback as Quantified Self Avant la Lettre

Philipp Hauss

While most articles in this volume look at the idea of the quantified self from a contemporary perspective, the following article looks into its history and argues that the biofeedback movement, which rose to prominence in the 1960s and 1970s in the US, can be identified as one of its immediate precursors. The quantified self and the Quantified Self movement integrate a number of different cultural practices that Gina Neff and Dawn Nafus convincingly divide into practices of "self-tracking" (measuring vital data), "life-logging" (writing diaries or record life-events others) and "self-experimentation" (exposing oneself to certain stressors and documenting reactions). Not all of these practices can be found in biofeedback training. However, never before was access to the body moderated by electronic feedback technology like this and thus, biofeedback training paved the way especially for self-tracking as it is known today. Through taking a historical perspective that focuses on the phenomenon of Biofeedback as it has developed, the risks of a hasty diagnosis of the present movement can be prevented. Moreover, this approach lends itself to tracing certain constants, which can demonstrate the promises of salvation that seem to accompany the development of both: biofeedback and the quantified self. Such a cultural analysis does not aim to classify these technical advances from the angle of ideology critique, but rather asks the Foucaultian question as delineated in his *Archeology of Knowledge* as to why a particular discursive event appears at a point in time and no other one in its place (Foucault 1981: 43).

In the 1950s, Joseph Kamiya at the University of Chicago and Barry Stermann at UCLA both succeeded in showing that the brainwaves of humans or animals (Stermann worked with cats) could be deliberately influenced. Not only brainwaves but also bodily processes like raising or lowering the body temperature, speeding up or slowing down the heartbeat, inner-muscular tensions – all proved to be controllable through feedback training. During the late 1960s to the late 1970s, biofeedback became more widely known as a method for pain relief, behavioral change, relaxation, and the enhancement of the quality of life. It aimed at teaching the client via written, acoustic, and/or visual feedback to recognize bodily processes and reactions, to control them, and to keep them within a designated target area.

The Quantified Self movement, as it rose to prominence in 2007, similarly established itself as a method for health improvement, behavioral change, optimizing physical and mental fitness. Vital data is tracked, stored and evaluated. Converted into graphic or sonographic representations, this data provides the user with insight into their bodily condition, documents progress or demands changes. Furthermore, the data is shared with other users or companies, which allows the user to locate themselves on a general scale. Biometric data is processed by relying on medical or scientific standards, yet can be altered and freely adopted by the user, thereby defining independent standards for each user group.

The measuring devices used in biofeedback obviously differ from those in self-quantification. QS devices have become smaller and increasingly more undetectable (e.g. they are now integrated in headphones, watches, etc.). Wearing comfort and smartphone compatibility proves to be more important than measuring accuracy. The digitalization allows the immediate exchange of data and a rapid networking in user groups.

Nevertheless, decisive features have persisted, illustrating a clear link between the biofeedback practices and the quantified self techniques of the 21st century. Both are coaching setups rather than therapeutic clinical interventions. Biofeedback having once developed from scientific research became an everyday phenomenon used in homes and private initiatives. Self-quantification originated as a subculture practice, and its potential medical uses are being discussed, but far are from established. Both include a target zone of some description and involve more than one training session, and are designed for long-term use. Most importantly, however, both directly translate vital processes into fragmented tasks and ascribe numbers, or discrete values, to them. They utilize and at the same time generate a new concept of the body that can be sketched as a transition from a thermodynamic model of activity – tire and rest – to a systemic model based on feedback, information management, and control. Furthermore, even parameters such as well-being, mental fitness, self-esteem are no longer determined by verbal introspection, but defined by an algorithmic product of correlating various data.

Gaining self-knowledge – one of the central projects of modernity – no longer depends on language and its self-revelatory slips, but can be gained through discrete information and numbers. The individual human in this setup is above all a transit area of data, as Stefan Rieger states (2000: 470), or as the Quantified Self pioneer Gary Wolf writes on the WIRED website, "We don't have a slogan, but if we had it would be 'Self-knowledge through numbers'" (Wolf 2009). Biofeedback and the quantified self both qualify as techniques of bypassing the conscious mind (cf. Rieger 2000: 466). A detailed analysis of the biofeedback movement not only provides a historical background of the quantified self concept, but also lays bare the discourses that enabled a new understanding of the human body and mind as an information processing control loop.

Before I discuss in detail what the biofeedback technique means, how it developed and, more importantly, which discourses it relied upon, namely the merging of cybernetics and feedback loops, stress research, and technological advances in the measuring of brainwaves, two remarks need to be made. Firstly, in the field of cultural studies, biofeedback and other 'mind-body medicine' practices, such as the quantified self, have been met with criticism. The focus has mostly been on pointing out its dark undersides like excessive self-optimization, pathologization, and addiction, regarding these techniques as means of achieving an economically viable homogenization while offering factitious individual freedom. The fundamental criticism, as for example articulated by Mattan Shachak and Eva Illouz, is that people's inclination toward financial gain naturally leads them toward self-optimization technologies offering positive effects such as well-being and relaxation, which in our economic system can be considered commodities themselves:

> This process can be conceptualized as the commodification of happiness, a process by which ideals and practices of well-being are integrated into the market, a process which includes two complementary aspects: It introduces the logic of market and efficiency to the cultural repertoire of happiness and inherently promotes the 'emotionalization' of economy, i.e. the conversion of an economic transaction and service into the 'real' psychological transformation of the self. (Shachak/Illouz 2010: 20)

These observations often trigger the introduction of heavyweight concepts such as 'surveillance', 'biopolitics' and 'governmentality', concepts that, as Illouz also recognizes, do not take the actor's ability to self-reflect seriously, and assume that individuals are incapable of questioning technologies of the self.

Instead, they passively surrender to a power imposed upon them, as for instance by the economy (Illouz 2009: 13). This position disregards the fact that in both cases – with the biofeedback pioneers of the 1960s and 1970s and the beginnings of the Quantified Self movement, such as its initial prominence in WIRED magazine – we are dealing with small elite groups whose initial motivation was to improve their own quality of life.

Of course, one should not ignore the tipping point when self-care is rendered mandatory within social and economic fields, but, as stated above, I find it more fruitful to look at it from a perspective that asks why these techniques appeared at a certain point of time and what utopian fantasies were linked to them. This becomes especially apparent when we look at the historical beginnings of both movements. One should not forget that in an environment of poor healthcare (it is safe to say that the US has a traditionally weak public health system) and with a general feeling of detachment from medical practices, most of the holistic health movements in the US at the time were characterized by a striving to reclaim active authority over one's body and to take care of one's own health. These were emancipatory projects that embraced new technologies and media, albeit in an occasionally awkward or superficial manner, but nonetheless, the momentum came from hippie and counterculture circles rather than as a means of creating bodies that conformed to market necessities. In the San Francisco Bay area, where biofeedback was used in the early wellness centers, and where later self-quantification emerged in Silicon Valley, alternative lifestyles and new techniques of self-care flourished. John W. Travis, founder of the first wellness center, summed up the characteristics of the ideal breeding ground for alternative well-being practices as "moderate-to-high income levels, a well-educated population, a work force subject to considerable stress levels [...] and sensitivity to the natural environment" (Ardell 1976: 69). Obviously, the WIRED scene also meets the same criteria. Therefore, if one wanted to use the theoretical framework of Michel Foucault, it would not be his notions of biopolitics and surveillance that are relevant in this context, but rather the so-called third period which focuses on the *souci du soi* (Foucault 1993a: 31), i.e. on technologies of self-care. As an extension of his interpretation of the dietetics of the ancient world, Foucault retraced the development of a very specific form of an "existential art" of "self-care" that goes back to a different concept of autonomy: one that has been diminished firstly by Christianity and later through medical, educational, or psychological practices (Foucault 1989: 16).

The second remark aims to underline this with an interpretation of an ancient myth, which anticipates the implication of biofeedback. The blind seer Tiresias told Narcissus' mother that her son will enjoy a long life "if he but fail to recognize himself," as Ovid puts it in the third book of *The Metamorphosis* (Ovid 2015: 87-92). In relation to biofeedback and QS, this would actually ban such techniques, since they revolve around the recognition of oneself via visual, acoustic and other technological reflections. If one follows the traditional reading of the myth, as with Freud or Lacan, we encounter a tragic self-importance. Narcissus falls in love with his own image in the mirror, ergo himself, and dies because of his insatiable desire (Macho 2002: 20).[1]

However, if we follow the cultural scholar Thomas Macho, one could also come up with a different reading, namely that the tragedy of Narcissus is that he discovers too late that this image on the surface of the water is actually himself. Hence, instead of boisterous self-love through self-recognition, it would be a case of tragic self-deception or an inadequate perception of oneself. Actually, we find this version not only in Macho, but in the writings of an influential figure for contemporary biofeedback practices, the media philosopher and media occultist Marshall McLuhan:

> [T]he wisdom of the Narcissus myth does not convey any idea that Narcissus fell in love with anything he regarded as himself. Obviously he would have had very different feelings about the image had he known it was an extension or repetition of himself. It is perhaps, indicative of the bias of our intensely technological and, therefore, narcotic culture that we have long interpreted the Narcissus story to mean that he fell in love with himself, that he imagined the reflection to be Narcissus! (McLuhan 1964: 45-46)

McLuhan's influence on the biofeedback movement – an influence so great that Joseph Kamiya even talked of a "McLuhanistic technique" (Hardt/Simmons/Yeager/Kamiya 1973: 31) in an essay on biofeedback that he co-wrote – would not have been of such great importance, if he had merely offered a diagnosis of his contemporary world. However, *Understanding Media* also offers what one could call a third non-tragic reading of the Narcissus myth: the young man sees the image, understands its medial nature, and uses it to reintegrate it into himself, thus improving the accuracy of his self-image. Or as

---

1   Used to accuse an egotistical society of narcissistic navel-gazing, this idea is rarely absent from modern discussions about burnout, food allergies, and intolerances, and any phenomena relating to excessive self-observation.

McLuhan puts it: "When we have achieved a world-wide fragmentation, it is not unnatural to think about a world-wide integration" (McLuhan 1964: 117). To conclude the McLuhan excursus, it is precisely the concept of media as extensions of man, of artificial senses, that forms the basis of the biofeedback and the QS technique. Measuring devices and computerized data processing perform a prosthetic function in the combined human-machine system.

Gary Wolf who hosted the initial gathering of the Quantified Self movement and set up the website quantifiedself.com together with Kevin Kelly, actually does seem to advocate this non-tragic reading. He defends self-tracking against claims that it cultivates narcissism and presents the subject in an idealized and optimized manner. Quite the opposite, in his blog, he identifies social attributions and flawed introspection to fuel a deceitful self-image, while he refers to the quantified self as a mirror revealing a clearer picture encompassing both 'order' and 'chaos' as well as things not anticipated:

> Spending a lot of time looking in the mirror is unhealthy for anybody past the age of adolescence. "The most fascinating thing in the world is a mirror." Isn't that statement kind of immature? And yet as far as personal data is concerned, I sympathize. The interesting thing about these unanalyzed numbers is the hint they give us that we don't completely know who we are. Suddenly realizing that you don't really know yourself; this is the pain of adolescence, and a great spur to growth. (Wolf 2009)

Having made those two remarks, let us now focus on the historical phenomenon of biofeedback and its actual implementation.

Biofeedback Practice

The biofeedback setup usually consists of a human (as with animals it is not quite so easy to distinguish between voluntarily or involuntarily action; in 1970 there were also experiments with groups of people) and a measuring device, an electroencephalograph, a thermometer, an electromyograph, a microphone, etc., which is attached to one or more body parts. Together with a trainer, an exercise is outlined and a target area defined. Deviations from that target area are brought to attention via a signal, usually a sound or a light

(Karlins/Andrews 1973: 30).[2] As a contemporary guideline says, the trainer should never ask the patient/client explicitly to raise the heart rate or to relax muscles but rather simply to avoid the beep sounding or the light dimming (ibid: 30). For instance, one exercise would be to raise the temperature in the index finger of the dominant hand to increase the blood flow in that specific area and thus reducing it in other parts of the body, such as the head in order to prevent or minimize migraine pain. Heart rate biofeedback reports back to the trainees if their heart rates exceed the target area and then consciously reduce it by calming down, breathing or whatever they find working. Exercises with EEG brain wave measuring train the ability to arbitrarily enter a state of low brain activity.

Within a few years, biofeedback research centers had been established all over the US, not only in universities, but also and quite numerously as part of private initiatives, health centers, holistic practices, and later in the country's living rooms, as feedback devices became less expensive and smaller, and a market for home feedback devices emerged. Among the different parameters measured and used in biofeedback training, electroencephalography (EEG) assumed a prominent role. Most of the home devices were (more or less reliably) designed to measure brain activity, i.e. brainwaves. The so-called alpha rhythm, whereby brain neurons oscillate within a frequency range from 9 to 13 Hz, is a state of mind that stood for relaxation, inspiration, and creativity. It quickly became the ideal in the field of mind-body medicine, as historian Anne Harrington calls the complex of holistic, alternative, and innovative approaches to healing, especially from the mid-20th century on. To "go alpha" became a popular expression in the US at the time.

It was not a given from the beginning that alpha waves would be at the apex of desired states. Initial research indicated that alpha waves were typical of the passive-dependent personality, and also linked to schizophrenia. However, within a few years, this notion changed and the cybernetic pioneer Norbert Wiener even considered the regularity of alpha rhythms to be a property of intelligence. Wiener envisioned alpha rhythms, as Cornelius Borck recounts in his history of the EEG, as a central instrument for the evaluation

---

2   The reward systems were not always the same. In David Shapiro's lab at Harvard Medical School the test persons who managed to decrease their blood pressure and light up a red light were rewarded with a Playboy pinup girl appearing on the monitor after 20 successful attempts (ibid: 30).

of EEG correlograms, including intelligence tests and career guidance (Borck 2005: 299).

Following the immediate and (widespread) embrace of EEG technology, there was something of a missionary tone and utopian scenario evident in the writings of biofeedback practitioners. Lewis M. Andrews and Marvin Karlins, authors of a contemporary book introducing the biofeedback method, speak of a turning point in the history of human psychology, as for the first time it was possible to show experimentally that man is his own master and not a slave to bodily fluids (Karlins/Andrews 1973: 105). Biofeedback has been understood as the first step towards the systematic exploration of human nature, comparable perhaps with man first setting foot on the moon.

The catalog of symptoms that could be relieved or potential areas of use seemed infinite: migraines, tension headaches, nervous tics, digestion problems, sleeping problems, restlessness, the Raynaud syndrome, and problems that medicine has come to call functional disturbances, to name but a few. All of these afflictions were deemed to be cases that could be improved or tackled by biofeedback. Significantly, many of these functions stem from the autonomic/sympathetic nervous system, so they are essentially pulled out from the darkness of the body and brought into the light of the conscious mind. As soon as you are able to see your heartbeat or hear your own brainwaves, you have enough information to start controlling them (ibid: 14).

From the collected audio or visual feedback, a cybernetic loop is created that bridges the gap between arbitrary and non-arbitrary, between conscious and unconscious processes (Green/Green 1978: 75). According to Elmer and Alyce Green, who in 1964 founded the biofeedback center of the Menninger Foundation, this paves the way to inner self-regulation. Instead of numbing (like medication does and – as in McLuhan's reading – media can do), biofeedback allegedly raises sensitivity to processes within the body. Through training, this raised level of awareness can become a permanent ability, thus the outer-body feedback loop then becomes superfluous (ibid: 71). The question, of course, is whether this really enhances one's perception of the body or causes its deterioration. Does the McLuhanistic prosthesis, be it the signal of the biofeedback training setup or the reward notice on the smartphone display, lead to an atrophy of the natural senses? Certainly, for both biofeedback advocates and Quantified Self activists the answer is clear – the hybrid human machine system is the ideal setup for self-knowledge.

The continuous references to cybernetics follow along these lines, which will be analyzed in detail later, but in guidebooks and brochures one also finds a strong affection for the meditation practices of Zen monks or yogis. The alpha state is seen as comparable to immersion during meditation. Since meditative practices often require years of training and complex instructions, biofeedback can supposedly offer almost instantaneous success and simple exercises. As the title highlights, it is "Instant Nerve-ana" (Karlins/Andrews 1973: 71), a machine that meditates for you, an idea that many religious groups would object to. Nonetheless, reports of monks who by the mere power of thought are able to renounce food, make their hearts stop beating, and lower their sensitivity to pain to almost a threshold of feeling no pain, recur in biofeedback literature as a cross-cultural analogy. These references also add tradition and 1,000 years of wisdom to the 'new technique' of biofeedback. David Boxerman and Aron Spilken provide a rather extreme example in relating how a yoga master could control his sphincter to such an extent that he could reverse the direction of flow and take in water through his anus or penis (1977: 66). These examples show that the autonomous functions of the body are seemingly not only able to be controlled, but can also be remodeled.

What were the utopian scenarios foreseen by the biofeedback advocates? Never too modest in their epoch-defining rhetoric, they mapped out the future of the biofeedback practice in technicolor. The benefits were claimed to be transferable to other medical problems and advocates claimed that one day "it may be possible to teach the body to stop a cancerous growth by closing off its blood supply or letting it starve" (ibid: 65). They also said biofeedback practices could enact changes in social behavior: "Poets have long pondered the nature of love. In the near future we may be able to provide an answer in cycles per minute" (Karlins/Andrews 1973: 52). Boxerman/Spilken report on a homosexual, who in their terms suffered from his rampant promiscuity and through biofeedback learned "to withstand longer phases of solitude and was thus able to build a stable relationship" (1977: 79-80). The healthcare system in the future was envisioned as one where every community would have a computerized self-help system. The patient can consult his or her computer doctor as often as he or she wishes, and go through his or her programmed biofeedback routine until he/she has learned to eradicate the defect (ibid: 74).

Biofeedback enthusiasts also saw education and work environments undergo major changes. Not only could students and workers be monitored and monitor themselves on individual EEG screens, but their eligibility could be tested beforehand via brainwave scans. Karlins/Andrews spread the rumor (biofeedback disciples occasionally tend to be quite loose with their sources) that the well-known neurophysiologist Grey Walter suggested including a person's alpha-type in diplomatic passports (1973: 52). The British medical journalist Donald Gould is cited to make the following proposal in an article in the *New Statesmen*: "We should examine carefully the functioning of the brains of the men who rule over us and bring together politicians whose modes of functioning harmonize or find able translator" (ibid: 52).

Returning from this envisioned future back to the contemporary scene in the 1960s and the devices that were in use, it appeared to be an advantage to setup experiments in such a way as to provide the test person with an environment as natural as possible, e.g. by disguising the electrodes in a jacket to omit the "electric chair-effect," as Green and Green put it (1978:58). This had also proven beneficial in research on classical psychological techniques: leaving the person under examination uncertain of whether he or she is part of an experimental observation, or finding means to make subjects forget that he or she is being examined (Rieger 2000: 291).

These technological improvements in areas such as wearing comfort, ease of use, etc. not only advanced scientific research, but also supported another development. While biofeedback centers were opening all over the US and offering services that went beyond the strict realms of healthcare, the market for *personal* biofeedback devices also grew tremendously. In 1977, there were no less than thirty different producers of biofeedback apparatuses for home use. There were primarily three types of devices being offered: electroencephalography to monitor brainwaves, electromyography to control muscle tension, and advanced thermometers to measure the specific temperature of body regions (see Karlins/Andrews 1973: 66). The more advanced user could even utilize a combination of these three measuring techniques. An alpha-wave detector costs between $35 and $500 US dollars. A decent mid-range model would cost approximately $200. With a median income of $13,570 in 1977, these prices rendered biofeedback devices affordable purchases comparable to present day smartphone prices (cf. United States Census Bureau 1978).

In his study on the history of the EEG, the medical historian Cornelius Borck timidly mentioned the cliché of the United States of America as a pioneer nation, a place where technological innovations fall on fruitful ground (2005: 210). For biofeedback advocates Karlins/Andrews, it was clear that the use of measuring devices suits the American habit of happily taking advantage of technological innovations. Furthermore, Karlins/Andrews contend that many people who would normally never have been interested in controlling or dealing with their inner processes are more likely to accept a little apparatus as a bridge to their psyche (1973: 18).

In the history of the EEG, one major development was to minimize its size so that it could be utilized, for example, by air force pilots in operation. With home alpha detectors, a shift from the clinic and laboratory to use in everyday life and from pathology to optimization occurred, a decisive step on the path toward contemporary quantified self practices. Even the scientific tinkering of the German neurologist and EEG pioneer Hans Berger (1873-1941) was echoed in the computer magazine *Popular Electronics* (1973) with a do-it-yourself manual for constructing an "Alpha Brainwave Feedback Monitor." The headline was supplemented with the sentence: "You may be able to relax through electronics" (Waite 1973: 40).

Since the equipment was available to everyone, the obstacles were more of a practical nature. In large cities, the electrical infrastructure and the transformer units distorted the results (Borck 2005: 56). Incorrect use was another problem as results could be erroneously positive due to muscular artifacts (the user thinks he/she is producing alpha waves, but in reality the results are due to the strengthening of a nervous eye twitching) (Karlins/Andrews 1973: 66). With these cases being the worst side effects, for advocates, biofeedback seems to fulfill the dream of medicine without a dark side. Even defective or inefficient devices can still have a healing effect, since the concentration on one's inner life and the immersion into bodily processes is already beneficial (ibid). This pragmatism, i.e. maintaining "even if it doesn't work, it's still good for you" is prevalent throughout holistic or alternative methods.

Astonishingly, in spite of its distinct scientific positivism, biofeedback research did not fear drifting toward para-psychology. On the contrary, it was assumed that through biofeedback parapsychological phenomena could be experimentally proven (this is similar to the introduction of the EEG and the discovery of REM sleep which added to the seriousness of dream research in the 1950s). These types of phenomena included supra-sensory perception, psychokinesis, the psychology of plants, and extra-sensory perception (ibid: 88-90). This research also seemed mandatory in political terms. In the views of the US biofeedback pioneers, the Russians who were thought not to draw such a clear line between science and para-psychology were way ahead of the Americans (Karlins/Andrews 1973: 91). The book *Superlearning*, an instructive publication for better learning techniques (Ostrander/Schroeder 1979), tells the story of Nelya Mikaihlova who, according to the authors, was able to move the needle of a compass through psychokinesis (Karlins/Andrews 1973:

95). Karlins/Andrews cite a certain William Tiller, who saw a film that featured a different woman, Alla Vinogradova, moving objects weighing up to 200 grams by mere thought. Here we can conclude two things: firstly, that science, especially in the years of the Cold War, has always been political, and secondly, that the distinction between science and para-science is historically contested. Without delving too deeply into these Cold War narratives, we can concede that they do show that biofeedback is a perfect example of how different discourses were intertwined to allow a new technology to emerge.

There are primarily three areas in which the biofeedback movement can be traced back to (and which were also key in the conception and implementation of the Quantified Self movement): cybernetics, stress research, and the technological advances surrounding EEG.

Cybernetics – the Body as a Feedback-Processing System

Cybernetics is one of the biofeedback movement's explicit reference points. Karlins/Andrews declared Norbert Wiener to be a father of feedback research (1973: 14). The principles of cybernetics and Wiener's definition of feedback as the "control of a system by reinserting into the system the results of its performance" (ibid: 14) were considered the basis of biofeedback.

The central assumption that cybernetics of control processes in humans and machines were structurally the same allowed physical processes to be reconsidered as systemic, information theory-related phenomena. Without taking an overly detailed look at the history of cybernetics, it must be pointed out that Norbert Wiener, Arturo Rosenblueth, and Julian Bigelow had affirmed as early as 1943 that the body's nervous system does not function as an isolated organ that sends sensory impulses to the muscles. They found that the countless processes could only be explained as circular processes, as they went from the nervous system to the muscles and were then fed back into the process as reentry via the sensory organs or other proprioceptive mechanisms (Wiener 1961: 8). This led the authors to realize that the nervous system works as an "integrated whole" (ibid: 8). In 1948, Wiener suggested that "irritability" (ibid: 11) is a precondition for these communication processes and a fundamental life principle. Wiener sees the flow of information in circular processes as a characteristic feature of the nervous system. He suggested that if the 17th and 18th century could be seen as the age of the clock, and the 19th century as the age of the steam engine, then the present day is the age of "communication and control" (ibid: 39). The main interest of the system is no longer the economy of energy, but rather an accurate reproduction of a signal (ibid: 39).

According to Wiener, conservative physiology concerns itself more with "power engineering," while more recent developments are dedicated to "communication engineering" (ibid: 42). Information can be saved beyond its immediate use and retrieved at a later date. Muscles, for example, have a pronounced capacity to save not only energy, but also information (ibid: 94).

> In such a theory, we deal with automata effectively coupled to the external world, not merely by their energy flow, their metabolism, but also by a flow of impressions, of incoming messages, and of the actions of outgoing messages. (ibid: 42)

Feedback is the key pillar in the regulation and functionality of cybernetic systems. Information is fed back into the system, which then makes the necessary adjustments in a certain direction (e.g. by increasing temperature or flow rate, etc.), until new information forces it to readjust in the other direction (drop in temperature, decrease in flow rate, etc.). Exercising control via informative feedback not only allows the system to function correctly, it is also linked to the idea of being able to control it in a way to maximize efficiency and reduce energy losses. "When feedback is possible and stable, its advantage, [...] is to make performance less dependent on the load" (ibid: 108).

Yet, all information and transfers of information remain linked to energy consumption. Wiener states, "It may well be that this information is carried at a very low energy level. [...] Thus all coupling is strictly a coupling involving energy" (ibid: 58). Due to the very low energy consumption and subsequent lower increase in entropy, stability can be maintained for a longer period of time, resulting in metastability (cf. ibid: 58). These benefits provided by information processing can be applied to human bodies in the same way as they can with machines and other systems. Hence, by making its control system more efficient, the human body can also avert fatigue and exhaustion for a longer period of time – the specter of the thermodynamic working world of the 19th century (cf. Rabinbach 1990). The cycle of labor and regeneration through idling and resting, which structures the workday, the week, the year, even our entire lives, heavily relies on the idea of energy consumption and energy restoration. In contrast to that, the cybernetic dream is to minimize the dissipation of energy and to reduce the time needed for the restoration of energy via better regulation.

Yet, the aspect of regulation is where, according to Wiener, a new threat comes into play: the "system error." Various regulatory mechanisms, such as homeostasis, are in place to prevent such errors. All open systems are, according to Ashby, Wiener, and other cyberneticists, characterized by the fact that they can be *interrupted*, that the process performed will vary according to the input. They see stability not as the ability to maintain a fixed condition, but stability lies in invariance, that even when a number of different conditions pass through the system, something remains constant, not in the sense of a static balance (equilibrium), but rather as a multitude of recurring conditions (Ashby 156: 85). Stability is thus achieved when a system, following an interruption, reverts back toward its original state. Negative feedback (an error is reported) "corrects" the deviation. Errors form the outer limits to stability, a critical stage where the system is no longer capable of returning conditions toward the region of equilibrium. This condition of the continually recurring equilibrium is known as homeostasis. Using feedback loops, a system manages to process various external and internal pieces of information in a way that all functions can be maintained and the system is considered to be stable.

Under this aspect, biofeedback is therefore the outsourcing of internal bodily feedback loops with the aim of keeping the system stable and flowing. However, contrary to simple feedback (whereby an actual value is fed in to the system), the feedback obtained is then compared to a target value, and a systemic process (in the body, physiological process) is triggered – hence, biofeedback is more an attempt to change or (re)set the thermostat.

We can see the exact same mechanism in action with the quantified self. A measuring device provides information about the actual state, thus provokes the reaction of correcting this state to meet the target value, while the whole setup, e.g. the smartphone application, aims at improving – one is tempted to say optimizing – the system by sensitizing it to deviations and comparing it to other systems via data exchange. This last point is vital, as in quantified self and self-tracking, feeding information into a shared data cloud serves as an additional feedback loop. While in the biofeedback training parameters such as optimal heart rate and desirable brain wave pattern are externally defined, in the Quantified Self scene they develop a life of their own. Or as Neff/Nafus put it, they are being "crowdsourced" (2016: 149).

Age of Anxiety – Overcoming Stress

"The cybernetic mechanism (one might almost be tempted to say 'thermostat') has to be set at a higher level to maintain equilibrium in the face of such very excessive demands." This vivid description by stress researcher Hans Selye (1976: 84) clearly illustrates how the mechanism works. In simplified terms, Selye found that stress is ubiquitous, but also something that can be actively managed and his conclusions formed the premise of the idea of biofeedback and also inform its main areas of application. What were these "excessive demands" that he spoke of in the previous citation? What was it that stood so vehemently in the way of the flow of the system that it required better managers and technicians to maintain its functionality? What was required of a complex apparatus to return the malfunctioning bodily system to its flow?

The most vehemently disruptive input to humans conceived as open systems in the 1950s seems to have been a new kind of stress that arose in the 1950s. Science historian Anne Harrington considers the term to have been commonly used in American society during that time to express the mixture of emotions that the American middle classes felt amid the post-war prosperity, ranging from a fear of failure to fantasizing about success, juxtaposed with rigid corporate policies demanded mobility and flexibility. In short, she describes the stress of modern life (2008: 159). Fearful soldiers, concerned housewives, overworked bosses, suicidal students, and neglected children all represented a clear failure to adapt to modern life, and the adverse effect this failure had on their physical and mental health was evident (Jackson 2013: 144). In 1947, the Anglo-American writer W. H. Auden called his age by what became an oft-cited term: the "age of anxiety" (see Harrington 2008: 158, Jackson 2013: 141). The war was in the past, but the trauma it had left behind had been supplemented by the need to cope with the challenges of a new, rapidly-changing world, and this created fears, albeit no longer mortal fears, but rather everyday anxiety and concern.

Even before the time of Selye, Walter B. Cannon, amongst others, had already documented the body and mind's systemic reaction to stressors (1936: 1458; qtd. in Harrington 2008: 147). However, Selye also introduced an element into stress research that for Cannon and the others had played only a minor role: chronicity. The term stress had finally liberated itself from simply meaning "shock," and now described the pathological consequences of continual attempts to adapt to one's unrelenting environment (Jackson 2013: 83-84). The spectrum of potential stressors had expanded to affect all aspects of people's lives. Anything could potentially cause stress; it simply required certain negative factors to occur simultaneously. As the medical historian Mark Jackson observes:

> Increasingly construed as a normal feature of everyday life, during the postwar decades stress became a defining characteristic of the modern anxious self rather than merely an attribute of the modern environment. (ibid: 145)

This resulted in the creation of the term "stress diseases" for ailments such as high blood pressure, heart attacks, stomach ulcers, migraines, neck pains, various types of asthma, alcoholism, and other addictions, obesity and being underweight due to poor eating patterns (Selye 1976: 84). Here it can be noted that there is a distinct similarity in the catalog of stress diseases and the above-mentioned potential areas of the application of biofeedback. The rhetoric of the Quantified Self movement tends to describe the areas of application in less pathological terminology, but the central issues of modern-day Western self-care remained identical: weight, cardiovascular system, general physical relaxation. What has been added is that QS aims not merely at regaining a 'normal' state, but at an optimization that goes beyond attaining normality.

What could people do to counteract stress and its detrimental effect on their health? The techniques available, according to Selye, could be divided into two categories: supercompensation, i.e. fighting stress with stress, and deviation, i.e. break the stress-inducing routine and thus relieving stress. Heterostasis aptly describes a state of deliberate deviation from homeostasis:

> The most salient difference between homeostasis and heterostasis is that the former maintains a normal steady state by physiological means, whereas the latter "resets the thermostat" of resistance to a heightened defensive capacity by artificial interventions from outside. (ibid: 86)

Resetting the system is one response and of course, absolute rest is another possibility. Since the traditional "rest cure" proved to be no longer sufficient, Selye argues it could be improved with medicinal supplements, and that medication could be used to reduce stress levels in general.

> Prolonged sleep (e.g. that induced by barbiturates), artificial hibernation, Transcendental Meditation, and treatment with sedatives, such as chlorpro-

mazine and extracts of the Rauwolfia root, appear to act largely through this mechanism. (ibid: 403)

Nevertheless, these two coping strategies of medication-induced distraction or simply more stress (ibid: 417) did not seem fit to fight the cumulative effects of stress during the 50s and 60s. The groundbreaking aspect of Selye's stress concept is that it still holds one more option up its sleeve: overcoming stress. The idea behind it is relaxation that goes beyond simply being in an idle state and instead attempts to actively regenerate and take the system out of the wrong "groove" (ibid: 402), and thus return it to its flow. With this idea, Selye became perhaps the most important influence on the wellness movement and other mind-body medicinal practices, as he favored an approach that moves away from the immaturity of the physiological regulatory system and towards learning to manage stress. He portends that "the problem is one of excessive general stress. It cannot be handled either by deviation or more stress; the great remedy here is to learn to relax as quickly and completely as possible" (ibid: 420).

Biofeedback is ideally suited to stress management due to the fact the bodily system is taken to be a conglomerate of feedback loops in which dealing with stress will require its thermostats to be adjusted or reset. Equally relevant is that thanks to the research carried out by physiologist Selye on stress and its opposite state (relaxation), these states can now be mapped in a way that can be described physiologically and within discrete parameters. The ideal conditions for relaxation can now be determined based on one's pulse, blood pressure, breathing, EEG measurements, and metabolic rate, thus enabling the individual to avert the risk of stress. The sensory control a person can gain through such techniques can therefore allow individuals to experience relaxation despite the presence of stressors in their environment due to their lifestyle, etc. And fortunately, physiological parameters are able to determine the necessary criteria for the attainment of this condition.

Brainwaves

As aforementioned, the technique of electroencephalography played an especially prominent role in measuring relaxation, and it led to the discovery of electronic activity in the brain, most significantly the discovery of alpha brainwaves. Halbert L. Dunn, the 'Father of Wellness', described the alpha state of mind as a phase of creativity, as the ideal state of being:

> Science has discovered recently that there are electrical waves which seem to scan the cortical cells of the brain all the time. The most consistent is the so-called "alpha rhythm," with a frequency somewhere around 8 to 13 cycles per second. It appears to be constantly searching for pictures. It would seem that the alpha rhythm is associated with the formation of ideas. (1961: 105)

Yet, it is not only in Dunn's "High Level Wellness" (1961)[3] that one can find such descriptions, Wiener (1961: 141), Ross W. Ashby (cf. Borck 2005: 296), and countless other cyberneticists have referred to alpha waves as the providers of the brain's rhythm and as a state of visual absorption. The heyday of the alpha wave, however, would not begin until the second half of the 1960s. This was especially true in the USA, where the focus, according to Cornelius Borck, moved away from the basic research into the principles of neuronal function and towards its application on concrete issues and a pragmatic interpretation of the curve patterns (Borck 2005: 217).

Borck speaks of a rampant proliferation of electroencephalography, not as a diagnostic tool to identify and describe certain diseases, but to be directly (and financially lucratively) applied as a solution to a wide range of problems (ibid: 231). The attention was no longer merely on the sick brain; the challenge for electroencephalography was now to map the mechanisms at work in a "normal" brain (ibid: 229).

The EEG device became established as the ideal artificial sense (ibid: 289), which in turn led to the development of a portable EEG device (ibid: 287) that came into use starting in 1943. Without this stage of development, medical practices and centers would not have been as comprehensively equipped with EEG devices as they were, nor would they have become commercially available as household appliances so soon. This also led to the emergence of a control loop that, as it was more sensitive than the number-writing test and introspection, could guarantee the brain's functional capacity (ibid: 286). Borck saw it as a shift that would have far-reaching effects in the future at the point when the fields of technology, medical care, and physiological research would intersect with concepts of man-machine hybrids already being discussed at

---

3   Dunn already mentioned wellness in 1957 and 1958. In 1959 he held 29 talks in a church in in Virginia on wellness concepts, which were then published in a book two years later.

the beginning of the 1940s, and which many years later would be dubbed the "cyborg" (ibid: 283).

In the post-war years, these 'cyborgs' (before the term was widely known) were envisioned as being no longer only deployed in warfare contexts; on the contrary, the new regime of human self-assessment devices had now extended its influence to be used throughout society. Grey Walter, who is referenced by biofeedback writers (even though as aforementioned without verifiable sources) saw the technology as a potential path to electronic self-enlightenment (ibid: 311). Individuals could use these devices not only to learn about themselves, but also to set out on their own path towards happiness. Even today, modern neuroscience is like a technological revolution where the outcome is still unknown. According to Borck, Walter's "Practical Instructions for a Better Life" promised to literally create more free space in the brain through symbiosis with technology (ibid: 311).

EEG research also had other consequences, as it appeared to empirically prove the cybernetic assumption that the human brain and the machine/computer were structurally the same. This was the central point of early cybernetics: the control processes and the laws that regulate them were essentially the same for organic and technical systems, and these processes could be applied to any issues in any system that could be described as a feedback system. This could now be illustrated with the human brain thanks to EEG graphs.

Moreover, the EEG played an especially key role in sleep research. For example, Alfred Loomis and his colleagues had attempted to correlate brainwave patterns with sleep studies in the 1930s (2004: 3-4; see also Borck 2005: 191). The discovery of REM can only be indirectly attributed to the development of EEG, but the EEG was the first device to be able to show that brain activity is in fact greater during the REM phases than during the deep-sleep phases. If the thermodynamic century of the "human motors" (Rabinbach 1990: 45-46) recognized the two poles as "work with its associated fatigue" and "sleep with its associated recovery," then the brainwaves that can be recorded with an EEG point to activity and passivity within the brain, independent of the subject being awake or asleep. This creates the need to also optimize sleep to afford oneself better regeneration, and to actively recover. Instead of subjective introspection, EEG-based sleep research allows us to determine the precise amount of sleep required, the optimal sleeping rhythm, and the right ratio of different sleep phases. It allows us to make a more conscious decision of what should be regenerated when.

From the beginning of the Quantified Self movement on, sleep control, the recording of sleep phases, and the optimization of sleeping habits made up the majority of the programs. Apps have already been developed that aim at optimizing the duration and quality of sleep, the ideal time for going to sleep and waking up by synchronizing them with the different sleep phases. Nevertheless, this sleep monitoring, especially if carried out with a smartphone, is prone to render false results, since most applications distinguish between REM and Non-REM sleep by merely measuring the movements of the bed the device is placed on.

The End and Legacy of Biofeedback

These three fields – cybernetics, stress research, and technological developments – contributed significantly to biofeedback emerging precisely when it did at the end of the 50s and establishing itself in the years that followed. The cybernetic concept of control via feedback resulted in the setup where technical and bodily feedback loops were connected with each other, while stress research initially revealed a huge increase in stress and stress-related illnesses, but showed physiologically how stress could be overcome. The EEG device then took a look inside our heads and was able to map tension and, more importantly, relaxation in discrete values. However, biofeedback did not fulfill its promises as the perfectly constructed utopia of self-control and self-management. Once seen as the future of medicine, biofeedback – and all the centers and equipment associated with it – had largely disappeared from the canon of mind-body practices by the 90s.

The biofeedback pioneers could have never dreamed that one day recording devices would be so small and affordable that practically every household in the Western world would have unlimited storage space available to them and at the very latest, with the dawn of the smartphone people would one day always carry these devices around with them. For the first time in the history of mankind, this generation has the practical means of recording and evaluating their entire life on film, in sounds, and in terms of statistical data. Of course the implications of this innovation are still being discussed and will perhaps not become apparent until we can look back in retrospect, and (borrowing from Claus Pias's "What Was Media?") future media scholars will ask: "What were smartphones? What were quantified self gadgets?"[4]

One marked development is how laboratory-like conditions have become completely integrated into our everyday life (Borck 2005: 313). The constant monitoring of our own bodies via portable sensors housed within armbands, headbands or belts is not seen as a deadening (anesthesia) of the body's natural senses, but rather as an increased sensitivity of our perception that allows individuals to be even better informed about themselves. As Borck states at the end of his "Cultural History of the Electroencephalography," the technologically enhanced self replaces the pre-technological self that apparently once existed (ibid: 315). It is easy to conclude that the home devices that emerged during biofeedback's heyday in the 70s and 80s were stages in the development of medical technology and its introduction into our everyday lives. Technical measuring methods have permeated mainstream culture to such an extent that modern epistemes follow a logic of knowledge production where one can no longer differentiate between cognizance and technology (ibid: 321).

If we were to examine the historical relevance of the biofeedback movement for the quantified self and the present, the findings would be largely ambiguous. On the one hand, neither biofeedback nor the quantified self have yet succeeded in replacing traditional medical practices. The mass of data collected by tracking apps do pose a new challenge to doctors and practitioners, but their inaccuracy and schematism have made these applications an adjunct to conservative health care at most (cf. Drösser/Stillich 2014). This is equally true for the assessment of mental fitness and psychological disorders, where social media and telemedicine exceed the influence of health tracking by far. It is true that digital technology is omnipresent in our daily lives, but we are still a long way away from a Cyborg Age. Even the excessive use of smartphones – the Smombie phenomenon – cannot be read as a true symbiosis between human and machine as equal partners. On the other hand, the second half of the 20th century including the emergence of biofeedback fundamentally transformed our understanding of the body and the interaction between body and mind. And this goes beyond the fact that conceptualizations of the body as a computer processing information, running out of battery power, needing a reset, etc., determine how we reframe physical and mental states.

---

4   "What Was Media?" is a series of lectures that looked at the why, where, and when of media over the past 25 years and was given at the University of Vienna between 2006 and 2008 (see Pias 2010).

Preventive and predictive medicine, which heavily relies on data processing, seems to be able to diagnose an illness before it breaks out (cf. Borck 1996: 18). The individual is being fed with information as to what diet, behavior, sleep patterns might lead to potentially lethal malfunctions, and is under the illusion that changes in behavior, changes in diet, or improvement of sleep can prevent any physical harm. Thus, the focus has shifted from the ill patient to the healthy patient whose project is to optimize their bodily functions. Biofeedback as well as the quantified self both rely on the phantasm of control that the body and mind can be successfully managed. Since all data can be correlated, there is potentially no area of human life that cannot be taken into account as a playing field for cultural over-accentuation. The most elementary human activities such as breathing, eating, moving, sleeping, copulating – seem to raise questions that can no longer be answered without the prosthesis of data processing.

Works Cited

Ardell, Donald B. (1976): "Meet John Travis, Doctor of Well-Being." In: *Prevention* 4, 26, pp. 62-69.

Ashby, W. Ross (1956): *An Introduction to Cybernetics*, New York, Wiley.

Bagchi, Kumar B./Wenger Marion A. (1957): "Electrophysiological Correlates of Some Yogi Exercises." In: *EEG and Clinical Neurophysiology*, Supplement 7, pp. 132-149.

Borbély, Alexander (2004): *Schlaf*, Frankfurt/Main, Fischer.

Borck, Cornelius (ed.) (1996): *Anatomien medizinischen Wissens. Medizin Macht Moleküle*, Frankfurt/Main, Fischer.

Borck, Cornelius (2005): *Hirnströme. Eine Kulturgeschichte der Elektroenzephalographie*, Göttingen, Wallstein.

Boxerman, David/Spilken, Aron (1977): *Alpha-Wellen. Die Technik der elektronischen Meditation*, Basel, Sphinx.

Cannon, Walter B. (1936): *Wisdom of the Body. How the Human Body Reacts to Disturbance and Maintains the Stability Essential to Life*, New York, Norton.

Drösser, Christoph/Stillich, Sven: "Der Arzt am Leib," *Die Zeit* 38/2014, September 11, 2014. (https://www.zeit.de/2014/38/apple-digitaluhr-smartphone-ueberwachung-koerper)

Dunn, Halbert L. (1961): *High-Level Wellness. A Collection of Twenty-Nine Short Talks on Different Aspects of the Theme "High-Level Wellness for Man and Society"*. Arlington, VA, Beatty.

Foucault, Michel (1981): *Archäologie des Wissens*, Frankfurt/Main, Suhrkamp.

___ (1989): *Der Gebrauch der Lüste. Sexualität und Wahrheit 2*, Frankfurt/Main, Suhrkamp.

___ (1993a): "Technologien des Selbst." In: Luther H. Martin/Huck Gutman/Patrick H. Hutton (eds.), *Technologien des Selbst*, Frankfurt/Main, Fischer, pp. 24-62.

___ (1993b): "In a Conversation with Martin Rux: Wahrheit, Macht, Selbst." Ein Gespräch. In: Luther H. Martin/Huck Gutman/Patrick H. Hutton (eds.), *Technologien des Selbst*, Frankfurt/Main, Fischer, pp. 15-23.

Green, Elmer/Green, Alyce (1978): *Biofeedback – Eine neue Möglichkeit zu heilen*, Freiburg, Hermann Bauer Verlag.

Hardt, James V./Timmons, Beverly/Yeager, Charles, L./ Joseph Kamiya (1976): "Studying Power and Coherence Relationships in 6-Channel EEGs: A McLuhanistic Technique Applied to Zen Meditation." In: *Proceedings of the Biofeedback Research Society* 2, 7, p. 31.

Harrington, Anne (2008): *The Cure Within. A History of Mind-Body Medicine*, London/New York, Norton.

Illouz, Eva (2009): *Die Errettung der modernen Seele. Therapien, Gefühle und die Kultur der Selbsthilfe*, Frankfurt/Main, Suhrkamp.

Jackson, Mark (2013): *The Age of Stress. Science and the Search for Stability*, Oxford, Oxford University Press.

Karlins, Marvin/Andrews, Lewis M. (1973): *Biofeedback. Die Technik der Selbstkontrolle*, Stuttgart, Deutsche Verlagsanstalt.

Macho, Thomas (2002): "Narziß und Spiegel. Selbstrepräsentation in der Geschichte der Optik." In: Renger, Almut-Barbara (ed.), *Narcissus. Ein Mythos von der Antike bis zum Cyberspace*, Stuttgart, Weimar, Metzler, pp. 13-25.

McLuhan, Marshall (1964): *Understanding Media. The Extensions of Man*, London/New York, Routledge.

Neff, Gina/Nafus, Dawn (2016): *Self-Tracking*, Cambridge, MA, MIT Press.

Ostrander, Sheila/Schroeder, Lynn (1979): *Superlearning 2000*, New York, Dell.

Ovid (2015): *Metamorphosen*, übersetzt von Michael von Albrecht, Stuttgart, Reclam.

Rabinbach, Anson (1990): *The Human Motor. Energy, Fatigue and the Origins of Modernity*, Berkeley, CA, University of California Press.

Rieger, Stefan (2000): *Die Individualität der Medien. Eine Geschichte der Wissenschaften vom Menschen*, Frankfurt/Main, Suhrkamp.

Selye, Hans (1976): *The Stress of Life*, New York, McGraw Hill.

Shachak, Mattan/Illouz, Eva (2010): "The Pursuit of Happiness. Coaching and the Commodification of Well-Being." In: *Querformat* 3/2010: Weichspüler. Wellness in Kunst und Konsum, Bielefeld, transcript, pp. 16-30.

United States Census Bureau: "Money Income in 1977 of Household in the United States," December 1978 (https://www.census.gov/library/publications/1978/demo/p60-117.html)

Waite, Mitchell (1973): "Build an Alpha Brain Wave Feedback Monitor." In: *Popular Electronics* 1, 19, pp. 40-45.

Wiener, Norbert (1961): *Cybernetics or Control and Communication in the Animal and the Machine*, Cambridge, MA, MIT Press. 2nd ed.

Wolf, Gary: "The Most Fascinating Thing in the World is a Mirror." April 26, 2009 (https://quantifiedself.com/blog/the-most-fascinating-thing-in/)

Contributors

Stefan Danter is a PhD candidate at the University of Mannheim. His PhD thesis analyzes how critical posthumanist theory can be applied in a re-reading of literature ranging from realism to contemporary science fiction. It analyzes how concepts of autonomy have changed over time and how human agency can be reframed into a more relational concept taking nonhuman entities (e.g. animals, objects) into account. He was a member of the research project "Probing the Limits of the Quantified Self," which was funded by the German Research Foundation (DFG). His main research interests are posthumanism, monster studies, technology studies, theories of quantification, game studies, and science fiction.

Kristina Graaff is faculty at Humboldt University's American Studies Program, where she obtained her PhD in 2014, and is currently writing her habilitation treatise (postdoctoral lecture qualification) on the intersections of race and ability in interwar US self-help cultures. She has been a post-doctoral fellow at the DFG research group 'Mobilizing the Self' and a DFG doctoral fellow at the 'Transatlantic Graduate Research Program Berlin – New York'. As visiting faculty, she taught at the University of Washington, Fordham University, and the University of Minnesota. Her research interests include the US justice system and critical prison studies, spatialized inequalities, and psychological/advice cultures. Among her publications are *Street Literature: Black Popular Fiction in the Era of US Mass Incarceration* (2015) and *Urban Street Vending in the Neoliberal City: A Global Perspective on the Practices and Policies of a Marginalized Economy* (2015, with Noa Ha).

Philipp Hauss studied philosophy and media philosophy at the University of Vienna. He has completed his PhD thesis "Das Paradies liegt unter 13 Hz. Selbstmanagement und Steuerungsfantasien der Wellness" ("Paradise is a place below 13 Hz. Self-management and fantasies of control of wellness") in 2017. Philipp Hauss has held talks at the ETH Zürich, EIKONES Basel, the University of Vienna, and the University of Hamburg. He was a Junior Fellow Researcher at the MECS Institute at Leuphana University, Germany. His publications include "REST in Peace – on Floating Tanks" (together with Sebastian Vehlken, Konstanz University Press, 2017), "The Birth of Wellness from the Spirit of Statistics" (*Themenhefte zeithistorischer Forschung*, 2014), and "Human Range Anxiety" (transcript, 2020). Philipp Hauss has been working as an actor and director at the Burgtheater Vienna since 2002.

Jennifer Hessler is a lecturer in the journalism, media and film department at the University of Huddersfield. She received her PhD in Film and Media Studies from the University of California, Santa Barbara. Her current book project is a technological history of the Nielsen ratings that examines the role of audience analytics and consumer surveillance in the foundation and evolution of commercial television. She has published work in *Television & New Media*, *The Velvet Light Trap*, and *Media Fields*.

Dorothee Marx (née Schneider) is a research associate and PhD candidate at the chair of North American Studies at Kiel University, where she teaches classes in literary studies and works as a coordinator at the Center for North American Studies. Her PhD project is entitled "Bodies Irregular: Temporalities of Disability in Contemporary North American Literature" and examines renderings of time experience in American novels and comics, focusing on the difficult intersections between chronic illness, trauma and disability. Her past research includes works on the depiction of disability and im/mobility, the influence of toxic positivity on disability self-representation and the function of cripping up in contemporary film. She is the first recipient of the Martin Schüwer Publication Award for Excellence in Comic Studies for her article "The 'Affected Scholar': Reading Raina Telgemeier's Ghosts as a Disability Scholar and Cystic Fibrosis-Patient" that appeared in *CLOSURE. The Kiel University e-Journal for Comics Studies* in 2018.

Katharina Motyl is assistant professor at the American Studies department of the University of Mannheim. In her second book project, she investigates the loops of interaction between cultural, legal, and medical discourses on substance dependence and social minorities from the Early Republic to the 'War on Drugs'. Her publications include the edited volumes *Who Can Speak* *and Who Is Heard/Hurt? Facing Problems of Race, Racism and Ethnic Diversity in the Humanities in Germany* (with Mahmoud Arghavan, Nicole Hirschfelder, and Luvena Kopp, transcript, 2019), *The Failed Individual – Amid Exclusion, Resistance, and the Pleasure of Non-Conformity* (with Regina Schober, Campus, 2017) and *States of Emergency – States of Crisis* (with Winfried Fluck, Donald E. Pease, and Christoph Raetzsch, Narr, 2011). She is principal investigator (with Regina Schober) of the research network "The Failure of Knowledge – Knowledges of Failure," funded by the German Research Foundation from February 2020 through January 2023. She obtained her PhD with a dissertation on Arab American literature since 9/11 from Free University of Berlin in 2013. Further research interests include the sociocultural history of drugs and addiction in the U.S., particularly the hyperincarceration of lower-class Black Americans in the 'War on Drugs', African American expressive culture, Native American Studies, as well as decolonial thinking.

Stefanie Mueller is deputy chair of American Studies at Westfaelische Wilhelms-Universitaet Muenster and a former Feodor Lynen Fellow at the University of California at Irvine. Her research interests include law and literature, sustainability and aesthetics, financialization, and corporate storytelling. She has co-edited *Financial Times: Competing Temporalities in the Age of Financial Capitalism*, a special issue of *Finance and Society*, as well as *Poetry and Law*, a special issue of *American Studies/Amerikastudien*, and *Violence and Open Spaces: The Subversion of Boundaries and the Transformation of the Western Genre*, a collection of articles on the contemporary Western film. She is the author of *The Presence of the Past in the Novels of Toni Morrison*, which was nominated for the Toni Morrison Book Award in 2015, and she has recently finished a manuscript on the literary and cultural history of the corporation in nineteenth-century US law and literature.

Ulfried Reichardt holds the chair of North American Literature and Culture at the University of Mannheim. He studied at the University of Heidelberg, Cornell University, and the Free University of Berlin, was assistant professor at the University of Hamburg, visiting professor at the University of Cologne as well as visiting scholar at Columbia University, the University of Toronto and the University of British Columbia, Vancouver, York University and the University of California at Santa Cruz and Santa Barbara. He received his PhD at the Free University of Berlin in 1988 (*Postmodernity Seen from Inside*, 1991) and his Habilitation at the University of Hamburg in 1998 (*Alterity and His-*

tory: Functions of the Representation of Slavery in the American Novel, 2001). He has edited *Time and the African American Experience* (2000) and *Mapping Globalization* (2008), co-edited *Engendering Men* (1998) and *Network Theory and American Studies* (2015). Further publications include *Globalization: Literatures and Cultures of the Global* (2010) as well as essays on the dimension of time in literature and culture, on American Pragmatism, on music in America, on diaspora culture, and US-American authors of the 19th, 20th and 21st centuries. He was principal investigator (with Regina Schober) of the research project "Probing the Limits of the Quantified Self" funded by the German Research Foundation (2015-2018).

Regina Schober is Professor of American Studies at Heinrich-Heine-University Duesseldorf. She is author of *Unexpected Chords: Musicopoetic Intermediality in Amy Lowell's Poetry and Poetics* (Winter, 2011) and co-editor of *Network Theory and American Studies* (with Heike Schäfer and Ulfried Reichardt, *Amerikastudien/American Studies*, 2015), *Data Fiction: Naturalism, Narratives, and Numbers* (with James Dorson, *Studies in American Naturalism*, 2017), and *The Failed Individual: Amid Exclusion, Resistance, and the Pleasure of Non-Conformity* (with Katharina Motyl, Campus, 2017). She recently completed a book manuscript entitled "Spiderweb, Labyrinth, Tightrope Walk: Networks in US-American Literature and Culture." She was assistant professor at Mannheim University and visiting scholar at the University of California, Santa Barbara. She was principal investigator (with Ulfried Reichardt) of the DFG research project "Probing the Limits of the Quantified Self" (2015-2018) and is co-founder of the DFG research network "The Failure of Knowledge/Knowledges of Failure" (with Katharina Motyl, 2020-2023). Her research interests include literary and cultural network concepts, critical digital humanities, cultural negotiations of failure, theories of intermediality and adaptation.

Dominik Steinhilber is academic staff member and doctoral student at the chair of American Literary and Cultural Studies of the University of Mannheim. Before coming to the University of Mannheim, he worked as an academic staff member at the chair for American Literary and Cultural Studies at the University of Stuttgart where he also received his Staatsexamen in English and German in 2016. His research interests include contemporary literature (in particular the works of David Foster Wallace), modernist and postmodernist fiction, digitization, and intertextuality. He is currently working on a dissertation on "The American Epic Novel in the Ulyssean Tradition" in which he investigates Wallace's *Infinite Jest* and Thomas Pynchon's *Gravity's Rainbow* with regard to their response to James Joyce's *Ulysses*.

Cultural Studies

Elisa Ganivet
Border Wall Aesthetics
Artworks in Border Spaces

2019, 250 p., hardcover, ill.
79,99 € (DE), 978-3-8376-4777-8
E-Book: 79,99 € (DE), ISBN 978-3-8394-4777-2

Andreas Sudmann (ed.)
The Democratization of Artificial Intelligence
Net Politics in the Era of Learning Algorithms

2019, 334 p., pb., col. ill.
49,99 € (DE), 978-3-8376-4719-8
E-Book: free available, ISBN 978-3-8394-4719-2

Jocelyne Porcher, Jean Estebanez (eds.)
Animal Labor
A New Perspective on Human-Animal Relations

2019, 182 p., hardcover
99,99 € (DE), 978-3-8376-4364-0
E-Book: 99,99 € (DE), ISBN 978-3-8394-4364-4

All print, e-book and open access versions of the titles in our list are available in our online shop www.transcript-verlag.de/en!

Cultural Studies

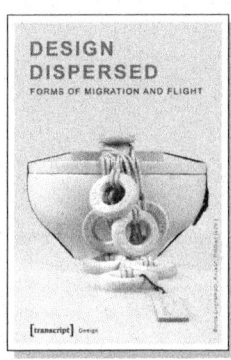

Burcu Dogramaci, Kerstin Pinther (eds.)
Design Dispersed
Forms of Migration and Flight

2019, 274 p., pb., col. ill.
34,99 € (DE), 978-3-8376-4705-1
E-Book: 34,99 € (DE), ISBN 978-3-8394-4705-5

Pál Kelemen, Nicolas Pethes (eds.)
Philology in the Making
Analog/Digital Cultures of Scholarly Writing and Reading

2019, 316 p., pb., ill.
34,99 € (DE), 978-3-8376-4770-9
E-Book: 34,99 € (DE), ISBN 978-3-8394-4770-3

Pablo Abend, Annika Richterich,
Mathias Fuchs, Ramón Reichert, Karin Wenz (eds.)
Digital Culture & Society (DCS)
Vol. 5, Issue 1/2019 –
Inequalities and Divides in Digital Cultures

2019, 212 p., pb., ill.
29,99 € (DE), 978-3-8376-4478-4
E-Book: 29,99 € (DE), ISBN 978-3-8394-4478-8

All print, e-book and open access versions of the titles in our list
are available in our online shop www.transcript-verlag.de/en!